D0852435

expanded
ORGASM

SOAR TO ECSTASY AT YOUR LOVER'S EVERY TOUCH

expanded
ORGASM

SOAR TO ECSTASY AT YOUR LOVER'S EVERY TOUCH

PATRICIA TAYLOR, Ph.D.

SOURCEBOOKS CASABLANCA™
AN IMPRINT OF SOURCEBOOKS, INC.®
NAPERVILLE, ILLINOIS

Copyright © 2002 by Patricia Taylor
Cover design © 2002 by Sourcebooks, Inc.
Cover image © Corbis

All rights reserved. No part of this book may be reproduced in any form or by any electronic or mechanical means including information storage and retrieval systems—except in the case of brief quotations embodied in critical articles or reviews—without permission in writing from its publisher, Sourcebooks, Inc.

Disclaimer: This book is not intended as a substitute for medical advice from a qualified physician. The intent of this book is to provide accurate general information in regard to the subject matter covered. If medical advice or other expert help is needed, the services of an appropriate medical professional should be sought.

Published by Sourcebooks, Inc.
P.O. Box 4410, Naperville, Illinois 60567-4410
(630) 961-3900
FAX: (630) 961-2168

ISBN 0-7394-2498-X

Printed and bound in the United States of America

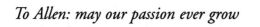

To Allen: may our passion ever grow

Table of Contents

Acknowledgments

I have long held a vision near and dear to my heart that women and men everywhere can begin to share in some of the exquisite joys and pleasure we have been fortunate enough to bring into our own lives. I thank all those who have supported me in helping make this vision a reality.

With deep appreciation I want to acknowledge in particular some of the people who have helped me bring my vision to fruition.

First and foremost, I thank my loving husband and partner of sixteen years, Allen. From the beginning, Allen has let me know that giving me pleasure is one of his greatest joys in life. He has taught me to value my own wants and desires. Allen's passion, joy for life, and commitment to expanded orgasm has infused me with a lifelong foundation of security, joy, and pleasure. It has been a joy to connect, play, and teach with him.

Next, I thank Jim Heynemann for our many years of friendship and success in working together. His gifts as a brilliant teacher are priceless and evident to all who know him. I am deeply grateful for the privilege of knowing Jim and working with him.

I thank my dear friend and teacher Lori Star for all she has taught me about Tantra. To this day, Lori inspires me to progress ever forward, through her own teaching, her love, her encouragement, and her friendship. I also thank Celebrations of Love, in Marin County, California. This community continues to nurture my soul deeply.

Thank you Victor Baranco and the many gifted teachers at More University for the incredible quality and quantity of information you have developed and shared on extended orgasm, relationship, community, communication, and pleasure. My life has been deeply and permanently transformed as a result of studying with you and meeting so many people in this wonderful community.

Thank you Bill Lamond for taking such a stand for turn-on and pleasure in the world. I am constantly amazed and inspired by your vision, integrity, and foresight, as well as your brilliance and warmth.

I thank Osho for his everpresent words of inspiration on Tantra and other great religious traditions of the world. Thank you for opening my mind up even further to the great power of spirituality and the variety of ways in which this precious energy can be experienced and enjoyed.

I thank Stan Dale and the Institute for Human Awareness for your information and your community. You have been instrumental in opening me up to the riches of intimacy and the beauty and power of win-win relating, in, as they say, "a world in which everyone wins."

I thank all my friends and clients who have taught me more than I can ever fully acknowledge here. Know that you live in my heart and that you teach me just as much as I could ever teach in return.

Finally, I thank my agent, Carolyn Grayson, for believing in this project when it was little more than a query letter; and my editor, Deb Werksman, for seeing the potential in this book from the start. Her vision for the potential of this book, plus enthusiastic encouragement and skillful editing, has played an essential role in bringing this book into print.

expanded
ORGASM
SOAR TO ECSTASY AT YOUR
LOVER'S EVERY TOUCH

Introduction

"Knowing I can expand gives me a tremendous feeling of power and calm."

"This experience makes me look and feel younger."

"It's like a kaleidoscope of delicious feelings, thoughts, emotions, and physical sensations."

"I feel refreshed, renewed, even reborn afterward."

"This practice has immensely increased my sense of well-being and self-worth."

"Men who never noticed me before now find me intoxicating. They can just sense how orgasmic I am, without my saying a word or acting any particular way."

What if there was something you could do that would reliably and dramatically increase your sense of well-being, give you great pleasure, improve how you feel about yourself and about life, and practically guarantee a great relationship? And suppose it was legal, free, and readily available?

What would you do to seek out this "something"? Would it be worth hunting it down? Taking the time to learn how to use it? Getting those you love to share it with you?

This book is for those who want their lives to be filled with these benefits—and many more. The "something" that yields these benefits is an experience called *expanded orgasm.* Building upon—and far beyond—"regular" orgasm, expanded orgasm is practiced by a surprising number of women and men who are finding deep fulfillment in it.

Orgasm is not an easy subject to talk about. To discuss a dramatically enhanced kind of orgasm presents new challenges. In order to make it easy for you to understand—and achieve—the benefits of expanded orgasm, I've employed stories about the practices and results of women and men who engage in it frequently. More important, you will follow two couples—Sam and Linda, and Kelly and Jason—through ten expanded orgasm lessons from our couples coaching. You will see how each couple learned to achieve great benefits for themselves and in their relationships.

This book will help you understand what this remarkable experience is and how it is different from "regular" orgasm. You'll explore your own motivations and readiness to learn to expand. As you read about each lesson, you'll learn how to achieve and enjoy expanded orgasm step by step. I assume you are working with a partner with whom you have a basically good relationship. However, much can be learned on your own, especially in the first four lessons. Don't let the lack of a willing partner dissuade you from such a pleasurable path! Let's get started!

Orgasms: Can We Talk?

Orgasm. The very word evokes deep emotions. What energetic crosscurrents do you feel just saying the word?

You've been told that your orgasms are important. Conversely, you've been told that they are unimportant and that you should go for the emotional connection. You've compared yours with others—well, with what others told you,—with descriptions in sex manuals, and with benchmarks promoted by magazines (don't tell me you haven't!). What a lot of fuss over eight to twelve muscular contractions, eight-tenths of a second apart.

If you've been unfavorably comparing your orgasms with some "ideal," you may have been taking this exquisitely pleasurable, sublime experience and turning it into yet another reason to beat yourself up, or another reason for performance anxiety?

I'm here to tell you there is another way. *What if we've simply been asking the wrong questions about orgasm?* What if there is another realm of orgasmic experience available, in which the pleasure is far greater, in which the orgasmic feeling is spread *all over your body*, rather than just localized in your genitals? What if you could have this powerful, all-over feeling for as long as you desired? What if this orgasmic state could have beneficial effects on your mind, your emotions, your intimate relationships—in short, on the rest of your life?

And what if this wellspring of orgasmic bliss was available to you—not after years of arduous study, but after consistently applying a few simple principles and practices? This all-over, whole-body, extended-in-time kind of orgasm is *expanded orgasm.*

What Is Expanded Orgasm?

It may surprise you to discover that there is more than one kind of orgasm. (We'll explore the typology of orgasm in detail later on). You are probably most familiar with *regular* or *climactic* orgasm. In fact, *climax* is often used as a synonym for orgasm. However, in addition to the orgasm you think of when you have a climax during sex (alone or with a partner) there is something more available. The climax-type orgasmic response evolved as part of the dance of procreation. You will learn that orgasm can be extended well past the limits that serve that biological function.

Expanded orgasm is a compelling, accessible *process* that anyone can use to enter a *state* of pleasurable expansion and flow. It is also a name for the orgasmic state people enter using this process. Here are some of the benefits they report. Expanded orgasm:

- feels surprisingly good.
- promotes partners to feeling better about themselves.
- revitalizes their relationships, in and out of the bedroom.
- creates a state of youthfulness in thinking, feeling, and appearance.
- offers practitioners health benefits such as stress reduction (stress can be linked to a variety of health problems) and general body toning.

This is a type of orgasm that is even more powerful and intense than regular orgasm. In one sense, it's orgasm expanded in both time and space. It lasts longer, and is felt more widely throughout the receiver's body. It is usually experienced not only physically, but in the emotional realm as well. During the experience, body and mind no longer feel separate, but part of a larger self.

Expanded orgasm can't be compared to the kinds of orgasmic experiences described in most sex instruction books. Frequently, these manuals focus on how couples can psyche themselves into feeling more sexual desire using techniques such as fantasy, deep breathing, and sensate focus (wherein the receiving partner excludes thinking about the giving partner while enjoying pure sensation). This information can do more harm than good when it directs people away from the most reliable source of true turn-on—intimate attention that is at once physical, mental, and emotional. Which would you rather have—psyched-up excitement or the profound experience of physical, mental, and emotional *connection* with a partner who is giving you full, intimate attention?

While some people have engaged in expanded orgasm spontaneously or via "secret teachings," it's a whole new world for most of us. Just like regular orgasm, information about expanded orgasm may have been repressed or simply undiscovered and unexplored through history because society feared the negative repercussions that open, expanded orgasmic sensuality might bring forth. It is time to challenge that assumption.

Both men and women are equally capable of experiencing expanded orgasm. While this book focuses primarily on women (and how they and their partners can create it), the exercises are applicable and rewarding to both men and women in a relationship.

Expanded orgasm can be learned on your own. We encourage single men and women to learn these skills on their own. However, most people find that the practice and the experience are made even more powerful when in a relationship. And, key attitudes and skills like communication and partnership are important in developing your ability to enjoy this new expanded sensation.

Women's Changing Attitudes

Attitudes about women's orgasm have done a complete about-face in a generation. When once orgasms were seldom discussed in public, it is now a suitable topic of conversation. When once a woman could plead ignorance and propriety as acceptable excuses for not knowing how her own orgasmic body functioned, she is now expected not only to be familiar with her genital geography, but also to claim and master her orgasmic expression.

Women can give themselves orgasms or receive them from a partner. In both situations, they link their orgasms with the broader activity of sex.

What is sex, if not a deeply intimate form of communication and self-expression? Orgasm is but one aspect of sex. It is not necessarily the most important. But orgasm does play a special role: it is a defining moment in sex, one in which the person having the orgasm experiences a singular symphony of events. Hormones course through the body, the nervous system becomes highly aroused, and pleasure washes rapidly through body and mind. I think of this series of events as the "little o."

Other times, if we're savvy or lucky, we catch a ride on the orgasmic wave. Progressively more intense feelings spread through the genitals, pelvis, abdomen, chest, face; radiate out through hands and feet. The river of sensation melts our cares away, so that our being fills with love for ourselves, our partners, and our world. Our breathing alters, our sense of time expands. We climax. Was that one minute, or ten, that we spent going over the edge? Our capacity for feeling itself expands and we find ourselves in wonderment. Was that another orgasm? Am I losing count? Who cares? And this I think of as "the big O."

Some women are pre-orgasmic. They have yet to feel their first orgasm. The word "pre-orgasmic" has thankfully replaced the word "frigid." It leaves room for the hope that someday, maybe soon, a pre-orgasmic woman will find her way into the club of the orgasmic. This hope is well founded; most pre-orgasmic women can learn they have an orgasmic capacity that simply hasn't yet been awakened.

Most women I know have a range of experiences with orgasm. At times they are as hot as a smoking pistol, and at other times, can barely feel a thing, despite all the right factors (great partner, great mood, desire).

When things go right, and that "big O" just keeps rolling in, is there any need to ask ourselves what we are doing right? We feel expert, as demonstrated by the outcome. It is only when the "big O" fails to materialize, or even more disturbing, when the "little o" is smaller than we hoped (if it comes at all), that suddenly our doubts motivate us to understand, and hopefully reverse, the situation.

This is the moment when most women will ask not "what has happened to my orgasmic capabilities?" but, "what has happened to my sex life?" And, in some ways, this is a most reasonable question. Our experiences with sex take place on the emotional, mental, and even spiritual—as well as physical—level. To analyze any of the component parts is like trying to determine where the fire in a diamond is coming from by peering through one facet alone. Is this the right facet to be peering through right now? What if all of the facets together create the fire? Then does it ever make sense to regard the fire through one portal alone?

It turns out to be useful to approach understanding our orgasms from both directions. To uncover clues to enhancing our orgasmic (and sex) life, it makes sense to focus on both the big picture and the details.

What questions do you ask when tonight's encounter with your pleasure center has fizzled? More seriously, suppose its has been a while since you felt anything to make you sing? You wonder what caused your experience to fall far short of its potential? *Was it me, was it him, or was it our relationship that somehow failed to perform?*

More specifically, we ponder:

How can I feel as much as I know it is possible to feel?

What must I do to stay interested in sex with my partner?

How can I get my partner even more interested in having sex with me?

Are my hormone levels adequate to support a rewarding sex life?

How often do I need to have sex in order to stay in good sexual condition?

Why does my desire for sex fluctuate so much?

To what extent is my partner responsible for my pleasure during sex?

You can ask these questions both at the big picture level and at the specific level. A consistent practice of exploring expanded orgasm will expand the number, variety—and usefulness—of your questions about your orgasmic response, your sex life, your relationships—in fact, your whole life. It will also vastly increase the number of answers.

These are excellent questions for women to ask. If you wait until things go poorly to start asking, then you've waited too long. If you'll start addressing these questions now, you can begin a lifelong learning and feedback process.

My Personal Path

It may appear that I've been an orgasmic *diva* my entire life, but nothing could be further from the truth. I still envy women who ooze with a remarkable inborn sensuality. For me, becoming and staying orgasmic has been a path of consistent, pleasurable discipline—and a little good fortune (don't worry—finding this book will be enough "good fortune" to get you started).

My orgasmic life opened at age eighteen. My older, more experienced boyfriend "touched me there" and I immediately yanked his hand away. The sensation frightened me. I assumed I was too oversensitive to be orgasmic. Based on this conclusion, I didn't pursue orgasm directly for the next ten years, despite having a succession of willing applicants and an otherwise healthy sex life. If you asked me, I would have told you how happy I was with my sex life, and how content I was with the extent of my knowledge. I never bought a vibrator, read steamy novels, or hoped for anything more than a satisfying sexual encounter, surrounded by plenty of loving and cuddling and touching.

Over time, my appreciation grew for what I learned to regard as "twangs" of pleasure. Within ten years of my first orgasm, I was ready to accept a certain amount of sensation without complaint. By age thirty, the idea of improving the quality of my twang lurked ominously in the background of my sexual encounters. Unfortunately, I seemed to have developed lockjaw every time I had sex. My inner world bristled with commentary: *Move your finger to the left, please. Could you go a little slower? Oooh, that felt good, why don't you stay there a bit longer? What's the rush?*

But I was paralyzed by the belief that merely to utter such directives would be to slam my partner's ego into a hard brick wall. After all, wasn't he trying his very best? And then there was the issue of politeness. How rude it would seem to imply that his offerings were less than delightful! I was raised to be a lady, and ladies didn't act like demanding tramps. If I were to reveal how much I liked what he did, that might cheapen me. And so my inner dialog continued. *How shall I fake my orgasm today?* I searched for that Goldilocks orgasm, not too big, not too little, but just good enough so that he would still respect me in the morning.

Finally the noise inside my head was so intense I couldn't live with myself another day. My success in the rest of my life was too greatly at odds with my bedroom lockjaw, and I resolved to right the situation. Incapable of saying anything in the heat of the moment, I waited until we were suitably elsewhere. We went out to eat the next night and I made sure we both ordered wine. Then I pulled out a book on sexual technique. The author advised couples to talk frankly about their needs, hopes, and desires in the bedroom. I showed him a particularly rousing passage encouraging such communication, and asked his opinion, remaining as ladylike as ever. Did he agree with such a modern approach to sex?

As he read the paragraph, he said, "Is there something you would like to tell me about how I touch you?" Through my haze of embarrassment, I admitted that I occasionally wanted him to touch me in different ways. He thanked me enthusiastically, and begged me to communicate from that point forward. He scored big points with me that night. Still, I never brought the subject up again, and most of my sexual lockjaw persisted.

Five years later, I was dating a new man. He wanted to practice something known as "extended" orgasm. He even brought a book with him on our second date. He read it like a man, from cover to cover, taking notes, underlining key principles, and setting up practice sessions. I read it with much less diligence.

In an hour, I'd skimmed through this big, fat tome on techniques. I then followed my partner's lead in exploration, enjoying his new attention more than his new techniques.

The book promised that extended orgasms could lead to one-hour orgasms. If a one-minute orgasm seemed immense, an hour-long orgasm seemed truly incomprehensible. My own orgasms lasted about ten seconds. I had (thank heaven) gotten far past the point of pushing a man's hand away as soon as the sensations felt too good. But it still took twenty minutes to lead up to the "little o," while my partner hunted, pecked, and rubbed me every which way. Despite his studious book learning, the end results bespoke a certain lack of real mastery. By the time I was ready to go over the edge, my attention span was gone. I felt sore and disinterested. I was grateful when the orgasm appeared—that was my permission to stop. As ever, my lips were sealed. He never knew that I wasn't having the time of my life.

Three years later, we became involved with Tantra, a practice of energy movement and ecstatic sexuality, where we had the opportunity to get our first real experience of expanded orgasm. Suddenly the world of orgasm exploded. With training, my partner learned how to give me powerful extended and expanded orgasms unlike anything I had ever known before. With my first expanded orgasm, a hot, white light electrified my entire body in a continual stream, and I remained in that state effortlessly. *I had been completely unprepared for anything ever to feel that good.* And when my partner was done giving me this pleasure, I looked at him as a woman newly in love. Right then, I dedicated my life to learning as much as I possibly could about an experience that had touched me so powerfully and deeply, and which had allowed me to connect with my partner in ways I had never imagined.

As I progressed in my studies, I found many other women who had had experiences with orgasm similar to mine. They and their partners were frustrated by the lack of good information. They were eager to learn more, and discovering that book learning wasn't giving them what they needed. Our eager interest and explorations attracted people to us who wanted to jump-start their own expanded orgasm programs. Most significantly, there was a juice, a joy, and a special glow in our connection, and everyone who met us could see it. That is what they wanted.

I trained by locating every eclectic source of information I could find. While my partner trained as a giver, I trained as a receiver. I began to enlarge my own orgasmic capacity through masturbation. I learned how to talk with my partner. Importantly, I began to recognize the extent of my power to create the experience of expanded orgasm. Eventually, I learned how to become an excellent giver of expanded orgasm as well as receiver, greatly to my partner's delight.

I have come a very long way. Today, I can go into orgasmic states at will, just by thinking about them. I can enter and remain in expanded orgasm for hours. But I developed this ability over time. My partner and I had to scour the sexual literature and learn from a wide variety of teachers (with dramatically varying abilities). We progressed as we stumbled through trial and error. If you follow the path outlined in this book, you will streamline your learning process significantly.

Today, I enter expanded orgasm at least five times a week. Sometimes I engage in it to keep my youth eternal, to have reasons to sing, to share energy with the stars, and to feel as if I am in love every day of my life. And sometimes, I do it just because it's two o'clock, and if I don't, I will never have this unique two o'clock chance again. Sometimes I use expanded orgasm to celebrate something special with my partner—a birthday, an anniversary, or an especially beautiful night. Increasingly, I access expanded orgasm to enhance my sense of pleasure in what used to be routine moments. Finally, I often do it just because it is my practice and it feels wonderful. I know instinctively that each time I thoroughly immerse myself in the vibrational awakening of my whole body, I grow younger and happier and more vital.

My ongoing, always growing practice has been a continual source of joyful learning and discovery. I have come to appreciate how much of our sexual pleasure is based on physical skills, and how very much lies in the non-physical domains of mind, heart, and spirit.

Expanded orgasm has given me a leg up on pleasure. I am far more ready to have pleasure, or at least consider having pleasure, in all areas of my life. And yet, I must confront the same issues as every other woman who wants to keep a lifelong relationship vital and juicy and authentic. I have found that the practice of expanded orgasm is not a panacea that will answer all my questions about love, turn-on, sex, orgasm, and pleasure. In fact, I ask more questions than ever. My orgasmic capacities serve as a barometer to how well I am doing with the rest of my life. This barometer has guided me often into returning to pleasure when I have been lost. Today, with the fresh passion and anticipation of a teenager, I eagerly anticipate the many years of learning and growth that still lie before me. Expanded orgasm is a path for life.

Our Coaching Practice

Our personal path to orgasmic pleasure led to an interesting development. Given our rather unique training in expanded and extended orgasm, friends and acquaintances who knew of our pursuits began sharing with us that they, too, had been facing some of the same challenges and rewards that we had experienced. Some had been given little or no information about how to pleasure themselves or their partners before partnering up. As a result, they were shy, afraid to communicate, or lonely, simply because they didn't know what to say or do. A few lessons invariably opened up whole new avenues of pleasurable relating; all that was needed was the information.

Others we knew had made significant progress toward expanded orgasm on their own, and yet were eager to add more information to the already rewarding progress they had made. We found our style and method of teaching worked well for those who didn't want therapy, but rather new ideas and techniques that would increase the depth and fun of relating together intimately.

Over time my partner Allen and I joined forces with others to teach workshops and private sessions to individuals and couples wanting more information, and as such, we became coaches in this art.

Today I work with various teaching partners in a variety of settings, with individuals and couples who seek to enhance their sensual identities and relationships. We work with people from all over the country and in all walks of life. Some people prefer going to a class or workshop, where they can see and hear ideas to take home and try in private. And yet there is also a demand for private sessions, in which we work couple-to-couple and delve more specifically into the optimal course of learning. We observe what they are feeling, reposition them, open up their personal dialog, and get them started. Our goal is always to train partners how to train each other.

We know that no matter how good our teaching is, each client is always the final expert on what he or she wants and likes the most in every moment. Once we open up that dialog between couples and get them started powerfully down the road to giving and receiving exquisite orgasmic pleasure, we know we have done our job well. They now have the tools they need to develop and maintain a lifelong practice of expanded orgasm.

Who Learns Expanded Orgasm?

Most couples have a honeymoon period in which everything they say and do works like magic on their partner. A velvety touch, a furtive kiss, or a finger tracing a squiggle down an arm is enough to send a lover into paroxysms of rhapsody. During this honeymoon period, sex happens in a state of grace. The juices start flowing before the clothes are off. Like two halves of a pair of gloves, two lovers cleave together as a part of a greater whole. Who hasn't met that new couple, aglow with confidence, and secretly wished them well for as long as it lasts? Honeymooners are the experts at effortless, meltdown sex. Predictably, we have yet to see honeymooners as clients.

The vast majority of clients coming to us to learn about expanded orgasm are couples in established, long-term relationships. I used to think of these relationships as being three years or longer. These days, however, relationships come and go so quickly that long-term relationships now start at about the six-month point, and that is about the earliest time that couples start coming to us to learn expanded orgasm training.

Time works both for and against long-term couples. On the one hand, as they continue to share dreams, snuggle, cuddle, laugh, cry, eat, sleep together, and feed each other in every possible manner, hormones of bonding, like *oxytocin*, kick into action, ensuring their continued attachment to one another. Like comfortably worn shoes, old family traditions, trusty hairdressers, and favorite restaurants, our partner's very existence reassures us that life is worthwhile.

On the other hand, nature has designed other hormones such as *phenylethylamine* (PEA) that have us bond just long enough to make that special, hot, sexual connection. These hormones create that love at first sight, romantic longing that we crave, usually for about six months before mysteriously vanishing. As the oxytocin builds and the PEA wanes, couples trade in the hot sauce for a security blanket. Fortunately, while PEA goes down as the length of time in relationship goes up, PEA also peaks during orgasm. Couples who practice expanded orgasm can access all those wonderful feelings of giddy, I'm-in-love euphoria as often as they wish. Thankfully, they are not bounded by the seeming constraints of how long they have been together.

A shared expanded orgasm practice will not solve all of a couple's problems. A bevy of factors contributes to the ease or difficulty with which we can have ongoing honeymoon sex with our long-term partners. Still, assuming the couple is reasonably happy otherwise, the expanded orgasm practice promises at a minimum to bring back the magic, sweetness, and sparkle of the honeymoon. Regular access to these feelings gives long-termers the fuel they need to keep their relationships vital and to resolve any other problems that invariably arise.

Expanded orgasm training satisfies those who like to improve their relationship, and those who like to improve their sex life. This training rivets their mutual focus on fun and pleasure. Many couples have viewed this training as a major investment in their future together. It offers them a natural antidote to sexual boredom, some wonderfully good times together now, and technicolor promises of even better times tomorrow.

Singles also have good reason to pursue expanded orgasm training, as it can—and should—be practiced alone as well as with a partner. Such practice confers a sexual radiance and fulfillment that others clearly sense.

Rather than feeling needy and deprived, such single practitioners appear brim-full with an inner presence that's attractive to potential partners. Furthermore, they offer partners those eternally desired qualities of a slow hand and an easy touch. They are confident in and out of the bedroom. Through training, they become an attractive catch to prospective partners, and they know it. They learn volumes about what to look for in a partner, too, thus ensuring that future partners will satisfy their ever-rising standards of sensual excellence.

We are always single people first, whether we are then also dating or in partnership. No matter what your partnership status, your solo practice of expanded orgasm will dramatically enhance your sensual and sexual life. Your own sense of fulfillment emerging from this practice will blossom into all the areas of your life. People who are fundamentally happy with themselves and their partners will enjoy this practice. Those who reap the greatest gains from it have the mental and emotional energy to make an essentially good sex life better. For those who still feel they have serious sexual problems to address, we recommend sex therapy. Couples should plan to begin expanded orgasm training only once these therapeutic issues have been addressed and resolved.

Anyone can start expanded orgasm training as long as his or her attitude is healthy and positive. We have worked with many grateful pre-orgasmic women, older couples, and even those who have disabilities, to enjoy a far greater range of orgasmic capacity.

Many long time practitioners of expanded orgasm work with us too. Following the adage that "the rich get richer," those who already have practiced expanded orgasm independently for years are eager to learn more from others who promise to further their development. They are often our most avid clients.

An Art Form and a Practice

Expanded orgasm practice may or may not occur as a separate activity from lovemaking. However, for teaching purposes, we do wish to separate it from lovemaking. We do this because:

- People often have fairly stable patterns of lovemaking. These patterns may be hard to break if they have been going on for a long time.
- People are reluctant to be completely honest with their partners for fear of hurting the other person's feelings. Additionally, they resist total honesty because they themselves don't want to admit their vulnerabilities in revealing their wants and needs.
- People feel that lovemaking is a sacred, special act of sharing love between two people, and that "lessons" or "practice" would spoil the act of opening their hearts fully in the moment.

For these reasons, we never teach expanded orgasm as a way to make love, even though it may be considered one. As we teach it, expanded orgasm is both an art form and a discipline. Like cooking, yoga, or painting, you can immerse yourself in learning the art, fully reaping rewards from the practice itself.

By viewing expanded orgasm as a practice, both partners can feel that they are not fixing lovemaking problems of any kind. They are simply learning a new skill. In this way, they are creating a new framework that values open, honest communication, precise attention to what one is giving and receiving, and more.

We liken learning expanded orgasm to building a new wing on the already existing house of your relationship. We never suggest you tear the old house down. If you build, and occasionally inhabit, this new wing, you may find you like spending time there. Then, you have a choice as to where you wish to spend your time together.

How to Use This Book

What can a book on orgasmic development really contribute?

People will learn from a book if it is enough fun and if they can relate to what is being presented. Therefore, I have presented an opportunity for you to look inside other expanded orgasm practitioners' lives. You will get to know us and some of our clients (all of whose names and identifying data have been altered).

In our professional practice of helping couples achieve expanded orgasm, we utilize ten lessons, or steps, that are easy to master and fun to practice. This book explains each lesson in detail, in such a way that you will be able to use it to practice and master expanded orgasm.

You will see what we teach and what we've practiced ourselves over the course of ten steps. Each step represents one of the lessons we typically give the couples that choose to work with us. Together, the ten steps give an excellent foundation for developing your own expanded orgasm practice.

You will follow two couples through the entire training process, and observe as they run into obstacles and celebrate their successes. You will find exercises throughout the book as well. These exercises will help you learn much more quickly than you could by only reading examples. We strongly recommend that you create your own story by actually doing the practice sessions.

Take pleasure in exploring this world, much the way you might plan a trip to a new part of the world. Take inspiration in those moments where you see yourself in someone else's similar situation, learning to achieve greater levels of orgasmic pleasure and mastery. Take new ideas back into your solo practice and into your relationship.

Step One: Getting Ready

Step One starts with an "informational interview," very similar to the ones we conduct when we talk with prospective clients.

Then, we will share with you the qualities we have found in those that make the best candidates for an expanded orgasm program and why. We will invite you to conduct your own "informational interview" by considering your own motivations. Soon, you'll meet two couples—Sam and Linda, and Kelly and Jason. You'll learn about their unique issues and reasons for learning expanded orgasm, and follow their progress over the course of the ten lessons they take from us. Through them, you will get an additional experience of what it is like to pursue the path of expanded orgasm.

Step Two: Connect with Yourself and Your Partner

I have spent innumerable hours puzzling over how I should classify my orgasmic range of experience. From the days of feeling little twangs, I have wanted to give words to my experience. Did I just have an orgasm? What kind was it? Was it extended? multiple? Did I go "over the edge," or was it even an orgasm at all? It sure felt good, no matter what it was. Can it feel good, even if it wasn't one? Even now, I love being able to identify just what kind of orgasm I am having.

By describing in detail the main varieties of this experience, this chapter will empower you to set words to your experiences of orgasm. Let's take a tour of the orgasmic landscape, and learn what types of orgasm you have been having, and can look forward to having in the future.

The exercises in this chapter will prepare you and a partner for an expedition of learning and pleasure about a woman's most intimate secrets. Most men and women know surprisingly little about this area. As a result, they don't appreciate it fully, understand the full extent of its capabilities, or know just how much to expect from it. I know when I began learning about my genital area, I couldn't even tell whether my partner was giving me up and down, or circular strokes, or whether he was on the top or bottom of my clitoris! No wonder I was unable to ask for what I wanted.

By the end of this chapter, you will have learned a new language for describing past experiences and requesting new ones.

Step Three: Build the Right Mindset

In this chapter, you'll lay the foundation for the most effective non-physical mindset for practicing expanded orgasm alone or with a partner.

Recently a couple came to see us with a fairly simple and typical concern. Elena had a tiny clitoris. Charles would try everything he could think of to give her orgasmic pleasure, but, since he couldn't locate her clitoris very easily, reported only occasional, random success. We coached them on the various mental and emotional techniques Charles could use before he even touched her genitals.

Using what you will learn in this lesson, he set up the environment, created a pleasurable focus, and got her deeply into the mood, ready to surrender to bliss.

By the time he was ready to touch her clitoris, it was quite engorged, triple its original size, and very, very ready for sensation. In his first moment of contact, he found her clitoris easily and gave her immense waves of pleasure.

Like Charles and Elena, many people skip the "non-physical" aspects of learning this art. Since they have been "non-physical" their entire lives, they reason that they don't need lessons on this aspect. Nothing could be further from the truth. Learning the non-physical aspects of this practice will open many doors for even the most experienced lovers. This chapter will enable you to vastly enhance and improve everything that you do on the physical levels as well.

Step Four: Erotic Development

Many clients expect us to train the man to give more pleasure to his partner. They assume that if the man knew what he was doing, the woman would be having a much better time. The man's "contribution" is, of course, crucial—but (as in any dance) the woman's is equally so.

In our culture, *erotic self-development* is rarely ever mentioned or discussed. Our ancestors often viewed this practice with shame and aversion. Traditionally, women might masturbate, but only as an answer to the problem of missing a partner. Today we have the option to revisit those assumptions and choose how we want to be with our own bodies.

This lesson focuses on giving you a larger container to fill—it's about dramatically increasing your capacity to experience orgasmic pleasure. Expanded orgasm first and foremost is an individual path. To the extent each of us masters it on our own, we become a more exciting partner to be with. The inspirational stories and exercises in this chapter help to jump-start women on their own path of erotic nourishment and enhancement.

Step Five: The Opening Strokes

Men could save so much time, and have so much more fun with their partners, if only they understood and mastered the three opening strokes.

Engorgement is as important to a woman as it is to a man. Just as men enjoy the feeling of a hard penis, with nerve endings stretched out to receive so much more sensation, so women notice that an engorged clitoris feels more of every sensation you deliver.

Opening strokes is a technique that when mastered will enable the man to let a woman know he is about to take control of her pleasurable nervous system, locate her clitoris, get it engorged, and go right to her favorite spot. This approach will save him from trying to find her clitoris when she is not engorged. Men, these strokes will help you become the confident sexual hero she wants you to be, right from the start.

Step Six: Thrilling Caresses

No matter how wonderful something is, after a certain amount of repetition, we seek novelty. The drive to experience the new and different appears to be hard-wired into us at the biological level. Fortunately for those studying this art, expanded orgasm practice engenders the emergence of endless creativity, generating an ongoing fountain of deliciously novel moments.

Here's why: because expanded orgasm develops simultaneously in the dimensions of mind, body, emotion, and spirit, it is expressed in words, deeds, intentions, emotions, and energy. The expanded orgasm experience builds in momentum through endless variations in speed, pressure, location, rhythm, timing, communication, and desire.

This step enables you to identify—and practice—all of these variables. With enough experience, the combinations of these variations in new and novel ways will allow men and women to achieve a quantum shift in their abilities to expand orgasms.

Just like snowflakes, no two expanded orgasm sessions are alike. If your current lovemaking, love-creating sex has become routine (and over time whose hasn't?), then this lesson will impart a wealth of new and very powerful ideas and skills. You will learn how to expand your repertoire dramatically, so that every session deeply engages both of you on all levels possible.

Step Seven: Feedback Loops

This step helps you to develop the communication skills essential to giving and receiving expanded orgasm.

With communication, the details of technique and anatomy can be mastered in a relatively short time. As you become more facile with these aspects, communication—both verbal and nonverbal—becomes increasingly important in powering your experience of expanded orgasm.

You can expect to encounter certain communication conundrums along the learning path. You might wonder, "If I talk too much, how will my partner ever learn to feel and respond at the bio-energetic level? If I don't talk enough, how will my partner ever know to do what I want him to do at the right moment? If my partner can feel everything I am thinking, why do I need to talk at all?"

This powerful lesson will show you how to use effective verbal and nonverbal communication during your expanded orgasm practice.

Step Eight: Spreading the Sweet Spot

A great musician uses two hands. A great golfer uses two hands. A great actor uses two hands. A great cook uses two hands. How many hands are you men using to create the expanded orgasm that will thrill her to her toes?

If the answer is even slightly less than two, then this step will change that forever. Using both hands will give a man the ability to create a much vaster range of experiences that last longer and take his partner much higher. The hands, too, are just extensions of his body. As he masters using more of his body, he will eventually learn how to deliver expanded orgasm from his head to toe, to hers!

Step Nine: Live a Turned-on Life

If expanded orgasm were just about acquiring technique, then progress would occur in something of a straight line. The more you practiced, the more you learned. The sky would be the limit. However, technique alone cannot bring about a steadily increasing level of expanded orgasm pleasure.

Technique must combine with turn-on—that combination of desire, enthusiasm, and sensuality that makes even the slightest furtive glance come alive. To the turned on woman, everything he does will seem inspired and creative. Turned on, our partners are heroes before they even walk through the door.

In long-term relationships, turn-on often suffers a slow death. Your jaded mind stamps as "routine" the familiar sounds of your lover's compliments, the tried and true way he looks at you lovingly, and even the gentle, knowing touch. All too often, your lack of turn-on for a partner reflects that lack of turn-on you have in your own mind, for much or all of what you see, hear, and feel in all areas of life. Are you destined to watch your turn-on slowly drain away? Not necessarily. Turn-on can be valued, and thereby cultivated.

In this step we discuss how expanded orgasm practitioners deliberately bring turn-on back into their lives, and in so doing, infuse their expanded orgasm practices with the kind of oozing sensuality and excitement that they would like to experience on an ongoing basis from this point going forth.

Step Ten: From Here to Further Mastery

It's practically a mantra to our clients: achieving expanded orgasm is 25 percent physical technique and 75 percent non-physical. We train clients relentlessly to develop both the physical and non-physical aspects, only to find them getting lost in the non-physical parts of this practice. What really shifts a practitioner into mastery is the ability to create pleasure using *both* the physical and non-physical aspects. This is why we always start with a strong foundation in the non-physical aspect of giving expanded orgasm pleasure to a woman.

Recently, a client couple had been rehearsing the physical technique for some time, but continued to find themselves stalled with the non-physical. This is quite a common occurrence in expanded orgasm training, similar to the experience of pursuing any true discipline. Learning typically occurs in accelerated phases and plateaus. Our clients did not advance significantly until the man had a breakthrough in claiming his personal power. Suddenly his ability to give his partner expanded orgasm progressed in a quantum leap. With his newly found deeper understanding of non-physical technique, the training in the physical domain took on an intense new flavor. His newfound understanding about himself allowed him to pull together all he had learned in the last six months. His every action became guided by instinct, intuition, and boundless joy as well as deep proficiency, and his performance seemed effortless.

In Step Ten, you will learn about mastery—how to go beyond technique, and into pure artistry.

Meet Two Couples

Expanded orgasm is best when directly experienced. How shallow my words some-times feel to me, as I seek to express the many ineffable qualities of this experience. I do my best, but in the long run, it is the stories of instructive and revealing moments of real people that best share and communicate what expanded orgasm is. I could tell you that expanded orgasm is simultaneously a state, a world, a prac-tice, a way of life, a period of time in which it occurs, and so on. Expanded orgasm is so many things! But you will truly encounter expanded orgasm by engaging in it yourself, and by sharing the stories of your experiences with your partner or with other expanded orgasm practitioners.

Thus, in each chapter, in addition to talking about topics in an instructive way, we look in on the inner lives and dynamics of several clients as individuals and as couples. Their experiences will help you create a deeper and richer aware-ness of expanded orgasm to complement what you learn from the "chalk talk" and discover on your own from exercises.

Since expanded orgasm really is a process that unfolds and grows over time, we want to introduce you to two special couples that we'll be following through-out this book. We have chosen these couples primarily because they represent very typical but contrasting issues of couples who have entered into expanded orgasm training. Both couples are happily married and committed to building and enjoying a full, rich life together. While they are not "in trouble," and are not likely candidates for marital therapy, each couple has some serious challenges that make what appears to be the simple goal of giving and receiving enormous, sus-tained pleasure seem at times almost impossibly out of reach.

By following these couples all the way through ten sessions, we hope to give these lessons an additional critical perspective. You will see for yourself what ups and downs expanded orgasm training introduces into practitioners' lives. You will see expanded orgasm as a process that interacts within the greater framework of a long-term relationship; and you will see how couples work over time to achieve the goals that motivated learning expanded orgasm.

Thus, our approach is as follows:

We will lay out ten steps to help you develop specific attitudes and skills for dramatically expanding your ability to give and receive the enormous pleasure that is expanded orgasm.

To help you solidify what you've learned conceptually, the major points in each lesson are accompanied by exercises for you to do individually and with your partner.

We also illustrate how clients have addressed and learned the attitudes and skills in each lesson. Two couples (composites of, but unidentifiable as, real clients) will show you how they learned expanded orgasm through the complete series of steps.

Kelly and Jason

Kelly and Jason are a sweet couple who have been married six months. Each is on their second marriage. They are concerned about making this marriage a success sexually because of their experiences with their first marriages.

Kelly, thirty-seven, is a marketing director at a fairly large firm in town. Her first marriage, which lasted five years, was to an artist. The sex was very passionate, but he was a poor producer, and this caused endless arguments. She finally decided to go it alone. For Kelly, it had been more than the financial insecurity that bothered her—she wanted a man who had whatever it takes to take care of himself. She worries that in a relationship, you can have either sex and passion, or production and economic stability. She recognizes that Jason is a good producer and can give her the economic stability she craves, but she is afraid this means that their marriage will lack the passion she equally craves. In fact, Jason does seem to be preoccupied with his growing company. Kelly has a very high sexual appetite and is afraid that if unmet, her sexual desires will sabotage the marriage.

Kelly saw her parents go through a divorce and has been through one herself. As a result, she feels a certain amount of failure in her life. She wants security and stability in a relationship; she yearns to plan a life together with someone without having nagging doubts about whether or not they will be together to enjoy what they are saving for. And yet, another part of Kelly is a very turned on woman; she bristles with it. It scares her; is this turn-on friend or foe? How can having all that juice help her reach her goals?

She would like to use expanded orgasm training to help her communicate better with Jason, and, better yet, enjoy Jason's attentions sexually.

Jason, thirty-nine, is an engineer. His first marriage lasted seven years and broke up when his first wife left him to be with another man. He is concerned that there is something about him that he still doesn't understand that made his previous wife leave. How does he know it won't happen again? He worries that perhaps he was unattractive or unskilled as a lover. To compound this, he recognizes how important passion in a relationship is to Kelly. Jason wants to be able to express and increase his passion for her and be a "great lover." He believes that he needs to do this in order to make their marriage thrive.

Jason—also wounded in the process of divorce—wants more than anything to succeed in his relationship with Kelly. He feels deeply competitive with the other men who have been in her life; while he realizes this is irrational, this competitiveness seems to control him. He feels insecure, unable to unlock the depths of his passion; caught in the self-fulfilling cycle he fears most: insecurity coupled with failure.

Jason would like to somehow become "someone new" in the bedroom. He has no idea how this might happen, and is hoping that the expanded orgasm training might help.

They do not see it, but their marriage is at a critical point. The sexual issues are more significant than they may realize. Nonetheless, they both know that their sexual relating is a concern. To them, expanded orgasm feels like an important investment in their relationship.

Sam and Linda

This couple has been married twenty-five years; this is the first marriage for each. They have two sons, ages twenty and eighteen; the second has recently moved out to attend college. Now the issue of the "sexual spark," the passion they once had, has awakened after a long, deep slumber. They want to regain the passion. Their marriage faces new risks in light of the changes in their lives. Both Sam and Linda are motivated to learn expanded orgasm as a way to proactively address the relative lack of sexual spark in their marriage.

Linda, forty-four, up to now has always defined herself as a wife, mother, and homemaker, though she has done considerable volunteer work with the city's symphony orchestra. She is now thinking of going back to school in the fall and training in website design. Linda often finds it difficult to communicate with Sam. As she looks forward to ramping up her career life, she is finding Sam increasingly dull, but she loves Sam dearly and wants to reignite the fire she remembers. She senses that her sex drive has been compromised from having been relatively inactive for so long, but that deep down, it is waiting to be liberated from a deep, long sleep. Now that her last child is out of the house, Sam has become more amorous and she doesn't quite know how to handle his sudden increase in drive. She doesn't feel erotic; she certainly isn't driven, as Sam seems to be; and she doubts her sexual capacities.

Linda recalls the heat and passion of their early marriage—which rapidly cooled with the responsibilities of work, homemaking, and child-rearing. She is aware that she is still attractive. She hates to admit it, but her feelings toward Sam have turned more brotherly than passionate. This is not the way she wants it. She wants Sam to be romantically and sexually attracted to *her*, not just want to be with her out of a desire to fulfill his own sexual desires. She perceives that Sam thrives on routine, while she craves new experiences. But she doesn't know how to communicate what she wants in a way that would not rock the boat or threaten Sam. On those times in the past when she attempted asking directly for something sensual, she remembers Sam getting flustered and even less emotionally available.

Linda would love to be able to communicate with Sam in such a way as to ignite their passion and the fulfillment of her sexual desires. In fact, increased communication itself would turn her on. Her goal is romance—those knowing looks, lingering touches, times of baring their souls, taking each other to new places, and having new eyes with which to see each other.

Sam, fifty-two, owns a successful chain of small restaurants. He prides himself on having been a good provider for his kids. However, running restaurants has taken a lot of day and evening time, as well as attention on weekends. His traditional marital and work values have made them economically stable, but he's paid little attention to play or to fanning the flames of passion. Born into a poor and struggling family, he did not learn the value or importance of play or passion. Sam recently arranged for a full-time manager to oversee his restaurant operations, and is thus entering semi-retirement. With the business taking less of his attention, and with the children gone, he doesn't know how to relate with Linda in a stimulating or satisfying way. His sex drive seems to have increased as his responsibilities have decreased, but his more-frequent advances have not always been enthusiastically accepted.

Sam is afraid that as Linda "takes off" she is going to leave him behind. Like Linda, he wants to reignite the spark, but is afraid to take risks in their relationship. He wouldn't know where or how to start, anyway.

He's worried that at fifty-two he's past the point where he can learn anything new. In fact, he's having a midlife crisis: he wants his life to be sweeter and richer instead of the hard drone it has been. He wants to satisfy himself—and he wants to remain with Linda. Nevertheless, he has fantasized about meeting someone new with whom he could just play and not have to work at figuring out the relationship. He hopes that expanded orgasm training can help him and Linda to reconnect at a level of true passion.

Linda and Sam have a more stable marriage than Kelly and Jason. But, their marriage is at risk of becoming far more competitive, given the opposing natures of their desires. It's fortunate that they are coming to us now, while there is still plenty of love and desire to connect more deeply.

You will follow these two couples through the book, accompanying them on the journey they took with us as their guides. Even if your situation is very different, try to see how their experiences might apply to your life.

Ten Steps to Your Own Practice

Each step is designed to open your range of experience to include new concepts and behaviors. We strongly suggest that you follow the steps exactly as they are given and proceed through them sequentially. Even those of you who consider yourselves highly skilled in sensuality will learn much from each step.

How long should each step take? That depends on you. It could take ten days (for those of you who are devoting yourselves full-time to the study of expanded orgasm), ten weeks (for those of you who wish to take on the training as you would a weekly class), or even longer (for those who simply wish to meander their way down the path). The pace is up to you to set. We do recommend, however, that you keep up a forward momentum.

Once you have completed a step, you may want to return to earlier lessons before moving forward. It is possible to move forward and yet continue doing some of the practices you learned early on as well. In fact, many of the later practices will be much more powerful if you have developed a solid foundation on the earlier ones.

My husband Allen and I are still practicing these lessons, too. Just last week we took a mini-retreat for three days. We spent two hours a day doing practices from this book. Our honeymoon wasn't nearly as much fun!

What We've Explored

In our introduction, we have opened up the subject of orgasm. I have shared with you who I am and how I came to learn about, and teach, the art of expanded orgasm. I've presented expanded orgasm in many ways. Among others, it is a sensation to experience, an art form, as an ongoing practice, and a deeply personal journey that each individual, and each couple, can choose to follow.

I have introduced you to my partner Allen, and to two of our client couples, Sam and Linda, and Kelly and Jason. In addition, you also can look forward to meeting several of our other coaching clients.

Now we can go right into our step-by-step lessons in expanded orgasm.

1

Step One: Getting Ready

Looking back to when I first heard about expanded orgasm, I can see that at the time I was threatened by the concept. Expand my orgasm for an hour? Why, I could hardly imagine expanding my orgasms to twenty seconds. Why would I want to have a feeling that intense for so long? And anyway, if you asked me, I would have told you I was the last person on Earth who needed to learn anything about sex!

I had other concerns too. What if being an expandedly orgasmic kind of girl made me like sex more than I wanted to? That could certainly be inconvenient. What if somehow my espousing an interest in expanded orgasm caused my husband Allen to raise his expectations of me? What if I was not able to perform up to the standard? What if I had to learn more about giving as well as receiving, before I was ready?

It's one thing to find out that you were not born to be an Olympic level skier, but what if I was not, exactly, an Olympian in bed? Could I ever be happy getting feedback that my ability to give and receive pleasure could be not somewhat but unimaginably improved?

These what-ifs lurked at a subterranean level not directly verbalized. Overall, to my conscious mind, expanded orgasm seemed somewhat like a foreign land—distant, interesting, and definitely far away. Did I really want to go there? What was it like? Did I really have enough information to make a good judgment? I can look back now and appreciate that, like most people, I was already concerned about my sexual performance and worried about what my partner expected of me.

Fortunately, our own lessons covered a whole range of juicy topics, only one of which was orgasm. These other topics were actually pretty interesting to my conscious mind. This training promised to teach us how to give each other pleasure and to stay in deep, honest communication at all times. It encouraged us to connect with one another and to enlarge our abilities to enjoy pleasure.

And so, in addition to learning about expanded orgasms themselves, I learned that sex—and orgasm—can be far more pleasurable than anything I had ever experienced. And, I learned the integrity to practice out of a genuine desire, not out of real and imagined obligations.

Actually, our clients are usually far clearer about what benefits they want from expanded orgasm than I was when I began.

Interestingly, most people do not learn expanded orgasm strictly to expand the length or even the intensity of their orgasms. Orgasm is one of the many motivations which tend to fall into two categories, outward-focused reasons and inward-focused reasons.

Outward-focused reasons to practice expanded orgasm are those that impact someone or something outside myself, for example to:

- increase my partner's interest in sex
- increase my partner's ability to satisfy me sexually
- improve the level of communication or feeling of partnership
- add variety, romance, and juice to our relationship
- improve our sexual skills as we age (reduce the impact of aging)
- become a better lover
- be more attractive to others
- enjoy health benefits that result from flooding the body with hormones, deep breathing, and greater use of sexual musculature: the overall sense of well-being that comes from being more orgasmic increase self-esteem

Inward-focused reasons to practice expanded orgasm have to do with who I am, how I want to feel, and the kind of person I would like to become. For example, I:

- do it for myself because I want to live a turned-on life
- want to enjoy more sexual pleasure
- want to feel myself—be in deeper touch with myself
- seek to radiate the kind of joy and enthusiasms I had as a kid
- want to open up to life experiences rather than shut them down
- feel passionate about being on a path of self-improvement, personal growth, or "self-actualization"

No two people are alike, and no two couples are alike. Everyone will have his or her own reasons for wanting to learn expanded orgasm. These reasons may change over the course of learning.

Your priorities may change or they may become more clear and focused over the course of your expanded orgasm training. The important thing is that you understand your priorities and what motivates you at every stage of learning expanded orgasm.

Here are some questions to ask yourself:

What personal priorities do I have in learning more about expanded orgasm?

What do I think are my partner's? What do I think my partner thinks are my priorities and motivations?

Discuss this topic with your partner after you have answered these questions. Any surprises?

Establish Your Baseline

Our work with clients starts with an evaluation session. In this session we get a picture of the individuals, their relationship, and their hopes, dreams, and fears. We help them formulate goals and determine whether expanded orgasm training is right for them.

The lessons in this book attempt to simulate our in-person sessions as closely as possible. Let's start with some questions about your approach to sex and sensuality. In beginning the expanded orgasm learning process, it's very helpful to have a snapshot of where you are in important arenas in your sensual and sexual lives. This baseline will help uncover key issues and also function as something that you can refer back to at a later point in time, in order to evaluate your progress.

While we ask these questions of couples together, you may wish to answer these in privacy if you feel that privacy will enable you to answer more honestly.

There will be ample additional time for sharing throughout the book.

How important is sex to you?

How often do you tell your partner the truth about your sexual preferences and desires?

What are your obstacles to orgasm?

What are your obstacles to good sex?

What would you like more of sexually?

What do you wish you could tell your partner that you want more of in the areas of relationship, communication, and sex? What do you believe your partner wants more of in these same areas of the relationship, communication, and sex?

Think back to the quality of relating in the first few months of your relationship. What, if anything, do you miss about those times?

What do you want to get out of this program?

Are you taking any medications that you think might be impacting your sexual functioning? If so, have you consulted with your doctor to see if there are other drugs that might have less impact?

Do you have any other physical, mental, or emotional challenges that might make your expanded orgasm program problematic?

Our Two Couples Get Started

In our first session, we observed certain revealing dynamics between our two couples. Both couples found themselves being more candid than they ever had been about what they wanted from sex. Most people discover relief at being able to verbalize what's going on for them and what they want for themselves and from their partner. They are often amazed when they hear their partner's perceptions and desires.

Kelly began her evaluation by enthusiastically acknowledging her love for Jason. She is captivated by his ambition, his mind, and his acuity. She loves spending time with him. To her, Jason is a harbor in a stormy sea to whom she returns for love, nurturing, fun, and connection. While the sex isn't stellar, she has resigned herself to a life of "OK" sex in return for all that Jason has to offer.

Kelly admits that she doesn't always find Jason right for being who he is, just the way he is. She does compare him to her former husband. She doesn't regard herself as very verbal, so that even when she is enjoying Jason, she doesn't let him know. She admits to having an irrational fear about letting Jason know when he has given her pleasure. She knows that if she does, he might think he has found the magic pleasure formula, and then might stop trying to learn more about her. Jason is thus always in mystery as to how much enjoyment he is truly giving her and even sharing with her.

Jason is crazy about Kelly. He has never dated such a brilliant, vivacious woman. He loves her zaniness, her fire, and her energy. Still, he feels Kelly's doubts about his sexual performance, and responds accordingly. Her doubts magnify his doubts. His insecurities keep him from putting his attention on Kelly during sex, and she can feel his focus on himself. His attention on his performance makes her feel lonely and less inclined to want to verbalize her emotions while making love.

In our opening evaluation with Sam and Linda, she talks of a recent concern. Linda fears she is out of touch with her own *erotic energy*; that what she "brings to the table" is flat. She has a hard time with developing her own erotic energy. She admits that part of the reason she has shut down is due to the mixed messages Sam gives her about her sexuality. It seems to her that he wants her to be more sexual, but not to "become more her own person" in doing so. She can see that she needs to claim her own erotic self.

Sam, encouraged by Linda's refreshing honesty, also acknowledges that he has always gotten sex by pressuring Linda. He has helped to create an environment in which Linda does shut down, but it's hard for him to stop. He really does fear that he will lose Linda if she awakens erotically, and yet he wants more passionate sex with her. He's also afraid he wouldn't know what to do with her if she started wanting lots of sex. He would love to learn how to be inviting, not demanding. So he's caught in a paradox. He is surprised to discover in the opening session that her increased sexuality would be threatening to him. He commits to developing a deeper understanding of how to resolve his contradicting messages with Linda.

Learn Expanded Orgasm in Stages

We appreciate all too well the courage these couples have displayed in taking on such a new learning adventure.

For thoughtful, intelligent adults, learning something new is not the same as it is for children. Children are wired for learning. Show babies how to walk, and they will gladly fall a hundred times in the process of mastering this new opportunity for mobility. Show kids how to ride a bike. They may not get it the first time and may spend weeks trying to master this new challenge. Kids may happily accept training wheels to guide them until they are sure they can ride safely without them. Adults are very different from children in how they learn. They become frustrated easily and they let their egos get involved. Show adults a puzzle; if they can't figure it out in minutes, they often become irritated, and are ready to tear it up and go on to something else in which they believe they can succeed. They will now be more leery about the next puzzle. *Adults hate failure.*

But learning is an exciting process. We are designed to experience pleasure when we learn. As children, learning was an activity that was its own reward. However, for most of us along the way to adulthood, "staying in the comfort zone" replaces "testing my limits" as the priority. Comfort slowly becomes inertia, and before long, once-champion learners are bored and wondering, "What happened to all the newness that life seemed to offer?"

Here is what works in expanded orgasm—and in going to enormous heights of pleasure and depths of connection in your relationship: reverse this process of unlearning, and believe that learning is pleasurable. Expanded orgasm is pleasurable.

Let's look at how people learn. This model, which describes four distinct stages of learning, will empower you to reawaken the joy inherent in learning.

In the stage of *unconscious incompetence*, you know that something in your life could use fixing or improving, but you don't know how you are going to respond to the challenge. Adults may feel both fear and excitement at the prospects of fixing the problem.

This is often the point where an individual or a couple experiences frustration with some aspect of their sexual, sensual, or emotional relating. You know you need something, but not what. Or, you're not even aware of the need to learn a new attitude or skill.

In *conscious incompetence,* you come to realize your current actions are the source of your problems, but not enough to really know how to change them. In terms of expanded orgasm, this is the point at which most couples come to see us.

Conscious incompetence also shows up when you're aware of the new attitude or skill to be learned, but don't have the attitude or skill yet. For example, if you don't know how to fly a plane, but you do know such a skill is possible, you're in this stage. This is the stage at which our clients usually begin to consider learning expanded orgasm.

In *conscious competence*, you have made a quantum leap forward toward acquiring the new skills and behaviors required to solve the problem at hand. However, you've not yet fully integrated the new skills, and you still need constant reminders to use them. Do you remember learning to drive a car? There came a point where you knew how, but nothing came automatically or without thought.

In expanded orgasm, this is where the practice sessions come in. Expanded orgasm is a practice that develops over time. A year from now, you will be significantly more skilled than you are tomorrow. Expanded orgasm practice can bring great pleasure all along, but many of the victories will occur only after trial, error, and experimentation.

In the last stage, *excellence* (also known as *unconscious competence*), you have mastered the skills so thoroughly that you are utilizing your new attitudes and behaviors without having to think about them consciously each time. They now seem to be a natural addition to your life. They are fully integrated.

In expanded orgasm, this state of excellence occurs gradually. Most expanded orgasm practitioners find that they are simultaneously at several stages of learning. This is because expanded orgasm mastery incorporates many new mental and physical behaviors. They may be mastering some skills and new ways of thinking in the first or second lesson. Others may take more time and practice to master. While mastering some concepts, they will feel they are still in the process of learning others.

For this reason, we strongly emphasize that expanded orgasm is best viewed as a process over time. And, expanded orgasm is most fully embraced by those adults who thrill at the prospects of learning new things, even if the learning process can be frustrating at times. Like children, the most successful expanded orgasm students are the ones who are willing to brush themselves off and try again until they get it right!

In fact, those who learn expanded orgasm most quickly and enjoyably consider the feelings of learning not as frustration, but rather the sure signs of body, mind, and emotions signaling that they are, in fact, engaged in succeeding. For such students, learning expanded orgasm is rapid and very, very enjoyable!

Recall your experience of learning some new skill—one that you valued highly and that was, once mastered, highly rewarding. Was your learning path always easy and effortless—a straight line? What was it like just before you made "quantum leaps" in understanding or in acquiring the new skill?

The answers to relationship problems often come not from getting the right answer but from *finding a new way of being.* As we get older, the nature of problems shifts. In school, problems come in neat little boxes that can be solved neatly in an exam question. But in real life, problems are often multidimensional. Change one thing and other things change too. Our school-based problem-solving skills do not prepare us to solve real life problems.

Our couples, for example, embody "real life" problems. These problems often have the quality that makes people feel as if they are painted into a corner with no way out that leaves them any better off than where they are now.

Linda, for example, feels she can seemingly only advance at Sam's expense. To her, Sam seems stuck. But Sam is clinging to what he knows works. He doesn't know how to let go without losing more than he feels he can afford to lose. Linda doesn't want to rock the boat, and yet, is feeling stifled. What next move will leave them both better off?

Kelly, too, doesn't want to rock the boat, nor does Jason. Rather than express her precious turn-on, Kelly fears this energy and tries to suppress it. In so doing, she is subverting the part of herself that Jason loves the most. Jason craves her passion, and he wants to find it in himself, too. He dreams of being the man to show Kelly the universe—only he cannot seem to find it himself.

Win/Win Relating

There is no solution to these problems at a logical level. There is only one way to break out of these stuck places: when both partners can learn a way of being in which when one partner advances, the other clearly benefits, or wins, from it. We call this win/win relating. It is a way of relating, but also a way of thinking about relating.

I first learned about win/win relating from a business model for high-level salesmen working with sophisticated customers. In it there are four possible outcomes for every transaction. Either the buyer wins at the seller's expense, the seller wins at the buyer's expense, both the seller and buyer lose from the deal, or both the seller and the buyer win from the deal. Opposed to doing business in the "I win—you lose model," this alternate way of thinking promoted "win/win" as the best overall strategy.

It makes sense. If you cheat your customer, why would he or she want to do business with you again? If you yourself get the short end of the stick, why would you want to do more business with that person? If both of you lose, well, obviously, you're done. The win/win strategy is the only one that makes long-term sense.

Maybe you're thinking that win/win is easy enough in business, but when you live with someone, life is just one big chess game between two people who are intimate. But is it really different?

What if Sam were to find a way to win with Linda's becoming more turned on? What if Jason was to win each time Kelly's passion came out to play? What if Linda was to enjoy it when Sam gave her so much pleasure that she started making dates with him? What if Kelly risked acknowledging Jason for all the things he did right, trusting that he would continue to want to learn about what gave her pleasure? The list of win/win solutions is endless.

This win/win approach is strongly reinforced in expanded orgasm training. We ask both partners to engage in new cooperative behaviors. Often, this new way of behavior and the accompanying mindset unlocks many stuck solutions, in new and delightfully surprising ways.

Take a look at your relationship and answer these questions for yourself:
Where do you engage in win/lose relating (also known as a power struggle)?
Where do you engage in win/win relating?

Embrace Positive Attitudes

We conclude this lesson with one very special step forward, and that is the *commitment to learning expanded orgasm as a process, and not as a goal.* Many people who learn expanded orgasm know there is always another great orgasmic experience waiting just around the corner, ready to top all the great experiences up until now. Clearly, while the goal of bigger, wetter, longer, yummier orgasms is understandably a great goal, most practitioners will tell you that for them, the journey is the reward. They are on a learning path for the long term.

Men who are great at delivering expanded orgasm tell us that the most important advice they have heard is: "Let go of your ego." Most men are raised in our society to produce and to perform relentlessly. In expanded orgasm, they are suddenly asked to "go with the flow," ask for directions, let go of their competitive natures, and do all manner of "unnatural male acts." Fortunately, these same men who dread the very thoughts mentioned above also come to enjoy expanding out of these limiting prescriptions of behavior, especially when they also find that in so doing, they are bringing their partners untold amounts of orgasmic pleasure.

Women committed to expanded orgasm are most likely to advise other women starting down the path to "Honor your true appetite for pleasure, connection, and sensual gratification." As one woman pointed out, "In hindsight, I saw that I was living in a small box when I could have been living in a palace. I was the only one keeping myself in there. By learning to really feel pleasure, and to see how it spread so much joy through me and also to others, I have learned to live my life fully. Now I want other women to have for themselves what I have been able to claim for myself."

As you can see, Sam and Linda, and Jason and Kelly have some significant issues in their relationships. But they also have some things in common:

- feelings of love, respect, and friendship for one another
- a fundamentally sound relationship, despite obvious areas for improvement
- commitment to address those areas that promise potential for improvement
- desire to learn the skills they need to deepen their sensual and sexual intimacy together
- desire to have even more fun together in all areas of their lives

This is not a long checklist, but it is an essential one. You may assume that all of the couples you encounter in this book share this checklist in common. You will hear about our work with Sam and Linda, Jason and Kelly, and others, all of whom we have assessed as ready and open. It is important for you to remember that we are not therapists. Our work is not about going from bad to good, but if you've already got it pretty good and want to get it way better, the expanded orgasm program is for you!

Activity #1: Buy a Journal

Once you have committed to undertaking the expanded orgasm program, we suggest that you buy a notebook in which to engage in personal exploration. Each partner should keep a separate journal. Most bookstores and many card shops carry attractive blank books or journals. You may wish to make an entire pleasurable afternoon out of selecting one that is just right for you. It is essential that you have a special place to practice the art of *self-disclosure*. Self-disclosure is a fancy way of saying: telling the truth about yourself. In your journal you will self-disclose to yourself. At other times you may choose to self-disclose to others like your partner.

Since sex is such a highly charged subject, people don't usually talk about it with other people. With whom can you talk in detail about your deepest secrets? This lack of conversation partners for your deepest, most intimate truths comes at a price to you. You lose, or never develop, the ability to talk to yourself about your sexual feelings and experiences. If you cannot communicate effectively with yourself, you will have a much harder time communicating with others. Self-communication opens the doors of intimacy and connection. For these reasons, keeping a journal is an essential element of the expanded orgasm training program.

Be sure to buy your own good-sized and attractive notebook that will invite you to outflow your every thought, no matter how subtle, sensible, grandiose, or outrageous! You will keep your own journal and should share from it only as you please.

What We've Explored

Our first step is a "get acquainted lesson" in which you begin the process of thinking about your sensual and sexual lives in greater detail, establish a baseline, and also make a thoughtful commitment to the expanded orgasm program. In this lesson, we ask more questions than we answer.

We ask you to spend some time getting used to the idea that you will be embarking on a new learning adventure that will most likely take you to some strange and exciting destinations. We caution you that at times the journey will not be easy; and that once on the journey, the trip itself will become even more important than the rewards you seek.

You can be confident that the rewards of both the process and outcomes of the journey will be many. You'll learn wonderful things about yourself and your partner. You'll connect in marvelous depths that maybe you haven't dared hope for. You'll reawaken the joy and passion and true promise of an intimate relationship.

And—oh, yes—you'll expand your capacity for orgasm far beyond your wildest dreams!

2

Step Two: Connect with Yourself and Your Partner

Katie, a client of ours, was unprepared for the impact of her first expanded orgasm—it swept her away into a world of mind-altering, heart-opening, soul-satisfying bliss. A flash of recognition announcing, "This is it!" rushed through her blood. A core part of her being had arrived home.

From the moment her partner Ron had touched her, Katie knew this was going to be an extraordinary experience. They had already connected in a powerful magnetic dance of heart, mind, and spirit. Eagerly, she pulled him closer. Their candle-lit bodies glowed with anticipation.

Within three strokes he had securely cupped her entire genital area, parted her lips gently with lubrication, and located one small spot on her clitoris already pulsing with pleasurable sensations. He anchored the pad of his forefinger here, and began making tiny, swirling strokes. Smooth, steady, and consistent, his energy entered hers, waking her with the sweetest of songs.

Incredibly, Ron latched on to her pleasure precisely as her body moved through one realm of sensation after another. Playfully, he created and then gratified her desires with a variety of tantalizing strokes. Ron calculated his banter for maximum effect, in one breath threatening to stop altogether, and in the next, promising to take Katie yet higher. With intoxicating confidence and uncanny accuracy, he told her when, how, and where she could expect each new peak of pleasure.

As Katie's body's resistance melted away, she opened more fully to the sensations that swirled and flowed within, until she surrendered totally. She entered a prolonged climactic state effortlessly, as if floating up and into a dream.

At some later point, Katie noticed a hand on her abdomen, in addition to the hand still anchored to her genitals. Slowly, she focused on Ron. He glowed with happiness as he brought Katie in for a landing, softly, safely, and lovingly. A new level of turn-on surged through her as she reached for, and felt, the details of his muscles, and skin, as never before.

Katie knew deeply that this was not a one-time experience. She had practiced—alone and with Ron—many hours to reach this suddenly surprising high point. Now, having been there, she knew she would be able to return here any time she wished.

How did Ron and Katie arrive here? They had learned a reliable method, and a secure knowledge of the path of return.

Are you ready to have this experience? This chapter is about the basics—it will launch you firmly on the path of expanded orgasm. We'll first make some essential distinctions among the different kinds of orgasm; this will help you clearly identify expanded orgasm. You'll learn some skills essential to feeling much more pleasure, and how to ensure that you and your partner can learn expanded orgasm in a safe and comfortable environment. Then, you'll discover powerful and effective ways to get exactly what gives you the maximum pleasure. Get ready for a lot of fun!

When I began my explorations, I learned I would need a map of the territory of expanded orgasm. I would need to figure out where I was currently in my pleasure, then the exact location on the map of my expanded orgasms. Finally, I would have to learn the most effective and most pleasurable routes back to those expanded orgasms.

How could I learn all this? The answer lay in making certain *distinctions*. I want to share these distinctions with you because when you begin to understand them, you will be well on your way to creating powerful expanded orgasms for yourself.

Orgasmic Distinctions

In order to clearly identify the different kinds of orgasms, you must learn to make *orgasmic distinctions*. Once you understand these distinctions, you will be able to identify what kind of orgasm you are having. If you can identify the direction in which you want to move, you can flow from wherever you are to expanded orgasm—or to regular or extended orgasm. But it all starts with knowing what is on the map.

When presented as textbook definitions alone, these distinctions seem a little dry. Therefore, for each, I give a factual definition, and a "feeling" definition as well. And for those of you who like to "see" things, I have added a visual definition, too.

Regular Orgasm

Factual explanation: An orgasm in which climax is the goal. The climax is usually a series of ten to twelve contractions over several seconds. This climax is commonly called "going over the edge." The climax feels extremely good, though brief, and there is often a physical and mental letdown period immediately afterwards. It can be an effective tension release and, of course, it can create a sense of bonding with your partner.

"Feeling" explanation: There you were on the dance floor. Suddenly, the DJ played your favorite song. Your partner swept you into his arms, and the two of you danced the perfect dance. At the very crescendo, he swirled you gracefully around, and the world around you transformed into a spinning sea of color, sound, and breeze. Your heart sang in joyful innocence. After several seconds he gradually brought you back into the regular cadence of the dance, which ended soon afterwards.

Visual interpretation: A single mountain peak. You are climbing higher and higher in sensation, until you go over the edge (climax), and then begin to descend down the other side.

Multiple Orgasm

Factual explanation: Multiple orgasms are a series of regular orgasms experienced over a short period of time. Usually there is only a partial letdown after each orgasm or climax, before climbing up again, to go over another peak. The peaks remain at about the same level of intensity.

"Feeling" explanation: Your partner tonight is terrific, a real Fred Astaire. He danced that perfect tango with you, only to sweep you off your feet soon afterwards, in a fantastic fox trot. Another winner! And then, the two of you melted into a tantalizing and seductive rumba. You could have won an international contest for that one. And then a whirling waltz, and then…could there be any more to dance from this point on? Yes, a final dance, the terrific, frantic, electrifying two-step that swept you up and down the dance floor so many times, you lost count. At last, you both rested. Tired but gratified, there were many swirling highlights to remember from this evening. You spend the next day wondering which dance was your favorite.

Visual interpretation: A range of mountain peaks. You go up and over the edge once, come down somewhat but not all the way, and then go up and over again (second climax). You climax to about the same altitude with each climax. At some point, you descend down the other side.

Extended Orgasm

Factual explanation: Extended orgasm is a single orgasm that maintains the level of pleasurable sensation at climax over a period of time. The climax is often rounded or flat like a plateau. There's no limit in length of time; however, one does need to build up the length of extended orgasm. With practice, many people plateau for an hour or more.

"Feeling" explanation: You decided to go to a new dance hall. The music seemed to go on and on, and soon, you fell into a sort of trance dance. Your partner led, until even that seemed irrelevant. You were in the dance of the music together. There was a certain point, a certain drumbeat, where you looked into one another's eyes, and time stopped. You catapulted into a space defined by the fires of a compelling pleasure filling every nook and cranny of your being. For some time, you swirled around, as if gravity no longer existed, and only your desires to touch one another kept the two of you together. After a very long time, you found yourself slowly feeling the floor beneath you, and the rhythms of the dance once again became something you moved to voluntarily.

Visual interpretation: A mountain with a very long plateau, like a great mesa. You climb up to the top. Instead of going over the edge in a short peak, you linger up there, at the edge, for a long while, before heading down the other side. For single extended orgasms, there is one mountain peak. For multiple extended orgasms, there are several mountains, each with its own plateau.

Expanded Orgasm

Factual explanation: Expanded orgasm is a path of expanding both sensual awareness and consciousness while receiving genital stimulation. Expanded orgasm uses one's own pathways of body, mind, emotion, and spirit to create maximum expansion opportunities. The goal (and focus) of receiving expanded orgasm is simply to feel as much of that pleasure as possible.

Think of filling a container in such a way that not only does the container become more full, *but also the container itself expands.* The distinguishing expansion is in the *sense of space*. There is the sense of one's entire body experiencing the orgasm, of reaching for an even larger being in which to put all that orgasmic pleasure. In contrast, regular orgasms are felt primarily in the physical domain.

Expanded orgasms are an added dimension of experience during regular, multiple, and extended orgasm. A regular orgasm, for example, can also be an expanded one. The expanded experience is felt in the body, mind, emotions, and spirit, all at once. The focus is on the entire experience, and not just going over the edge.

You can experience expanded orgasm immediately after the session begins, or later in the session. It starts when you become aware of the expansion occurring. Think of expanded orgasm as a domain, a state of being, a realm of consciousness, a condition of feeling everywhere.

When you enter the expanded orgasm state, two things occur simultaneously. First, you leave your normal everyday waking state, in which your mental state, your physical state, your emotional state, and your spiritual state are typically separate.

Second, you enter the expanded orgasm state, where all of these parts of yourself reconnect into one whole experience of yourself.

"Feeling" explanation: You start with mutual touching and the electricity between you spreads, coursing through your blood and nerves. You are dancing; it matters not where, or to what music. From the moment of contact, your beings merge. The energy of your combined connection fills your body, and expands beyond you two to fill the room. The awareness of all the sensations of sound, sight, touch, taste, and smell fill your dance with further delights. Whether you whirl, or pull away, only to return, you are locked in an energetic *pas de deux*, glued together in the rapture of the moment, until some unknown future you know not when. At some point, filled with the delights of this dance…or was it ten dances…you float back to the floor. You thank your partner with your broad, bright smile and notice him glowing with ecstasy as well.

Visual interpretation: Picture yourself receiving orgasmic stimulation at a central point of input, possibly the genitals. Then picture that sensation radiating out like a glowing ember over the rest of your body, in pulsating waves. Or, picture tossing stones, in rapid succession, into the same place in a still pond. The ripples extend and expand in waves, gently outward. With increasing numbers of stones, the waves build in energy, and extend increasingly further out, until the whole pond is filled with waves lapping up upon the shores.

Differences and Similarities between Extended and Expanded Orgasms

Extended orgasms are those in which the length of climax is extended in time. They can last a minute, an hour, or even longer (with training). An extended orgasm very often becomes an expanded one, as well.

An expanded orgasm might be an extended one; on the other hand, an expanded orgasm session might take an hour, but the climax time could be brief.

Let's try one other way to clarify. Classically, the orgasmic model based on Masters and Johnson's identifies four sequential phases of orgasm: 1) arousal; 2) plateau; 3) climax; and 4) resolution. This model applies to regular, multiple, and extended orgasm. However, in expanded orgasm, the phases do not occur sequentially, but simultaneously. Thus, you can become aroused, continue to build arousal while in a plateau state, and even climax during a plateau. You can see, then, that both kinds of orgasm can coexist.

Other Orgasms

Women can experience orgasm anywhere in their body and mind. Non-genital parts of the body can experience orgasms—nipples, anus, curve of the neck, face—really anywhere the women has allowed herself or trained herself to feel orgasmic sensations. Women who can feel other-than-genital orgasms learned by connecting genital orgasms with sensations in another body area. Then, once the connection is established, the genital stimulation is no longer essential.

Women can have orgasms solely in the mind as well. In fact, the biggest sex organ in the body is the brain. With our minds, we can fantasize about orgasms, we can remember orgasms, and we can even create orgasms—consider a hot, wet dream. And, some women readily go into full-blown orgasmic states without touching themselves, and remain in this state for prolonged periods (this is something you might learn to do by applying the program in this book).

Perhaps you are one of these women, and perhaps not, or perhaps not yet. Remember that your entire body, brain, emotions, and mind are constructed to be capable of experiencing powerful orgasms.

As you read, I invite you to maintain an open awareness of what is going on in your body. Has reading any of this information so far made you tingle or shiver? Can you feel sensations now in your genitals? Would you like to feel some sensations, even if you haven't yet? What sensations would you like to feel, if you could feel whatever you desired, in any moment?

The point is that by putting more attention on how your body responds to "pleasurable offers" such as those I just mentioned, you will learn to refine the marvelous sensing abilities you were born with. As you read, notice how you feel in your body. The more you begin to notice the sensations you do have, the more these sensations will intensify, and the more orgasmic you will become. Yes, it really can be this simple.

Explore for yourself how many parts of your body are capable of generating orgasmic energy! Lips, nipples, the nape of the neck, the creases under the knees...the list goes on from here! In these ten lessons, we will arbitrarily focus on clitorally originated orgasms. The topic of giving and receiving clitorally originated expanded orgasm with a partner is large enough as it is. You are certainly encouraged to use all information presented here as a basis for further explorations of other related expanded orgasm on your own, since there will be plenty of information crossover.

What Kind of Orgasm Are You Having?

If you are not sure what types of orgasms you have, don't be alarmed. Many women haven't verbalized much about their experiences. They wonder:

Did I have an orgasm (especially if it wasn't a "standard" one, complete with contractions)?

Am I orgasmic?

Did what I feel really count as an orgasm?

Focusing on questions such as these will help you "take inventory" of your current orgasmic capacity. Yet, women who focus on having a certain kind of orgasm during the experience risk disappointment when their goals are not met. They may have failed to appreciate the wonderful feelings that they were having, and may have short-circuited the potential to experience what they most desired.

Of course, appreciation alone is not enough for a woman to enter expanded orgasm. Clearly, her partner still has to be touching her correctly. And she must know how to "activate the circuitry." We will discuss many actions to take to create and enhance expanded orgasm. Still, genuine appreciation for what you are feeling in any moment will always help you reach expanded orgasm faster and stay there longer. Since you enter the expanded orgasm domain through letting go of goals (or, more exactly, to have only the goal of feeling as much pleasure as possible), and appreciating fully the experience you are having, you will benefit far more with this strategy. Classify your orgasms, but only as a learning platform, and only after the experience is complete.

Activity #2: Journal Your Sexual Experiences and Begin Sharing

Once you have acquired your journal, you can record your orgasmic explorations. The more you can put your feelings into words, the better you will be at asking for what you want.

Women, take some time to record in your journal your answers to the following questions. Allow yourself at least a half hour, so that you can put some depth into your responses. And please let your poet out! Orgasms can be written about, sung—even made into poetry.

What kinds of orgasms have you primarily experienced?
What has been the range of your orgasmic experiences?
What has been your favorite kind of orgasm, and why?
What would you like to experience that would be new for you?
If you have had expanded orgasm, can you describe it? How were you breathing?
Were you relaxed or did you tense your muscles? Spreading the sensation?
Focusing on pleasure?

Share these observations with your partner. Men, you can answer these same question, from the viewpoint of what you would like to give a woman. In addition, you might wish to record your orgasmic experiences.

While you may find it hard or even somewhat scary to verbalize your experiences, proceed anyway. Anything the two of you do to increase the level of positive dialog at this point will help tremendously to open the doors of communication about orgasm further, and create an excellent foundation for later activities.

Here is an excerpt that Kelly wrote: "Over the course of my adult life, I have had a significant range of orgasms. One memorable orgasm felt like a stratospheric cloud stretching over half the sky; then in another one I climbed until I was totally sated, but I didn't go over the edge. Another time, I exploded within three minutes of my partner's touching me. That was really exciting.

"Many of my orgasms have ended with one big climax, although some have had smaller climaxes along the way; then they end the way a leaf floats from a tree, gliding effortlessly and gracefully to a final dance down. I think my most favorite ones have been the real explosions, though I have really enjoyed orgasms of all flavors immensely.

"With Jason, mostly I have had regular and multiple orgasms, not expanded ones. He usually takes about ten minutes to get me going, and about another ten minutes to bring me over the edge. I want to start experiencing more expanded orgasms. I think I have only had about five of them so far with him. Of course, we've only been married six months, so we need more time to learn about each other. But I would like for him to learn about the range of what is possible and really explore the range. I want them all. I want to have cloud-gasms, fire-gasms, water-gasms, you-name-them, I want them. And I want Jason to give them to me.

"I suspect that I could somehow take more control over whether I expand or not. I need to decide for myself that I am going to expand more, and then let this expansion take over. When I do expand, my breathing becomes very rhythmic and I can feel electricity spread from my body to Jason's, and then back again, in an endless loop. I live for moments like that."

Jason was intimidated at first by this exercise. He was not used to verbalizing about orgasmic experiences, and felt somewhat awkward about having to write about it. To ensure progress, we asked him to promise to write a few lines, which he did. They read: "I am not sure what kind of orgasms I give Kelly, since this is all new to us. I think we can start noticing more, now that we have had the lesson. Actually, the explosive regular orgasms seem easy to create. I can support Kelly in feeling more from the first stroke. I can remind her gently to breathe. Naturally, I want her to have all the types of experiences she says she wants—but I don't know how to extend my performance yet."

How willing are you to share what you have written with your partner? Kelly was reluctant to share her journal record with Jason, but sensed that if they were really to benefit from the program, they needed to establish an open and honest tone. She decided to read her entry to him, in our presence.

At first Jason felt uncomfortable hearing that Kelly had orgasmic experiences that he had not produced. He asked us whether he was justified in feeling inadequate and uncomfortable.

We pointed out that Jason was at the first of many crossroads on the expanded orgasm path. He could choose to focus on either positive or negative aspects of Kelly's communication. Since he had expressed a negative interpretation, we asked him to give us the positive one.

Jason admitted that rather than feel upset, he could be deeply honored that Kelly wanted to create these profound types of experiences with him. When he said that, we asked him to look at Kelly's face. Her eyes were teary from joy. With that feedback, Jason chose to focus on the positive interpretation of what Kelly had revealed. He then volunteered to read his entry to her. As each expressed their desire to create a more orgasmically exciting life, they felt a surge of warmth and turn-on.

This exercise is significant on several levels. First, it enables you to locate where you are starting in your expanded orgasm training. It's like taking your own personal starting inventory. Second, it encourages you to verbalize your experiences. The more verbal you can become, the more power you have to define and ask for what you want. We cannot overemphasize the value verbalization skills add to your expanded orgasm learning program. Finally, this exercise invites you to set a standard of honesty and self-disclosure about your experiences.

Create a Space for Honest, Playful Communication

Remember the sandboxes you played in as a five-year-old? You entered them just to play. You explored your world, alone or with friends. There was no real right or wrong to what you did. You just played, learned, and discovered. If you wanted your communal sandcastle to have an extra tower, you didn't worry about your partner's ego. You just added one on.

Imagine this: you are alone together at last. He pulls you in, passionately, and begins sensually kissing you all over. You reel from the waves of ecstasy streaming through you. Soon, his hand reaches to awaken your private areas, lovingly, gently. You want to merge so much, your bodies cry out in their longing to melt together. A nagging little problem interrupts your reverie. He is touching you in the wrong place. What do you do? If you are like most women, you either do nothing, hoping that he will correct his positioning, or you move his hand over to the correct area. Once you move his hand, however, then what? Has it registered? If not, perhaps you move your hips. Somehow, you don't want to break the moment of lovemaking. What can you possibly do?

If you were to ask me, I would advise: do nothing! Not now, anyway. Not at this moment of making love. Not unless you can ask for what you want in way that he can win with it. For now, his hunting and groping, and a little positive attitude on your part (at least he wants to be with you) are the most you can reasonably ask for.

However, the next day, I would strongly urge you to set up a program of deliberate training in communication and learning. Together, and with plenty of advance notice, you can enact such a program by *making sandbox dates,* so named in order to emphasize a space created for fun, learning, and play.

Activity #3: Set Up the "Sandbox"

Here's how to set up your sandbox. As you begin your expanded orgasm practice, use your sandbox dates to try some of these activities:

Take turns. Show your partner how *you* do something you enjoy. Then have your partner copy this same move. For example, the woman can show the man how she touches herself in various ways. Can the man replicate what she is doing? Experiment with one variable: speed, pressure, or location, for example. Explore the limits. Suppose you choose pressure. Go very, very lightly (feeling as much as you possibly can). Increase the pressure all the way to very heavy pressure (the limits are where it stops being pleasurable to the receiver). Notice the effects of your shifts in pressure and discuss them.

Practice dialog. One person talks, then the other. Maintain a steady stream of communication. Notice the effects on your overall pleasure.

Let one partner do all the talking. Try to maintain a steady stream of conversation. Notice the overall effect this has on your pleasure. Playing in the sensual sandbox demystifies the process of communication during sex. In your lovemaking you will find you have a rapidly increasing range of pleasurable options.

Create a safe play-space in which the goals are pleasure, learning, research, and communication about sexual experiences.

"Bracket": declare a specific time to be devoted solely toward this activity. For example, from 8:00 P.M. to 8:45 P.M.

Identify deliberate goals for the session. For example, genital touching using only very light pressure, or, talking continuously while touching, or exploring her G-spot.

Agree to leave all egos and issues of past and future outside the time brackets.

Understand that this is a very different activity from lovemaking. Lovemaking may follow this activity if you both choose.

Be on the lookout for those "break points" where you feel stumped as to how to proceed further. Often, going beyond this point is where you will gain your most powerful lessons.

Appreciate your partner and yourself for your courage and dedication to communication and learning. Be delighted you have committed to pursuing these goals as a team.

From this point forth, we will encourage all expanded orgasm training to take place within the context of the sandbox.

Allen and I have sandbox dates all the time. He loves them so much that he almost always wants to set up the next one right after one is over. Many of our sensual breakthroughs occur during sandbox dates. It is not uncommon that at some point during the date, we identify a place where we haven't fully explored our combined potential for creating maximum pleasure. In fact it is often a moment where we both want to quit! *That is the worst moment to stop.* Knowing the cycle as intimately as we now do allows us to continue with a sense of humor. We are simply at the "break" point. We will take a small break, have a glass of water, and then continue our sandbox date. When we persist like this, we almost always learn something dramatically new, and end the date on a high note. The last time this happened, he was experimenting with when to start adding variety to a foundation of basic strokes. We wanted to know how long to keep using a certain basic back-and-forth stroke before switching to a series of eight strokes of various types: circles, ellipses, or sideways strokes (I call them windshield wiper strokes). How would this switch time be evident? Would it be he, or I, who would accurately ask for the switch? A few times, I had asked for the switch from base building to variety (we will cover these principles in more detail in Step Four). But, each time he made the switch, my energy dropped.

After three attempts, I didn't feel I had the energy to engage in another round of investigation.

We were both feeling rather dejected by our failure to succeed with our stated research mission. This was the clear sign that we had reached our *break point*. I got up and changed the music. When I returned, Allen offered to continue. This time, he and I simultaneously identified the exact moment in which to make the switch. My energy climbed much higher and the switch gave us the breakthrough in pleasure we were hoping for. We ended the date feeling positively jubilant.

We strongly encourage you to plan sandbox dates. You may set the topic in advance or when you start. You will get ideas for sandbox dates throughout this book. Sandbox dates make perfect sense. We can teach you techniques, and you will find many throughout this book. But you will discover more about you and your partner from this process of self-discovery than you will learn from anyone else. Use this book, and all other information, as subject matter for your sandbox dates. Then you can optimize what information you wish to incorporate into your expanded orgasm training.

Ask for What You Want

Early on in my expanded orgasm training, I discovered a puzzling situation. When I was enjoying what my partner was doing to me, I could ask for changes in a variety of ways. I could ask politely, or I could belt out commands: *Go lighter! Don't stop! Stop! Move an inch to the left!* And my partner would enthusiastically comply. However, when I was not enjoying the experience he was giving me, no matter how nicely I asked, my requests would come across like the barking of a platoon leader: *Take this request under serious advisement now, whether you like it or not!*

Only one solution really ever works, and that is to be genuine in the appreciation you give your partner. The more you as the receiver can find a way to enjoy what you are given—even if there is considerable room for improvement—the bigger your partner's ears will grow to listen to the changes you ask for.

Is it any wonder that couples can read a dozen books on technique and never create much more pleasure? Books on technique impart strategies, but they don't change the nature of the game. Manipulation, scorekeeping, and second-guessing run the show. In a chess game, the winner experiences the pleasure of victory, not the pleasure of connection. Often, the physical pleasure is sharply curtailed. Power-struggle sex leaves the players hungrier than ever for any morsel of real engagement and connection.

Do you ask for what you want during sex? Or do you edit your requests? If you do edit, then you may be relating to your partner more like an opponent in a chess game rather than as a lover cooperating to create the most winning mutual experience. *In chess-game sex,* a request is not a request…it's a move. First one partner moves. The other evaluates the move and countermoves. The desired outcome is not pleasure, but power and victory.

Let's view the counterpoint to "power struggle" sex. (Consider expanded orgasm training as just one of many wonderful love-making practices.) *In lovemaking sex,* pleasure is the goal, and honesty (self-disclosure) is the way to get there. This honesty may run against everything you've ever learned about how to enjoy sex with a partner. Most of us have not been raised to be honest about pleasure. Therefore, we must override the conditioning in us that says, "Don't reveal your hand (and expose your vulnerability to the 'enemy'). Don't give him (or her) a chance to hurt you. Don't look stupid, or unappreciative, or demanding." The list of what *not to do* is endless. But you cannot weave an ecstatic lovemaking connection from the not-to-dos.

Sam and Linda were powerfully affected by this topic. Linda, usually a good communicator, made a list of the rules that determined when and what she would say to Sam. For example:

"Don't give a better compliment than I receive."

"Don't give more than one compliment to Sam for each one I get."

"Measure Sam's compliment against the last one I got."

"If I really want to gush with exuberant feelings, only gush a little at a time so as not to reveal the full extent of my emotions."

"Act indifferent if I want Sam to give me more pleasure (under the theory that this will motivate him to extra effort)."

Many people, like Linda, are surprised in learning expanded orgasm at how difficult it can be to break the habit of making love the way you might play chess or even wage war. Powerful people are used to being in control elsewhere in their lives. Suddenly, when asked to give a simple positive acknowledgment to their partner, they freeze. Such an act requires them to expose an inch of themselves, and goes against their survival instincts. And yet, this same act of vulnerability opens the door to greater love and pleasure...as well as to those memorable, soul-satisfying expanded orgasms. To really practice expanded orgasm, you must learn to shift from the power struggle, wage-war mindset, into a lovemaking, love-creating mindset.

As part of her commitment to greater self-disclosure, Linda wanted to show her "rules" to Sam. We encouraged her to think about the rules she wished that she and Sam would use. She wrote the following:

"Whoever appreciates the most, wins."

"Whoever appreciates the winner wins, too, since everyone can win together."

"The more love each of us gives, the more each of us will have to give."

"The more pleasure each of us gives, the more each of us will be able to receive."

Sam was uncomfortable with so much focus on feelings. This list sounded somehow threatening to him, though he could not say exactly why. We asked Sam to come up with a list of the rules he wanted to play by. He thought carefully before responding. "I guess I want the rules I wrote myself. Linda was pretty accurate in writing them down. This may sound odd, but I like the first set of rules. They've worked up until now and I am comfortable with them."

But have they really worked?

We asked Sam to reconsider the motives that led to his taking the expanded orgasm training. He had said he wanted to expand his sensual life, and to increase the pleasure he and Linda shared together. We asked him to evaluate how effective the first set of rules had been in achieving these goals. Sam agreed to think carefully about both sets of rules over the coming week, and to see if he might update his thinking.

Linda looked both upset and relieved at the same time. She promised to continue thinking about her motives. How committed was she to playing by a new set of rules? What changes might she have to make in order to live by them?

The Power of Positive Acknowledgments

Giving and receiving positive acknowledgments is the fastest way to make that shift from power struggle to lovemaking. What is a positive acknowledgment?

It is simply a statement of the good you feel or felt at a specific time and place. When given a positive acknowledgment, your partner responds with a simple "thank you" and acknowledges that he or she has heard you fully.

"I really appreciated it when you agreed to set up the date this afternoon."

"I think you look very sexy in that black silk bathrobe."

"I felt loved when you stroked my hand this morning."

If this all seems seriously simplistic, that's great. Hopefully, you feel comfortable giving and receiving acknowledgments with no strings attached. However, we have had clients who have had serious problems moving beyond this very basic level without extra attention. They have had to unlearn power struggle patterns of relating, and even acknowledging, that they have taught themselves over many years.

Activity #4: Trade Acknowledgments

Practice trading acknowledgments with your partner. Use any subject: housekeeping, work, family, physical appearance. Try to include a range of time frames (including the present) and subject matters. Give, then receive, five acknowledgments in a row. The receiving partner should say and feel "thank you" to each acknowledgment given. You can continue this by trading acknowledgments back and forth for several cycles if you wish.

Typical acknowledgments might be:

"I loved it when you noticed how busy I was and took out the recycling for me this morning."

"That color red in your dress really brings out the gorgeous color of your lips."

"You made me feel so special when you gave me a kiss before going to sleep."

"Thanks for asking me if I wanted a hug just now."

Once you have mastered the form of acknowledgments, practice giving them just for the pleasure of giving. Give them liberally, with no expectation of acknowledgment in return. This act of pure giving will shift you immediately into the lovemaking mindset. You will come to feel yourself as full and flowing over with "good."

Giving acknowledgments is a cornerstone of expanded orgasm training. You can practice this exercise for the rest of your lives. Here are some of the benefits you will enjoy:

- Each time you acknowledge, you tell the truth about how you feel. You and the other person know where you stand.
- Each positive acknowledgment reveals something about who you are, what you want, enjoy, need, hope, desire, appreciate, and notice, at some past or present time.
- Each acknowledgment sets in motion a process that takes you out of strategic (chess game) sex, and into pleasurable sex.
- People tend to want to be around people who acknowledge them and are having a good time!

Experiment with how many heartfelt acknowledgments you can give to your partner, when pleasure is your goal.

One day last month, an expanded orgasm practitioner named, Annette called with this story:

"Phil called me from work and started raving about the date we had the evening before. For the life of me I could not remember what date he was talking about. He went on and on about how good I felt, how responsive I was, how beautiful I looked, and how much fun he had. At first, embarrassed, and wondering if my memory had finally gone completely, I said nothing. But finally I figured it out. Phil was referring to the fifteen minutes of cuddling we had done before going to sleep. I had no idea I had given him so much pleasure. I made a mental note: If he is going to enjoy it this much, cuddle more with Phil, immediately!"

Express Genuine Acknowledgment

Here are some of my favorite sensual acknowledgments. Please feel free to use them liberally. The more you acknowledge, the more you will develop your own personal vocabulary. In the meantime, remember, even the simplest acknowledgment will sound heaven-sent to a partner eager to please you.

"Mmmmmm.............."

"I love what you're doing right now."

"Your touch is so sexy right now."

"I love the way you feel trembling deep inside me."

"I can feel you reaching right down to my core."

"You really know how to make me feel fabulous."

"Whatever you do, keep doing it!"

"Thanks for giving me such wonderful attention"

Sam brightened considerably when we went through this part of the course. "I would pay Linda to say just three of those comments on any date!"

Linda looked uncomfortable. "How am I supposed to say things I don't feel?"

The question of how Linda was going to start feeling more pleasure from any kind of touch from Sam was significant at this point. Instinctively, as a woman, I knew that Linda had some work to do in developing her own capacities to feel pleasure. That training would come soon enough. I encouraged Sam and Linda to practice giving acknowledgments while trading non-genital massages for now.

Use Acknowledgment to Ask for What You Want

Now that you are mastering acknowledgments you can combine it with requests for what you want your partner to do with you sexually.

In order to make requests that are sure to boost, not damage, your partner's ego, we recommend the following simple three-part format:

"That feels really good." (Or some similar *genuine* appreciation for something your partner is doing right.)

"Would you please go a little _____ (softer, harder, slower, faster, to the left, to the right, higher, lower, etc.)?"

(Wait until they make the change.) "Thanks, that feels good (or wonderful, or really nice, or whatever positive words you can say about the change)."

Why is this a winning formula?

You sandwich your requests in acknowledgments. If your partner is feeling that he is producing a good experience for you, he will be much more open to learning about what he could be doing even better.

You are only asking for a *small* change in any given moment. People are likelier to respond to requests for small as opposed to large changes; it implies that they "weren't too far off" in what they were doing to give pleasure, and that it won't be too difficult to satisfy the request. You are letting him know that the small change has contributed even more to your pleasure.

You are more likely to engage in more honest communications when you know that your requests are pleasurable.

Ask for Feedback

The alternative structure for giving requires the giver to ask the receiver what feels the best. Here is the format:

"Would you like me to go a little _____ (softer, harder, slower, faster, to the left, to the right, higher, lower, etc.)?"

I recommend that when asking change-oriented questions like these, use those that elicit a yes or no. Questions such as "How am I doing?" or "Do you like this?" take the receiver out of the experience.

Imagine for yourself: your partner is giving you pleasure, and asking you yes/no questions. You are slowly relaxing your mind, and starting to feel more with every stroke. You are melting, going into a realm of pleasure. It feels so good to be climbing this ladder of sensations. It's not a straight climb up; your partner has to use exquisite biofeedback sensing to figure out what next best way to take you higher.

Suddenly you are asked: "How do you like the pleasure I am giving you?"

This question may come as a shock. Suddenly the mind is engaged. *What should I say? Should I be diplomatic? Lie? Okay, I'll be perfectly honest. I am climbing, and it is feeling progressively better.*

Even in this fairly idyllic scenario, you will have been taken out of your feelings. It will take a moment, or two, or maybe even ten, to get back out of your mind and into a climbing feeling state. Not all scenarios are so immediately pleasurable. You may be wanting or needing some time to relax into the experience. Now, it takes even longer to think about the appropriate response and to re-enter that warm, climbing feeling state.

The simple solution to this potential problem is for the giver of pleasure to avoid asking questions that don't evoke a yes or no. If, as the receiver, you are given this type of question, just say, "I'd like to stay with yes and no questions."

Activity #5: Communicate Through Massage

When learning how to honestly ask for and acknowledge pleasure, start on non-genital body areas like the arms, legs, feet, hands, face, scalp, back, or chest. It's much easier to ask someone to rub our elbow or our ears a little more gently than it is to request a change in genital stimulation. (If you don't believe me, experiment for yourself!)

Set up a sandbox date in which you and your partner give each other non-genital massages. Practice asking for what you want as receiver, and asking what your partner wants, while you are the giver. Both partners should take turns as giver and receiver of massages in a single sandbox session.

Ask for a steady stream of changes, even if you are enjoying what you are receiving. Remember that the goal is to improve your communication skills. Many people are so hungry for pleasurable touch that they either forget to pursue the communication aspect of this exercise or they are afraid to break the magic of the moment.

To prevent partner "space-out/bliss-out," agree in advance that each of you may coach the other in doing this exercise correctly. Arrange a separate date to enjoy each other's massages in silence, if you're having that much fun!

This exercise is an important one. It is much easier to communicate about a non-genital experience than it is to communicate about sexual desires. If you can get comfortable with general sensual communication, you'll find yourself communicating with far greater ease about your sexual wants and needs. You may wish to do this exercise several times before proceeding.

Fake It until You Make It

There. We finally used the four-letter "f" word. "F" stands for "fake," of course. In the first few years of learning expanded orgasm, I trained myself to notice when I faked orgasm and to put an end to this unproductive practice. From the school of bad habits, I had learned that I could psyche myself into feeling more by making lots of pleasurable sounds, deep breathing, and other displays of orgasmic pleasure. The problem was, faking never felt as good as a real bliss pool of increasingly hot, juicy feelings.

Faking can increase feeling temporarily, but it also prevents you from giving the accurate feedback your partner needs to give you optimum pleasure. Ideally, give feedback in the moment you realize you want something different.

However, when used deliberately, faking does have some positive value. In order to get value from faking, you must learn to psyche yourself into experiencing pleasure, and yet stay in touch with yourself enough to know the difference between faking and real feeling. Sometimes a little self-psyching can get you going in the right direction. Just stay in touch with what you are really feeling, and then use faking to move in your desired direction ("fake it 'til you make it"). Then you use faking for your pleasure.

Activity #6: Count the Ways You Fake It

Next time you are practicing in the sandbox with your partner, notice the following. How honest are you? Where did you hold back from saying what you were feeling? Where did you fake it for your own benefit? Where did you fake it and avoid honest communication? Remember to journal your responses.

Kelly noticed how much faking she had been doing with Jason. She reported in her journal: "I noticed that when I started faking my feelings, I did so in order to extend the good feelings, so my intentions were honorable. I wasn't aware of my actions; the faking was practically a reflex that came into play when the true feelings started to fade.

"Faking had a good side and a bad side to it. I'd extend the feelings by breathing more heavily, and moaning more. I'd put on a convincing show for Jason. However, neither one of us could tell you exactly when Jason stopped doing what felt good. At some point I felt like the Road Runner after he had run way past the cliff. Suddenly I'd looked down and there was no support of pleasurable contact underneath me. With no continuing stream of good feelings, and just my faking, I'd deflate. Then I just lay there, totally flat, without any really good sensations to enjoy.

"Jason would be thoroughly mystified. After learning about faking, I vowed to myself that I would have far more attention on my true feelings. Since that time I have come to see how ingrained my faking habit has been. It will take time for me to learn to fake only when I am sure it will take me further in the direction I want to go."

Men can learn to identify when a woman is faking her pleasure. We will cover more on this topic later. For now, men, begin to attune yourself to how you are feeling while giving your partner pleasure. If at any time, you begin to wonder if she is feeling less, rather than more, ask her if she would like some other stroke or pressure. You too will train yourself to have maximum integrity while giving expanded orgasm to your partner. And, you'll become more attuned to your ability to "notice where she's at."

Women: Experiment with deliberately faking pleasure. Notice whether you can use faking to actually feel more pleasure by hamming it up. Also notice what happens when you withhold honest communication and fake it in order to create a substitute. Repeat this several times until you feel comfortable identifying exactly how honest you are being in any given moment.

Men: See if you can tell exactly when your partner begins faking her pleasure. Ask her when you think you have felt her faking her pleasure to see if she verifies your intuition. Turn this into a fun experience, and open an ongoing inquiry.

Get to Know the Female Anatomy

Pleasure is the goal, and truthful sharing is the path to the goal of expanded orgasm. The more you know about your partner's experience, the easier it will be to achieve this goal. With this reminder, let us talk about a woman's genital area.

Consider these questions, alone and with your partner:

Women, when is the last time you got out a flashlight and mirror and took a tour of your private parts? Men, when is the last time you got a really good look?

Do you have a nice, loving name for this area? (I do, but since everyone's naming tastes vary so greatly, I will use the word "vagina" here, even if it sounds a little clinical.)

Is your vagina something you treasure, like a secret garden or great feast?

Please consider these questions seriously. No lecture is going to change overnight the feelings you have carried about a woman's genitals all your life.

Most likely, unless you have had some sensuality training, you will find you could have more positive answers to these questions. Wouldn't it be nice, for example, if you really did think of your vagina as a lush, fertile garden?

A Visit to a Woman's Genital Area

A major barrier to positive feelings in a woman's genital area is mystery. The vagina is often hard to see. The clitoris may be hard to locate. The whole area, surrounded in folds of flesh and mounds of hair, may seem intimidating. Ending the mystery is an excellent way to warm up genuinely to the landscape and the beauty of this territory. We strongly encourage men and women to become intimately familiar with the woman's genital area. I encourage you to privately journal your thoughts on the following questions, and, for extra credit, set up a sandbox with your partner to disclose and explore.

Women, how would you like to think of your genital area?

Men, how would you like to think of a woman's genital area?

Linda observed the following:

"I had never examined my genital areas carefully. I was afraid to discover something I didn't like or want to see. Maybe the skin around my genitals would be slimy, or feel like a slippery fish. Sam never looked there for long, so I figured that part of me must not be very attractive.

"I was assuming the whole experience of looking at myself was going to be unpleasant. I also knew that if I did nothing to reverse this attitude, certainly I wasn't going to like what I discovered. So before I even looked, I spent some time visualizing my private parts as something I would be proud to visit.

"What would they be? A mysterious fern cavern, dark, wet, lush, and moist? Or perhaps a seashell, vibrant with hues of opalescent pinks, pearly whites, and glistening rouges? I finally settled on being an exotic feast. My clitoris was a plump grape, my inner and outer lips succulent pear slices, and my insides, like the inside of a perfect melon. Suddenly, I wanted to visit myself. I spread myself out, with a mirror in hand, and stared in fascination at everything I could find. I thought I was so beautiful. Just looking helped me feel certain that my partner would also enjoy the chance to admire my luscious platter of delectables."

Activity #7: Learn More about Her Genitals

Remember, for all your exercises, we encourage you to set up a conceptual sandbox as a first step. Then, get a flashlight or other strong lighting source. Spend some time relaxing. When the mood seems right, "play doctor."

Did you know that very often a woman cannot identify many of the sensations she feels in her genital areas? A man can be stroking her, in a precise location, and in a precise way, and she will not be able to tell whether he is on the left or right side, or top or bottom of the clitoral area. Sometimes, she will even find it difficult to determine whether a man is giving her circular or up-and-down strokes! (You are really going to have to try this out for yourself to believe it.)

Men and women: Look carefully at the parts of her vagina. Explore them with a slow and soft touch. Name the parts. You should locate and name the outer lips, the inner lips, the mons pubis, the clitoris, the urethra, the introitus, and the anus.

To the partner, these are some of the types of movements that a woman can experience:

Location of touch: right side, left side, top of clitoris, bottom of clitoris.

Types of movement: moving up and down, diagonally, elliptically, and with circular strokes.

Touch her in different ways. Identify what kinds of touches you are giving her.

Then, continue to give her a range of touches and see if she can identify what you have done.

This exercise can be performed several times. The more you do it, the more a woman will develop a sense of where you are and what you are doing in her genital area. It will make it easier for her to request changes when she knows where you are now.

We encourage you in this exercise to use your hands. However, in a more advanced session, you might use your tongue or penis.

In this exercise, Sam and Linda found lots of ways to be sexually intimate and have fun at the same time. This fun was a welcome change to their old behavior patterns.

Linda was stunned to discover that she could not distinguish when Sam was giving her circles or up-and-down strokes. Nor could she tell whether Sam was on her right side or left side while touching her. After several times, Linda's guess rate became far more accurate. In the process, she learned not only where Sam was, but also how to ask where she wanted him to place his finger next. She delighted in playing "the guessing game" and in improving her accuracy.

Engorgement

When a woman becomes aroused, her pelvic and genital areas fill with blood. This is called *engorgement.* This is the same phenomenon that makes a man's penis hard, and we all know how much men enjoy having a firm penis. For both sexes, engorged genitals are capable of feeling more. Thus, a man will always want to get his partner engorged.

An engorged clitoris can be three times larger than an unengorged clitoris. Since an unengorged clitoris is often quite small, it can be hard to pleasure. Thus, by engorging the clitoris first, a man makes it easier to find the clitoris, and the woman feels more pleasure. Men, think about what happens to your ability to feel pleasure when you are engorged. Do you need any more reason to always engorge her before proceeding with stimulation?

Activity #8: Study Engorgement

Set a goal of studying engorgement. Notice what unengorged genitals look like.

Men: Repeat the exercise of "playing doctor," having your partner identifying a wide variety of your genital strokes. This time, however, practice verbal acknowledgments while you investigate. Tell her exactly what part you are touching. Tell her every stroke you are making. Notice as you do this how her level of engorgement changes.

Her inner lips will begin to swell. Often one side will begin to change size first. Notice this and comment. For example:

"Now I am touching your outer right lip, near the top. I'm moving down slowly, toward your introitus. Now I am at the introitus. You're starting to lubricate. I see little glistening drops of moisture just starting to form. You look most inviting. Now I am going up your left inner lip. Your left inner lip has become larger than your right lip was, starting out. It is puffy and soft. Looks very inviting!"

She may begin having genital contractions, which look like subtle or not-so-subtle clenching motions in her labia. Some women naturally contract more than others. Not all women are aware of any, some, or all contractions they are having. Starting out, if she is having contractions, they may be too subtle for her to feel, but easy for you to see visually. Note: contractions are not necessary for the experience of pleasure. Notice and enjoy them if and when they show up, but don't worry if you don't see them, either.

The coloring of her clitoris, lips, and introitus will also change from a light pink to a duskier rose. Eventually, as she becomes very swollen, they will often be dark red, or even purplish in color. Notice her color changes, her contractions, and anything else you can. Comment as you notice. A steady stream of comments is the most effective.

"Your clitoris is glistening like a pretty pink pearl. It is coming out to play."

"Your lips are getting softer and fuller. They feel nice and cushiony."

"Your outer lips are about 50 percent more engorged than when we started just ten minutes ago."

"The color of your inner lips has gone from a dark pink to a deep red."

"I see you are starting to contract very gently. There's one now."

"There's another contraction. This one was stronger, too."

"Your clitoris has tripled in size since when I started touching you. I find that very attractive."

Men, when you put this kind of attention of a woman's genitals, you are complimenting her and approving of her at a very deep level. You are supporting her in feeling sexually desirable and deserving of all the pleasure she can possibly consume.

Women, notice how it feels to be receiving so much feedback and attention. Communicate with your partner the pleasure you feel in receiving these gifts.

"A pink pearl…what a lovely image."

"Engorged? Already? That's great to know. Thank you."

"Yes, I can feel my outer lips swelling to reach for the wonderful sensations you are providing me. Please continue."

"I am so enjoying all your descriptions of what is going on. You are focusing my attention on my pleasure in the nicest way."

"Thanks for noticing those contractions. I didn't feel the contractions, but I love to know when they are starting."

By talking in this way, ladies, you are rewarding your man for his actions. He will want to give you increasingly more pleasurable attention when your sandbox date starts out this enthusiastically.

What We've Explored

In Step Two you have learned the basic distinctions necessary to identify expanded orgasm and to distinguish expanded orgasm from other kinds of orgasm. We discussed the *sandbox*—a valuable setting for safely and comfortably learning about pleasure. We have also learned some simple communication skills and taken a tour of the female genitals. Remember that the more precisely you communicate what you are experiencing and what you want your partner to do, the easier it is for him to give you what you want. We also have discussed why behavior you might use successfully in the rest of your daily life may not serve you in your expanded orgasm training, and we have suggested ways for you to interact to further your expanded orgasm goals the most quickly.

With the foundation of these skills laid, it's time to create the most effective mindset for expanded orgasm.

3

Step Three: Build the Right Mindset

The moment you "set the date" for an expanded orgasm, you start to open a door. In your mind, you must prepare to leave the old room and enter the new one. This preparation, or transition, occurs when you begin thinking about the date— whether it is five minutes or five days from now.

The "room" or "space" metaphor is an apt one. Consider that for most of our lives we inhabit a room that is a like the stage in a theater. In it we play out the dramas of work and play, family, survival, and competition. We have been living in this room all our lives and will continue to live here until we leave. Most of us live here by default—without having deliberately selected this very place to be.

The room we enter to practice expanded orgasm is going to be quite different. We will select and design this room in advance of entering it. In so doing, we will create for ourselves the optimal *mindset* for enjoying this exquisite experience.

You have certainly made many transitions in your life. Consider:

When you left a hectic, frustrating day at work and then met an attractive someone for a first date.

When you got off the freeway where heavy traffic has made you a half-hour late, to take your precious niece out for an ice cream sundae.

When you finished weeding the long-neglected garden and got ready to chair the annual charity ball.

When you dried the last dish from a botched spaghetti dinner, and then delighted your spouse's client with stories from your days as an exchange student in Paris.

In each case what happened? Most likely, when the first activity cycle came to an end, you pulled your thoughts together and said something like this: "Now look here, inner self. It's been really intense doing what I had to do already today. However, I have a new activity to do and the current frame of mind simply won't do. Put on a smile, leave the last set of activities in the past, and focus on what is coming next. I want to focus on the fun there is to be had. If I need to revisit issues from this part of the day, well, then, I'll just have to wait until I'm done with these current plans."

What striking transitions have you pulled off? What did you do to make the transition? (Yes, this is an excellent time to journal.)

If you have successfully made transitions in other areas of your life, then you grasp the mechanism:

You take stock of where you are now by acknowledging what you have been focusing on and how it has made you feel.

You declare that you have stopped that activity, for now.

You focus on the activities you will be starting, and the frame of mind you would like to have.

You begin dressing up, freshening up, and summoning up a cheerful attitude. You emerge ready to feel your best, have fun, and shine in the situation.

If this sounds reminiscent of what you did on your first date with someone special, then you are really catching on. Every expanded orgasm date can—and should—be treated as if it is a special first date, with a very special person.

In an optimal expanded orgasm world, or space, or mindset (there are many ways of looking at this), every moment becomes another opportunity to experience the best orgasm of your life. This chapter will tell you exactly what mindset will enable you to create the most rewarding expanded orgasm space. This mindset includes both attitude and the easily developed skill of communicating while you are giving and receiving pleasure. You will learn just how attitude and communication together make a potent brew that will maximize your abilities to create a world in which expanded orgasm thrives.

Practice the Principles of Pleasure

In many ways, this will be the most important chapter in the book. These principles will enable you to magnify the effect of every action you take. In fact, just adopting the expanded orgasm mindset delivers a vast increase in pleasure. In this chapter, we'll explore the why, the what, and the how of making the transition to expanded orgasm.

Get into Present Time

The present is where the presents are.

Another way of saying this is that the gifts we have to give and receive from expanded orgasm are available right now (and only right now). If either you or your partner is mentally or emotionally stuck in the past or the future tense, your attention will be diverted from appreciating these gifts.

These days, it's tempting to want to juggle many things in our minds at once: home, family, work, relationships, friendships, and other obligations compete for our mind-share. By multitasking and thinking about many things at once, many of us hope to get more done, more quickly, so that at the end of some point in time (hopefully soon), we will have more free time to just relax. Have you noticed how that time never arrives?

It takes real discipline to stop thinking about everything but the pleasure you wish to give and receive during expanded orgasm. But, that is exactly what we are asking you to do.

Today more than ever this is an essential mental skill to develop. Couples with busy lives often need to schedule expanded orgasm dates days in advance. And perhaps, they will only have an hour or two. If they know how to make the transition into *present time*, then most of the available time will be spent pleasurably. Otherwise, it will be spent on trying to make a transition occur.

There are several ways to get yourself into present time:

Make a firm mental decision to leave all your past and future thoughts outside while you enjoy the present moment. While this is easier to say than to do, I strongly recommend that you proclaim this decision both to yourself and your partner.

Ritualize the transition. Acknowledge to each other, perhaps with a hug or poem, that the transition has started. This will bring you into the present moment and "separate" this special time from the past and future.

Take turns talking while the other partner listens for a few minutes. Talk about whatever you want to bring yourself into the moment. After you have both done this a few times, you will have unloaded your concerns and feel more ready to transition into something new.

Start doing something that moves you in the direction of enjoying the present. Touch the other person and enjoy the sensation. Feed each other grapes. Appreciate the music. Dress provocatively. Dance for your partner.

You can train to refocus your mind just as you can train your body to lift weights. And, as with the physical, you will become progressively more facile with this over time. You also will become aware of the extent to which you are not in present time, and become increasingly able to relate your "being present" to your level of pleasurable feelings in your expanded orgasm dates.

A checklist for bringing you both into present time:

- Do whatever needs to be done to enter a present-time state. This can include a check in, hugging, a walk, setting up the room together, a bath, etc.
- Out of this, confirm your decision that you are in present time and are willing to feel as much as possible.
- Begin the sensual part of the date.
- Keep the whole system in present time with ongoing communication.

Francine and Robert are two clients who chose to become avid expanded orgasm practitioners. Both of them alternate between traveling for work and working at home. When both are home, they set up daytime expanded orgasm "lunch" dates. They have learned to use transition skills to rapidly enter into present time. This enables them to start off immediately creating pleasure. Francine says, "I have learned that *my decision about how much I am willing to feel* determines how much pleasure both of us have in the date."

Recently, Robert was upset when his date with Francine was extremely low energy. She barely rose above the level of a few mild contractions now and nearly fell asleep at one point. He did everything he could conjure to please her…except one key thing. He forgot—right in the beginning of the date—to check in with her. Francine, it turns out, had had a very rough morning, but did not want to bring her frustrations from work into her date, so she didn't mention it. Robert spent the rest of the day puzzling over what he could have done to make the date better—and where he could have done a better job pleasing her.

Francine ended the mystery that evening when she apologized to Robert for not getting sufficiently into present time for their date. Her motives were respectable enough. A client had delivered several urgent and unreasonable requests minutes before her date was to begin. Since she didn't want to ruin the potential for fun with her problems, she hadn't mentioned this to Robert. Clearly, in retrospect, her bravado and good intentions had backfired. After her apology, Robert realized that he could have inquired about Francine's state of mind and emotion at the start. Perhaps they could have rescheduled the date if that's what it took to "arrive" at the date in the right frame of mind.

A Strategy for Passion

In romance novels, movies, and TV, sensual encounters are always spontaneous and the participants are so overwhelmed with the magical presence of the moment as to make the notion of *planning a date* seem antithetical to pleasure. As a culture, we have bought into this ideal of spontaneous romance and sex. However, romance in the media always involves people who have just met. Popular romance stories do not portray couples in long-term relationships (and certainly not where one of them has had a miserable morning). If you desire a thriving long-term relationship that brims with passion, you will need to deliberately create strategies (dates) for pleasure. Then, inside those created dates, you will discover immense opportunity for serendipity, exploration, and deep passion. These qualities flourish in present time.

That's why we offer a strategy for passion as essential to learning expanded orgasm. The strategy is made up of several specific steps. If you rush over any one step, you will probably find you do not get the results this program promises. Too often, an expanded orgasm practitioner will think that his or her skills or general level of responsiveness are somehow inadequate when the real issue is something really simple, like failing to fully enter into present time.

Of course, not all dates—no matter how much "in present time" will or should include expanded orgasm. If you are really in the moment, really connecting with what each of you desires, you may want to trade massages, cuddle, or go for any of the vast menu of sexual experiences. What we're saying is that getting into present time is a necessary condition for expanded orgasm, but by itself it is not sufficient for fully experiencing any kind of pleasure.

Since the transition into the expanded orgasm space is an essential concept of learning expanded orgasm, we have contrasted the everyday state and the expanded orgasm state, and given some examples to give you an even better mental picture of the differences between the two spaces (which we also refer to as rooms, and even worlds).

Life in Your Everyday World

Not always, but typically, and often enough in our daily lives we create mental labels and categories that help us make life more manageable. Our labels of identity seem real and unchangeable, and we create behaviors that seem to fit the labels. Already carrying such labels as *devoted wife, virtuous daughter, giving mother, sharp businesswoman,* and far more, many wonder: is there any room left for a *foxy lady* or *sexy guy*?

Power struggles between the "parts" of each of us often erupt, and cannot be easily solved. Someone might want to experience pleasure but is also very nervous, for example. Their nervous self can cancel out their pleasurable self. Without even being aware of these tendencies, we can unconsciously divide ourselves into such small parts that we lose the greater picture of who we are right now. We become just "a businesswoman" or "just a mother" and forget about the part of ourselves that is a sexy lady, warm, turned on, and eager for pleasurable life experiences.

Practitioners of expanded orgasm learn to define themselves ever more broadly, so that they can comfortably allow the many different parts of themselves to peacefully coexist. I am, for example, an author, a devoted wife, and a fun-loving, highly orgasmic woman, all at once. How about you?

Life in Your Expanded Orgasm Space

We are all vastly greater in terms of our potential. The expanded orgasm space is just one such space that allows us to expand our identities beyond those of normal day-to-day living. We learn, and also rediscover, very different sets of rules and behaviors. For example, in the win/win space, both parties have to win in order for either one to win.

In this expanded space, our labels of identity seem fluid rather than cast in stone. For example, I can easily become a juicy lover any time I choose to. It is who we are in this moment, and not some other time, that matters now.

Expanded, we have access to worlds of new ideas, connections, and insights. For example, in this space deep relaxation occurs. Compassion, love, and a sense of being a part of a greater life force all arise naturally, and flood and feed your soul from a seemingly unlimited supply. Those qualities were there all along, inside you, just looking for an open door through which to enter into your awareness. Neither the everyday life nor the expanded life is better or worse than the other. They both offer all of us many rich, wonderful experiences. We like to ask our clients to develop the ability to notice which space they are in, when. This awareness helps develop their ability to understand, and to access, expanded orgasmic states more easily.

Expanded Orgasm Is an Art Form to Learn

Can you name any art, sport, or complex endeavor that can be mastered in a few lessons? Does your ego suffer as a result? Of course not! No one gets to be good at something without discipline, practice, and a strong desire to achieve mastery. Now ask yourself: why is it that when it comes to giving and receiving sexual pleasure (and we include expanded orgasm in this category) we are supposed to be completely void of experience until our wedding night…and then, suddenly, experts? Yet this is exactly what our culture does expect of us, in so many subtle and not-so-subtle messages.

Our solution is not to disagree with the prevailing culture. It is to separate lovemaking from expanded orgasm *training*. In so doing, you will give your vulnerable, impressionable ego much more space for the trial-and-error learning process inherent in learning anything worth mastering.

Expanded orgasm training requires the same dedication necessary to perfect any creative and rewarding endeavor. Is *training* the best word? Does it sound clinical to you? We use the word in order to emphasize its role as a true discipline—and a road to mastery. Most people we know who engage in expanded orgasm training have a lot of fun with it and create a lot of love in the process. These are the "extra benefits" of engaging in this learning process. And, lovemaking after practicing expanded orgasm can feel profoundly engaging and unusually pleasurable.

Activity #9: Are You Willing to Practice the Basics?
In your journal, consider the following questions:

How did you react when we advised you to "train" in order to learn to experience expanded orgasm?

Do you prefer other words (practice, home-play, study)? What would your words be?

When you see basic exercises (such as those presented in Step Two) do you skip over them, with the rationale that "you've already been there, and done that—let's get on with the good stuff"?

Have you ever assumed that you know all there is to know about what you have to offer another person? What was the result of making that assumption?

And then:

Do you feel your partner could benefit from practicing the basics with you? What would you like his or her attitude to be about learning or reviewing basic information about your sexual landscape?

Consider these questions carefully. Like masters of archery or opera singing, true masters of expanded orgasm practice the basics with as much enthusiasm as they practice the advanced information.

Jason noticed in his review that he felt impatient going over the basics. He said, "I've been married twice already. I don't need to examine my wife. I've done this plenty. This basic stuff is boring. I want advanced material."

What do you think Kelly had to say about this? "Jason doesn't know half of what I like. I myself am learning all the time. I'm not some machine that came with a complete set of operating instructions on our wedding night! I don't know how to bring this up to him. I have wished many times that he would ask more about me, if for no other reason than to get us both feeling more comfortable together. If he would compliment my genital areas, I would feel more proud of them too, and would act sexier.

"I have often fantasized that he would ask a lot of questions about me and my desires. I want to know if he realizes just how much my preferences can change from moment to moment. I would get very turned on just having that much of Jason's attention. And I know Jason would really like that!"

If you find you have had a jaded attitude, then you have not been in present time with your partner. In present time, it wouldn't matter if you'd done something once—or many times—before. *What matters most is how much pleasure the two of you are ready and eager to create right now, in whatever way feels best.* Welcome this discovery. It will open the door to fresh fun and exploration.

Commit to Pleasure

So far, we've explored the attitudes and behaviors fundamental to setting the stage: an appreciation for making a transition to expanded orgasm practice, getting into present time, a learning attitude, the recognition that mastery will require discipline (however fun) and practice, and the willingness to engage in an exploratory mind and emotional set with your partner.

You may be thinking that these are the very same attitudes and behaviors that are required to succeed in any complex skill that involves mind and body—

tennis, golf, or dance, for example. We agree. But there is something else you must realize and practice—different from the requirements of sports or art—in order to realize the benefits of expanded orgasm. You must be willing to expand the amount of pleasure you are capable of feeling.

The price of pleasure is eternal vigilance. When you understand this statement fully, you may never drop your guard again. You will always have to be on the lookout for those (including your own inner spoilsport) who will be trying to rain on your parade. On the other hand, once you truly embrace this idea, you will see to it that others don't rain on your parade, and you will live a much happier life.

The room in which expanded orgasm is created is a room built on the joy of pleasure. Expanded orgasm is a concentrated process of heaping one pleasure upon another. As you add on more pleasure, the amount you experience increases geometrically. At any step along the way, either one of you can stop the process by deciding to stop enjoying pleasure. Those who take expanded orgasm to the highest levels learn to steer a course in which pleasure is their truest guide. All other tempting thoughts, including guilt, blame, shame, awkwardness, shyness, boredom, anger, embarrassment, fear, and impatience, will take you away from your experience. Here is where your steadfast commitment to pleasure will save the day. Commit to this as a policy—once and forever. As other thoughts try to steer you off course, return your focus to pleasure. You are not in the room where these thoughts are meant to thrive.

It's very important to realize that this deep and abiding commitment to a "path of pleasure" is not the same as mindlessly (or heartlessly) following a course of immediate and self-centered gratification, especially at the expense of other important goals in your life (which presumably will also bring you various kinds of pleasure and fulfillment as well). It's just that our daily lives are already so full of worry, regret, tedium, and power struggles. Why bring more of this into the bedroom?

Activity #10: Commit to Pleasure

Take ten minutes apiece. First the woman receives pleasurable attention from the man. Women, decide in advance that you are going to appreciate everything the man says, does, and gives to you. Let this attention be a mixture of verbal and physical attention. Be sure to do this exercise at least once where the physical attention is non-sexual and at least once with some form of sexual attention included. When you find yourself giving way to doubts about your attractiveness, your worthiness of pleasure, your judgments of your partner, and your mind latching on to unpleasant thoughts, replace these thoughts with pleasurable ones. Record in writing or share with your partner what you notice from this exercise. How big of a "container" for pleasure did you have during the experience? What do you suppose the experience would have been like if your "pleasure container" were doubled in size (this is an excellent idea to discuss with your partner)?

Men, after the woman has received, it is your turn to experiment with how much pleasure you can receive. When you are done, once again record in writing or share with your partner what you notice from this exercise.

"Win" in Every Moment

I don't have to tell you that sexual communication can be highly charged. In expanded orgasm we experience a range of powerful emotions: joy at a touch that reaches deep into our core, gratitude for the one who is allowing us the chance to surrender to our deepest pleasures, and yet also anger at a wrong stroke, or hurt at a momentary lapse of attention. All emotions become intensified as our level of arousal builds. The receiver who falls sway to negative emotions begins a negative cycle that will certainly lead away from expanded orgasm.

Janet, a recent graduate of our program, knows all too well how this process works. She was brought up with a strict, work-oriented ethic. "If I didn't get As on my report card, I was grilled about where I had gone wrong. I took this same work ethic into my sex life, with disastrous consequences. Every time my partner gave me a stroke, I would report to him how perfect it was. Strokes that fell short of my perfect 'A' were graded, as were Bs, and Cs. I even had a Z for 'That was horrible!' Then, since this seemed a little hard on Jon's ego, I switched to numbers. 10 was the best, and 1, the worst. I thought I was being a good and honest communicator but it sure wasn't getting me the goals of increasing pleasure and a growing hot connection with my partner. Instead, Jon became terrified of touching me. Our dates grew less frequent. When he declined having one with me on our anniversary, I knew that my attitudes about expanded orgasm and Jon had hit rock bottom. I decided then and there to turn the situation around. The real challenge for me was going to be finding some way to enjoy every stroke, even if it wasn't—in retrospect—the absolute best.

"My desire for lots more fun with Jon forever changed the way I evaluated what was being given me. What if—I asked myself—I changed my reference point to eliminate the past and future? What if my only goal was to see how much I could enjoy each stroke? As an experiment, I challenged myself to enjoy what I was given, rather than challenging my partner to please me.

"Now I was able to get lots of 8s, 9s, and 10s, although, to be honest, I dropped the number scale pretty quickly. As I entered the expanded orgasm space, or room, I increased my focus on pleasure. I lost interest in judging everything so heavily. I also found out how to do a much better job as a communicator. My partner didn't want to hear a score for every stroke. But he did want to hear my expressions of pleasure, coupled with requests I made for changes to make it even more juicy and fun."

Seek Out Risk

The expanded orgasm room is full of risk. Granted, other rooms, like the one you inhabit daily, are also full of risk. But in the expanded orgasm room, risk is special, something to invite, to expect, to manage, to enjoy. You want to live high on the risk scale when there is such deep pleasure to be had!

Exactly what is at risk? Here are some examples:

- Wanting to do something spectacular for my partner and falling short.
- Rocking the boat—saying something that would challenge our normal patterns of relating. For example, "Why do you want me to do all the talking? I'd prefer it if both of us talked during our sessions."
- Trying something new that didn't work well, like giving my partner a rhomboid-shaped stroke that brings his (her) energy way down instead of up.
- Asking for what I want, even if I have asked before and haven't gotten it, like asking that we touch each other's bodies more during our dates.
- Letting my ego get in the way when something doesn't go just as I planned, even though I know I am not supposed to let my ego get in the way!

If you are lucky (or smart), you will build an expanded orgasm "room" full of this kind of risk. Remember that getting to expanded orgasm means you have to step outside of your usual comfort zone. You will want to speak buried truths as well as feel as though you must brace yourself to hear truths from you partner. At times you will wish you bought the easy book on orgasmic gratification (the one that gives you one simple technique and promises you will be an overnight sensation).

In this practice, risk is a good thing. It is what takes you and your partner to increasingly new levels of pleasure. It is your ticket to a fulfilling sexual life and, like all other tickets, it does come at a price. The price is your attitudes and practices that do not support expanded orgasm.

Have I had to pull together though moments of truth? You bet. I've been told that I have dropped the energy at the wrong moment; that I have forgotten to do what my partner asked me to do seconds earlier; that I've allowed my mind to drift off instead of paying close attention to the pleasure I am giving and/or receiving. Having been the recipient of truths more times than I could ever count (the kind where my stomach gets queasy and my insecurities skyrocket) I can share with you what I do. I find that when I invite the truth (Allen's self-disclosure) in at the very start, I am much more open to hearing it. When we start, I either say something like:

"Please tell me everything, and don't hold back comments."

"It's more important that we communicate than that we look good."

"If I look like I am going down on what you said, maybe give me an extra compliment or hug...but don't stop the communicating."

"Let's both learn to take feedback as opportunities to give each other more pleasure than ever."

"Let's practice using the *training cycle* (described below) so we learn to give each other lots of acknowledgment as we speak honestly, from our hearts."

Allen will usually make the same types of requests of me as well. Then, when we get each other's self-disclosed truths, we can feel good that our partner has honored our requests, rather than upset at getting uninvited feedback!

Saying these things proactively has made a huge difference. When I get a comment, I know that I asked for it. I feel that I am creating good communication rather than doing something wrong!

Risk is essential to keeping a relationship alive and thriving. The rough spots are always the knotholes which, when passed through, are the platforms for exponential growth in love and turn-on between partners.

Are you taking on enough risk in your practice of expanded orgasm? What would you like to say that you haven't?

Activity #11: Practice Total Disclosure

Practice some of the techniques outlined in Step Two. This time, during the session, notice for yourself where your ego feels threatened, challenged, and even delighted. Reveal these observations in a matter-of-fact tone of voice, as you notice them. The recipient of these observations can thank his or her partner for sharing, but should continue on with the date.

Then ask yourself these questions: *How does your ego influence the ability of both of you to give and receive pleasure? How do your insecurities take your attention off pleasure and onto yourself? How do your insecurities stop you from full communication?*

From Pain to Pleasure

One of the challenges—and great benefits—of expanded orgasm is learning how to communicate honestly and remain appreciative at the same time. What if you really aren't having fun? Are you supposed to be dishonest? Are you supposed to cover up your feelings and go into denial?

To answer that, you will need to examine why you are not having fun. Ask yourself:

Did you start the date in a bad mood? Then you didn't make the adequate transition. *Was your partner not doing something the way you want, and you could not find a way to find something about the experience to appreciate?* Then you did not make the appropriate transition. *Did negative emotions arise, in the moment, during the experience?* Feel them authentically. Then find a way to make the transition back into a space of pleasure and gratitude.

In expanded orgasm, just as in life itself, we always have the choice in every moment of winning with the experience or losing. Force of habit alone is enough to tempt us back into the survival-oriented, competitive world we often occupy when not in our expanded orgasm practice. Fortunately, just as losing is a habit, winning can be a habit too. You can teach yourself to remain in gratitude by recognizing when you are starting to fall "out of appreciation." Make it a policy to acknowledge true emotions like sadness and anger.

Your expanded orgasm practice may not be the place to dwell on these emotions. I only enter the expanded orgasm room when I feel reasonably confident that I will be able to cocreate fun and pleasure with my partner. If I don't feel certain of being able to do this, I will handle what is coming up for me emotionally and then begin.

We are not suggesting you be a Pollyanna. Part of being in present time is being real and authentic, and sharing from your deepest self. However, another part of expanded orgasm really is about creating pleasure. It is a discipline with goals. Just as meditating creates peacefulness and cooking lessons great food, so expanded orgasm creates fun, joy, and great orgasms.

Participate Fully in the Experience through Talking

Some people talk during sex, others don't. Those who do have often done this as a natural part of their full sexual expression. The words and sounds flow from a cornucopia, enhancing all the good feelings and selectively magnifying the best moments. Sound becomes an intoxicatingly delicious part of the experience.

Imagine hearing:

"Oh baby, that feels so good. You're really touching me in a good place. Mmmmm, I'd love it if you'd move a little higher now. Wow, that's great. Whatever you do, don't stop, yes, keep going. Okay, good, you lightened up, I love that!"

And mixed into that:

"I've got you babe, just where I want you. I am going to make this feel really wonderful for you. That's right, let go. I am going right into your core. You feel so hot, my hand is almost melting. Keep going, I'm not letting you down just yet. There's more where that came from..."

The talkers of the world know how to utter these wonderful words and sounds. The non-talkers, however, are usually aghast at the very thought of uttering a peep. "How could you even suggest that I say anything? That would take me out of the experience. What would I say? I just want to feel."

Talking serves some very useful functions in expanded orgasm: it keeps you and your partner in the experience. Expanded orgasmic energy can be intense, especially in the beginning. A typical reaction to the intensity of sensation is for givers or receivers to "space out," that is, lose full awareness. They go off into a dream world. While the dream may be pleasant, going into dreamland diminishes the total sensation you could be feeling. Like faking, dreamland is a step away from increasing the expanded orgasm experience.

We don't necessarily suggest that you talk continuously during your expanded orgasm sessions. Most likely, if you have practiced talking and can do it easily, you will find that on some days, you talk, and on others, you are more likely not to. You have learned through practice to avoid the spacing out. However, it is essential that you learn to talk as a part of your expanded orgasm repertoire of skills.

Activity #12: Talk It Up

Do this exercise twice. The first time should be when you are giving your partner a non-genital massage, and the second, when you are giving genital massage. (If the men and women are both going to act as receiver, they can both have a turn as the giver.)

During this exercise, both the woman and the man should make an effort to talk continuously. Talk just for the sake of talking. Include lots of acknowledgments, requests for changes, and sounds of pleasure. Notice what happens to your level of sensation when you do talk and when you don't. Also notice what happens when your partner talks to you.

Be alert: this exercise can be much more difficult than it sounds. Non-talkers especially will have to overcome significant preexisting programming to begin talking. You may wish to repeat the non-genital version of this exercise several times before you feel you can successfully progress to the genital version.

Learning to talk and feel at the same time may feel like rubbing your head and patting your tummy simultaneously. It is an acquired skill, which should get easier with practice.

Record your experiences in your journal, and share them.

Linda noted: "I have always been the talker in our relationship. Sam is practically monosyllabic when it comes to sex. This time, rather than start out upset at Sam for all the times in the past that he didn't say much, I just decided I would start talking even more. I asked Sam a lot of questions about what he was noticing about me, about how he was feeling, about where the energy was going. That really helped him start to verbalize. Finally, I think we are starting to work together rather than blame each other for what does or does not happen. Hey, we have twenty-five years of old habits to reconsider. Of course there are going to be changes. One thing I appreciate is that this course is not an overnight sensation. It is something where we develop our skills over time."

I couldn't help but smile at hearing her comments. Who was it (Sam, of course) who had just been complaining that his spouse was not talkative? It seems each of them wanted to talk a certain way, and hear that kind of talk from their partners. Sam wanted to hear Linda talk about her sexual experiences explicitly. Linda wanted Sam to talk about how he was feeling, and feel his attention fully on her pleasure. As both of them began talking more, they were satisfying both themselves and their partners, and loving every minute of it!

What We've Explored

Steps Two and Three constitute the building blocks of a solid foundation for learning expanded orgasm. In fact, the attitudes and skills you acquired from doing the journaling and exercises in these lessons will create a far more pleasurable, fulfillment-oriented life for you—in or out of the bedroom.

In this step, you learned that to make an effective transition into the "room" of expanded orgasm takes a certain mindset—one oriented toward honesty, self-disclosure, your willingness to enter present time, a path of mastery, and, above all, a powerful commitment to pleasure and fulfillment.

To reiterate a key point, the price of pleasure (or fulfillment) is eternal vigilance. You must be willing to win in every moment, not from a Pollyanna position of spineless optimism, but because you know you have the power to positively and joyfully transform how you view your present circumstances. Now get ready to learn how you can dramatically increase your capacity for orgasmic pleasure!

4

Step Four: Erotic Development

How do you go from wherever you are today—from however much orgasmic pleasure you are currently capable of enjoying—to this promised land of expanded orgasm? In this step you will learn how to dramatically increase your ability to fill your being with deep orgasmic pleasure. And, best of all, you will discover that you already have the most important skills you need to succeed.

Once I had a Cajun dance lesson at a music festival in a park. A crowd gathered, enjoying the exuberant, wet-kiss energy of the band. A very handsome and skilled man asked me to dance. He whirled me around with such grace, skill, and artistry, that someone asked me afterwards if I were the teacher. Having danced to Cajun music only a few times, I was flattered. But I knew that I was not really a great dancer (much less a teacher), and that I had much to learn. If I was going to dance consistently thrilling dances, I could not spend the rest of my life depending on others to emerge out of the blue to sweep me off my feet. I was going to have to learn how to be a great dancer myself.

This thinking made perfect sense when it came to learning an art (or skill) like dancing. However, I'd never applied this reasoning to my orgasmic life. There, I assumed that my partner was the only one fully responsible for (and capable of) giving me pleasure. If I had any problems "getting off" (which I often did) it was, of course, his fault and never mine. The thought that I might routinely give myself sexual pleasure had never crossed my mind.

I certainly had an excuse for my lack of orgasmic responsibility. While growing up, I must have received powerful messages saying that touching my genitals was wrong. I can't recall anyone sitting me down and imparting this message explicitly, but I certainly acted as if that had happened.

I can recall the first time I touched myself sexually, at age thirty-six— in a homework assignment for a course in sensuality. As instructed, I found a place where I could be alone. Then I climbed into bed, ready to explore myself genitally. But first I felt compelled to get up, double-lock the door, and put a chair in front of it, just to be "sure" no one would enter the room. Then, to be triple certain of my privacy, I dived under the covers and turned out the lights. I lay there with myself, terrified, wondering if I would be discovered, and if I would be an exciting lover. I also wondered where all this baggage came from, why I felt like I had to hide, and why I was so afraid of my own inadequacy. I never found a specific answer, and concluded I must have picked up these messages from general social conditioning.

Despite the shaky start, my date with myself turned out to be a smashing success. I delighted myself thoroughly! I knew just what to do to get myself warmed up. I knew just what to tell myself to make myself feel good. I knew exactly when to go to the next level of feeling, and how long to stay there. In short, I was just about perfect.

That night I had blown away the societal "hex" about touching myself to give myself pleasure. I had learned that I could be a terrific lover on my own. However, I didn't do too much with this information at that time. It was not until I committed myself powerfully to developing my expanded orgasm capabilities that I took my sensual alone-time practices to the next level of ongoing self-exploration. I learned one concept that opened the door to sensual self-exploration wide open for me: *everyone is 100 percent responsible for their own orgasm.* This is just as true for men as it is for women. The assumption that anyone else (including your partner) is more responsible than you will detract, not add, to your power to create the maximum pleasurable experiences, alone or with someone else.

We ask all women who enter our expanded orgasm program to develop their own erotic energy, independent of anything they may do with a partner. A turned-on woman continuously enlarges her capacity to feel and sustain large amounts of pleasure. Her "pleasure container size" is increasing as she develops her erotic capacities.

In addition, a turned-on woman ensures that expanded orgasm dates she has with her partner will be more fun and satisfying, for the following reasons:

When the woman is turned on starting an expanded orgasm session with her partner (as she will be when she does these practices), she will feel much more pleasure from every touch. The more winning experiences two people can generate together, the more likely they are to continue.

A turned-on woman will give more accurate (and more pleasant to hear) feedback to her partner.

A turned-on woman will have an engorged clitoris that is easier for her partner to find and stimulate pleasurably.

She'll enjoy stronger bonding and overall pleasure.

Container vs. Contents

The *erotic container* is a concept to describe how much sensual, erotic pleasure you are willing and able to have at any given moment. Your erotic container is how much pleasure you can allow yourself to feel in any moment. You can do this through two essential practices: erotic self-development and practice with your partner. The erotic self-development you learn now will launch you rapidly and powerfully into enlarging your erotic capacity.

There are two ways to increase the amount of "pleasure energy" you can contain. You can make your existing container more full, or you can enlarge your container. By enlarging your container, you will be able to hold—experience— much more erotic energy.

Enlarging your erotic container is a core skill for exploring expanded orgasm. You can expand your container size through physical training by yourself and with a partner. You also expand it through mental training and affirmations, every time you affirm that that is what you intend to do.

We are born in a state highly capable of orgasm. Our bodies are wired from head to toe to experience full-bodied pleasure. Tickle a baby's little toe, and waves of sensation shoot through her head and fingers. Growing up, however, we engage in the process of shutting down our mind/body erotic connections. By adulthood, most of us have localized (restricted) genital sensations physically and mentally. In essence, we have shrunk our erotic containers from covering our whole bodies to covering just certain areas, at certain times.

Every woman has a unique way of processing orgasmic pleasure's spreading fire of sensation. When a man touches her clitoris, some women will perceive the sensation as "too intense." Rather than expand and spread, and thereby reverse the localization, these women will push their experience further away from the sensation. By doing so, they reduce the size of their feeling container to something more manageable and familiar. Other women will feel very little at all when touched genitally. And they too can learn to expand their container size by enlarging and spreading sensation—even if by a seemingly small amount.

Yet another type of woman is naturally orgasmic. I have always marveled at such women. Touch them anywhere, and their skin shivers and spreads the sensation of pleasure along the central nervous system. Within seconds, they are cooing, purring, and reaching for even more touch. This behavior extends to genital touching: with a single touch, they are awake, alive, and inviting in whatever may be offered next. I admire these women for the way their natural erotic energy flows so effortlessly. I would envy them more if I weren't so busy taking notes on how I, too, could be like them! They always remind me how attractive a turned on woman is to others.

I have at various times found myself in all of these "erotic container" categories. As a teacher and student of eroticism, I like to notice what is happening to my body with precision. On any one day, I am likely to go through a spectrum of different responses. I expect this, since all women vary naturally in their responsiveness depending on the time of month, the time of day, and the mood they happen to be in.

Still, I have been expanding my erotic container for years, and I can also say that it is larger now than ever. Metaphorically, my container has gone from a thimble to a swimming pool, and I intend to expand it much, much, further. The erotic energy it holds can vary from a thimble-full to a swimming pool–full, but the container size stays relatively constant. My container size expands over time— with intention and with ongoing expanded orgasm practice.

A client, Bethany, was very shy. Her husband Ken loved her dearly but felt unable to communicate his love adequately to her, since her shyness would short-circuit his attempts to create greater intimacy. Fortunately, Ken was very patient. Each day he went out of his way to compliment her on some way in which he felt she was becoming more open to being appreciated and valued. With all his loving attention on her flowering (which she herself would not have noticed), she learned to look forward to his attention. At first his attention was expressed verbally, but in time, Ken added in more cuddling, massage time, and sensuality. Eventually, Bethany had a far greater capacity, or container, for "being loved and adored."

By the time Bethany and Ken took our training, she was ready to expand her container size even further. It was easier for her to make the decision to take actions that would be consistent with the erotic container size she now realized she wanted. Using the erotic development approach we are about to describe, she found she was not only able to feel more sensual pleasure, but that she was able to sustain very high levels of pleasure longer and longer. Once she had expanded the limits of how much erotic pleasure she was able to give herself, she become more willing and able to enjoy more erotic attention from Ken. By the time they had completed the course, Bethany radiated with a sense of such grounded erotic turn-on that Ken started teasing her that she "glowed in the dark." Bethany, of course, loved this teasing, and invited Ken to keep noticing how attractive she was becoming. She thanked Ken for his ongoing and consistent support for her own erotic development. Ken accepted these acknowledgments, while also realizing he had benefited far beyond his wildest dreams too from expanding her container for love and attention.

Are you, and your partner, ready to take positive action to enlarge your container?

Now let's turn our attention to what you can do with yourself to expand your ability to enjoy and explore your erotic experience.

Activity #13: Set Up a Date with Yourself

For many women, arranging the time and space to have a date in which you stimulate yourself to orgasm is going to be the hardest part of this lesson. Here are some actions you may need to take in order to begin:

You may have to resolve hidden and/or open negative judgments about what it means to self-stimulate.

You may need to locate available new sources of time and space where you can be alone. This can be challenging when you're not sure you want to do this in the first place!

You may need to resolve doubts about your ability to expand your erotic container size, if, at the start, your container size is smaller than you think it should be.

You may need to address and resolve fears about being alone with yourself.

You may wish to resolve fears about your abilities to satisfy yourself.

Each woman will have her own set of issues to resolve. Kelly, for example, was thrilled that we instructed her to take time to develop her erotic energy. But even Kelly discovered that starting this program was not as easy as it first sounded.

She wrote in her journal: "I am grateful for the chance to develop my erotic nature further. It seems funny, since usually I turn on so incredibly easily. That's my nature. But I have been afraid to develop my turn-on openly. I think I'm afraid that Jason would feel threatened, or left out, or somehow judge me. No— I'm certain. I am really afraid that Jason will discover that I get myself off better than he can get me off."

She brought this up at our session in front of Jason. As Kelly read from her journal, Jason seemed to fly silently through a range of emotions. Finally, since he didn't volunteer any information on his own, we asked him if he'd be willing to share how he felt.

He agreed. "Kelly, when you got the assignment, I guess I didn't think much about these issues. When I heard the homework for you, I assumed I would love it if you gave yourself pleasure. But I listened to your concerns, every one of them seemed real to me. Yes, I think I would feel threatened to see you get yourself off better than I could. But now I feel like a real heel. How can I be so selfish? Still, I am sure I would wonder if your other partners consistently got you off better, too." Jason looked at us, pleading to throw him a rope out!

"Have you started your erotic development practices yet, Kelly?" we asked.

"No, and it's just like you said. It's harder than I thought it would be to start," she admitted.

We suggested Kelly begin her program, despite her fears, and Jason's. Expanded orgasm training intentionally takes us to our sexual limits—and then beyond them. Hence, the training was working, just as planned.

We suggested that Kelly share with Jason details from every session she had with herself. By doing so, she would bring home the fact that her training is occurring with herself *now*, in present time. Jason would see that it is her own erotic energy she is developing. This energy is hers to develop as she wishes. Rather than feel jealous, Jason could decide to enjoy the fun she was having. After all, he (and not the imaginary others he feared) was married to Kelly, and the one with whom she planned to live a more erotic and turned-on life.

We always ask our clients to bring a calendar to sessions. Since Kelly hadn't found a way to make a schedule on her own, we suggested she plan time right now for at least five erotic sessions. And suddenly, she did find time. It was at that moment that we knew she was really ready to begin.

Are you ready to commit your erotic session time to a calendar? If so, do it now! Plan to spend anywhere from twenty minutes, to an hour per session. This time can vary according to the other demands of your day. With more time, of course, you will have more opportunities to go deeper in your practice.

Activity #14: Practice Stimulating Yourself

Ladies, set up your "erotic development space" thoughtfully before you start. For most women this will be a bedroom, but other places like the bath or the study may work, as long as you can lie down comfortably, and be assured of privacy.

You'll want to have a hand towel, some lubricant, and, if possible, a dildo. Prepare your physical room with as much care as you have created your mental expanded orgasm "room." You are about to entertain a wonderful and important visitor! We ask that you not bring a vibrator into these sessions. It is a mechanical device that will reduce the nuances of sensations you can feel. We want you to feel more, not less, nuance.

Bring music, flowers, candles, scents—and whatever else pleases you to make the room your personal space. Once you are comfortably supine, lie on the hand towel and bring enough lubricant to your genital area to enhance fluid movement of your hands. We recommend using liberal amounts of lubricant during all expanded orgasm sessions.

Now explore yourself. If you have never done so before, get a hand mirror and examine your genitals, much the way your partner did earlier. Notice the location and feel to the touch of various places: inner lips, outer lips, introitus, and clitoris.

Imagine a vagina as if there were a clock directly over it, facing out. Looking down, a woman would see the 3 o'clock on her left, the 9 o'clock on her right. The 12 o'clock would be at the top of her clitoris, and 6 o'clock would be at the bottom.

Be sure to investigate how you respond to stimulating the "two o'clock" area of your clitoris. Recall, this is the area just to your left of center, near the top of your clitoris. This spot is the one many women find most pleasurable to stimulate. If you have not been already stimulating yourself here, put on your explorer's mindset. How might you awaken feelings here in various ways? It took me a few times before I really awakened this spot. It was certainly worth the effort!

What if you don't feel much of anything? This is a typical concern when starting out. But of course you feel something. Focus your mind directly on what you do feel. Find something to appreciate, even if it is just the fact that you are giving yourself pleasurable attention right now. Remember that it takes time to wake the body up from a long period of inactivity. Any attention you give yourself is positive. Be patient and allow yourself to look for ways to enjoy the slightest pleasurable sensation.

What if you feel oversensitive? This is a good problem to have. It means you are already feeling sensations strongly. Appreciate these feelings and start to explore ways to spread the sensation out. You might try using the entire side of your finger instead of the pad or fingertip alone. Try putting two or three fingers over the area to spread the sensation. Slow and deepen your breathing. Many women find that if they allow their breath to slowly fill their abdomen, and slowly release, they feel more.

Experiment with different strokes, speeds, and pressures, in various locations on and around your labia and clitoris, and clitoral shaft. At some point, when you feel your inner and outer lips are sufficiently engorged, you can slowly and luxuriously insert a dildo into your introitus. Discover how you respond to having the added sensation inside. You will be able to stroke the bottom half of your clitoris at the same time you are stroking the top, in effect creating a "clitoris sandwich." This is a time to experiment in all ways possible. You get credit just for doing the exercise. Know that some days will yield very different results than other days—just as when you are with a partner.

Please record your experiences faithfully in your journal. You are learning how to express yourself erotically each time you make journal entries. This enhanced ability to describe what you are noticing and feeling will add considerable power and zest to the rest of your expanded orgasm training.

Can you identify your own range of experiences? Is it a small range or a wide one? How much would you like to expand your range?

Start by Feeling More

Lining bookstore shelves are many methods of teaching women how to become more orgasmic. Are they all the same? I divide advice on women's orgasm into two camps. Camp One is "Do more now." Move your pelvis. Squeeze your PC muscles. Talk to your partner. Fantasize being at the beach with a gorgeous stranger. While you're at it, keep your cell phone by your side so that if you're not busy enough, you can also call your mother and thank her for the nice color of ceiling paint she recommended two years ago. Seriously, Camp One advice on how to be more orgasmic has you very, very busy. It's the way that is comfortable for modern day gals, perhaps. If we just do enough, we'll succeed.

Camp Two advice goes like this. "Stop doing and start feeling. Stop being so busy. It's your busy mind that helps you negotiate children and contracts and freeways, not orgasms. Start feeling. Begin to let go. Turn off that phone! Melt into the bed. Just allow yourself to breathe deeply. Feel your whole body expanding, feel the sensations in your genitals, feel them spreading and flowing throughout your body. Feel, feel, and feel some more." In case you haven't guessed already, having tried the methods of Camps One and Two extensively, I am a raving fan of Camp Two.

These two camps have been in existence since ancient times. They are really two ends of the spectrum that represents what there is to learn about women's orgasms. Camp One came into focus and popularity in the 1950s and '60s, when researchers first got societal permission to study sex methodically. Scientific researchers examined women who were enjoying full-blown orgasms. They got out their plethysmometers (which measure PC muscles that tell them how many contractions a woman is having) and noticed that in full orgasm, women contracted a lot. They noticed that these women breathed deeply and fully into their abdomens, since they were so relaxed. They noticed certain rocking movements in the pelvis. Like good scientists, they decided if a woman could replicate the outer signs of physical orgasm, then she would soon have a real orgasm. This is an advanced way of saying, "Fake it 'til you make it." Lots of books have been written—and sold—that tell women exactly what to *do* in order to become orgasmic. Very few books, however, have discussed how to *be* orgasmic, so that everything a woman does *is* orgasmic!

What has been your pattern of getting into an orgasmic state? What additions would you like to make to the strategies you already use and enjoy?

In all fairness, the information in Camp One isn't necessarily inaccurate. During your orgasm, you will squeeze your PC muscles, secretly remember hot dates, and rock your pelvis. However, if you start out busily thinking about all these things, where will your attention be? At a minimum, it will be split between doing and feeling. As a result, you will not be starting out feeling as much as possible. And, then you will only be partially feeling.

If your orgasmic development program has been *doing*-focused, congratulate yourself. Anything you have ever done to bring yourself orgasmic pleasure is excellent. Now, consider yourself a researcher focusing on how you are *being*. After trying both *doing* and *being*-oriented approaches, you can choose the combination that gratifies you best.

My experience, after my research, strongly led me to favor the being-oriented principles advocated in Camp Two. Here's what I have found: when I am in a deeply orgasmic state, I don't need to do anything. Initially, I lie very still as I focus entirely on feeling. The more pleasure I feel, the more the orgasmic state of being takes over. The orgasm itself somehow creates a *me* that breathes increasingly deeply. Eventually, when I have surrendered deeply enough and the feelings reach a certain intensity, waves of orgasmic energy pulse through me. My jaw opens and relaxes, and my neck wants to be free, so that my whole body, from head to pelvis to feet, can pulsate, ever so gently. The movement is autonomic, that is, occurring without me consciously directing it to do so.

Begin to Welcome Letting Go

In this orgasmic state, I fill my awareness with the good feelings I am having. I follow them in my mind the way a monk might follow a flame for hours. But what a compellingly luscious flame! The more I relax, the more intense the feeling. The more I then allow the orgasmic wave to flow through me, the deeper my breathing comes, and of course, the more ecstasy fountains through me and out of me.

Just as you trained yourself as a toddler to gain control over your body, so in expanded orgasm training, you must learn to loosen your grip on yourself, and relax. *What you will enter is an increasingly profound state of surrender.*

The state of surrender takes time to develop. Our minds must learn to welcome this feeling, which may seem a bit foreign at first. Surrender? Relax? Certainly these ideas are otherworldly to a busy woman's mind. You may want to *tell* yourself that it's okay to surrender. You will want to invite surrender in by giving yourself permission to melt, to feel, to open.

Letting go can feel like falling backwards off a cliff and landing in a cloud that's floating ever up and away. This feeling may seem unnatural at first. Your mind says, "What? Let go? Fall backward off a cliff! Hmm, I don't know about that." It helps to remember that this all occurs in your mind. Place yourself on a bed, lying flat on your back, and tell yourself that the only way you can possibly fall will be up, not down. You fall by floating upward, as if you are dreaming, in the most sensual, graceful manner. After you try successfully a few times you will get the hang of it. After that, you will most likely develop a passion for this way of letting go.

Develop Your Ability to Contract

When you are contracting, you are naturally and effortlessly squeezing your PC muscles. As you relax and surrender more into your natural orgasmic energy, you will begin contracting more. At first, contractions might just occur when you are going over the edge. You may not even notice them, as they can be quite subtle to detect. Gradually, you can learn to notice little contractions occurring whenever your mind allows you to feel turn-on. They feel like little darts of exquisite genital pleasure. In time, you will be able to relax, and allow yourself to contract as lightly or heavily as you wish. In time, you can learn to feel fluid waves of contractions all over as soon as you begin to turn on.

I was one of those women who had great expanded orgasms while barely contracting. With time, I have gone into so many expanded orgasmic states that my contractions have now grown very strong. I have never had to deliberately strengthen them, since the act of being in orgasmic states did that for me. There is a full circle effect. The more orgasmic I am, the more my PC muscles strengthen. As my PC muscles strengthen, the more potent transmitters of my orgasms they become.

So far, much of Linda's expanded orgasm program has focused on Sam, what Sam did right, or didn't do right, and how the two of them have communicated. Since in the beginning, Linda had told us her own erotic energy was much lower than it used to be (and that was so long ago that even on that point she was relying heavily on memory), we were not surprised to hear that she had stumbled on this challenge.

In front of Sam, she reported to us: "I had no problem putting the erotic dates in my calendar. That was easy for me, since it was an action. I am very good at doing…especially good at doing things for others, but for myself, too. So I did everything correctly. I set up the room, I put on my music, and I told myself to relax and to feel. But—and here's the hard part—I can't seem to feel very much. I rubbed and I hunted and I went softly; nothing seemed to work. I tried having gratitude and yet I was, quite honestly, disappointed. I have had three sessions with myself. I guess somewhere I was expecting to have some sort of orgasm. I wasn't planning on getting bored. I was relieved when the time was up and I could stop."

In their beginning evaluation session, we had carefully checked to make sure Linda was not on any medications, like birth control or some anti-depressants, before she began her training. She wasn't. We now suggested she have her testosterone level checked, since she was over forty. Nonetheless, even without testosterone, we were a little puzzled by her experience. We asked if she had always had these results when touching herself?

"How should I know?" she sniffed. "Sam has always been the one to initiate sex. Since he starts by touching me, I have never had to touch myself. That's just not something I have done on my own."

"Is there any reason Sam might feel threatened about your getting yourself off or developing your erotic energy?" I asked.

"Are you kidding? Sam would love it if I would develop my erotic energy. He'd pay you big money right here and now if I got myself off like gangbusters."

There was something in her response that simply didn't ring true for me. I turned to Sam. "Sam, what have you done to encourage Linda to explore her erotic energy?"

Sam had been looking proud a moment ago. Now his face grew pensive. "What am I supposed to do? Isn't that something Linda is supposed to be doing for herself? I've been giving her the time to go off and do all this erotic play by herself. I thought I was being supportive. Is there anything else you want me to do?"

Sam wasn't watching Linda's face, but I was. She was broadcasting a sense of loneliness. Here was a moment in which to promote greater mutual support. "Sam, you're entirely right, of course, about this being Linda's process. As I see it, the two of you are in a profound transition in your marriage; you are exploring ways to be together more, as well as ways to be apart. You can explore these things together. So this is about connecting more *both* with your partner *and* with yourselves. Between now and next week, how willing are you to become more involved with Linda's program? I don't want you to actually go in there and take over. But are there ways in which you might communicate how happy you would be to hear of her successes? How supportive you would be of her attempts? Perhaps you might consider joining her after one of her dates and sharing her experience with her. I think you could be a great support to Linda right now. She's got twenty years of learning to unlearn, and reprogram. I really believe you could help here."

With Linda's agreement, Sam agreed to play a more active role in being a support for her erotic development program. They both felt that they were going to be breaking new ground over the next week with this very simple intention. Even with some trepidation, and a sense of risk imminent, they looked excited, as if something new and different might actually happen.

Relax...and...Breathe...

As you pleasure yourself, ladies, you want to heighten your feelings, your sense of gratitude, and your awareness. The more you let go into relaxation, the more you will be able to do all of this. You can use your breath powerfully to help you expand your orgasmic capacity. The deeper you breathe, the more you will relax. And, the more you relax, the deeper your breathing will become.

Breath is a mind/body activity. We breathe at the body level, and yet, we can follow breath with the mind. Some women can get into powerful orgasmic states from breathing alone! A breath orgasm activates the orgasm in the brain. However, a genitally originated orgasm incorporates this breathing, and tends to be experienced as more of a full-body orgasm. So we will focus here on breathing as an adjunct to heightening your orgasm, and not as a means of creating orgasm.

Breathing through your mouth may bring your awareness more fully into your body rather than your mind. Sometimes, I will shift focus like this: breathe, feel...relax, enjoy. Breathe, feel...relax, enjoy. Just breathe and focus on these actions in your own natural rhythm. As you feel comfortable with this cycle, you might improvise with the sequence. Breathe, breathe...relax, feel...enjoy, relax...relax, relax...breathe, enjoy...breathe, feel...feel, feel...enjoy, enjoy. Any combination of these words will be perfect.

Whatever you do, don't do what I do when I am not willing or ready to relax. I issue commands like *"Relax!"* And when that gets no response, I try a slightly more manipulative approach: "Relax, already! It says right here in the book, *you have to relax now.* Quit being so tense."

If I am going to get anywhere juicy in my session, I have to coax myself into letting down my guard. I find that if I talk to myself very nicely and sweetly, I get the best results. "Oh, aren't you good to be lying down now," I'll say solicitously to myself, much the way I enroll my aloof cat into playing with me. My voice drops to a purr. "Yes, you are so very, very good…that's right, how about a little pleasure? One stroke? Can we have one little stroke of pleasure here? Come on, just one…Oh, that's good, you're so good, that's what I am looking for, good girl!" You may find this amusing, but I suggest you remember this strategy the next time you find yourself resisting pleasure. It seems I am not immune to falling for my own sugar-coated lines, and you may find the same is true for you.

How to Stream Your Energy

As you increasingly explore this state of surrender, you will discover a current streaming through your body. This current will intensify over time. You will soon notice this current, at first feeling like an electrical charge, segue into a series of waves of energy washing over you. Whether this occurs in a day, a week, or a few months is going to be unique to you.

In your ordinary state of awareness, your body/mind system is usually so tightly strung that this charge cannot flow freely through you. When you relax enough to allow this charge to flow, you are "streaming." Streaming is a highly pleasurable state that may feel like a subtle, energetic shivering. You activate your body's chemical transmitters and electrical current to flow. You intensify pleasure throughout your body/mind system.

Many practitioners of expanded orgasm believe that the streaming is a powerful healing force. They cite, among others, medical data on psycho-neuroimmunology, Tantric yoga texts, and personal experiences as support for these beliefs. When I stream, I enter a state of wholeness and bliss that gets progressively more powerful and wonderful. I know from personal experience that I emerge from the streaming state feeling more whole, more healed, and more refreshed and renewed.

Here is the Catch-22 about streaming. The more you relax, the more you will stream. So you cannot try to stream. You are better off trying not to do anything. The problem is trying. Trying will stop the streaming.

If you want to increase streaming, notice even the tiniest stream of current going through you. Even if you wonder if you are imagining your streaming, notice it anyway. Enjoy it. Even if you are not streaming at all, imagine yourself opening ever more to your stream, and continue your cycle of breathing, relaxing, and feeling. Remember that the stream is already flowing, and so you only need to notice and surrender into it.

You must retrain your body/mind system to stream. You can expect to get progressively better at streaming with practice. In time, you will find yourself able to stream any time you like. As long as you can relax, you will be able to stream. You will be able to stream in line at the bank or on the phone with a friend. Imagine being able to stream the moment your partner touches you!

Activity #15: Relax Deeply and Then Explore Yourself
Get in a comfortable position for pleasuring yourself. Lie down and allow yourself to become relaxed. Before touching yourself, breathe, meditate, and do whatever you normally do to unwind. Get as relaxed as possible. Notice whether you are streaming already, as streaming can occur with the relaxation alone. This process should take at least ten minutes.

When you feel thoroughly, undeniably relaxed, start touching yourself very lightly, almost imperceptibly. You may start anywhere on your body that feels erotic to you. See how much you can feel with as little pressure as possible. Note that "pressure" is *not* the same as "contact." Explore how you can maintain and increase contact without increasing pressure. Experiment with how high you can take yourself in feeling pleasure using the subtlest touches. Eventually, begin to touch your genitals, and perform the same types of experiments in pressure and contact. Notice how much more you can feel from the first stroke. Begin a full range of clitoral, labial, and inner vaginal exploration.

At some point, when you have satisfied your curiosity, you may continue your regular style of pleasuring as you wish.

This exercise guides you to expand your range of feeling to include very light, subtle strokes. It also gives you a reference point for what it feels like to touch yourself (and be touched) when you are in a deeply relaxed state. After this, you may wish to make relaxation a more integral part of your self-pleasuring ritual.

You may also find that you felt more starting from a more relaxed place, and were able to go higher than usual, more quickly. If this is the case, make note. When you are with your partner, you can then bring this awareness with you. If you are not relaxed, you may wish to find ways to relax together before starting (and during) the date.

This is only one way to begin to self-pleasure. It can also be quite fun to start by touching yourself, and then noticing the relaxation develop.

Spreading the Sensation

As you touch yourself, allow the sensations in your clitoris to spread. How? Imagine you are developing feelings extending outward from the point of contact like the concentric ripples from a pebble tossed in a pond. As you feel more, your clitoris will engorge and its pleasurably sensitive area will grow. Begin to touch your clitoral shaft, your inner and outer lips, your introitus, and then your G-spot (which we refer to the as *G-area*) and you will quite literally feel this expansion occurring as it feels increasingly pleasurable to touch these areas. This is pure Camp Two stuff—surrendering and allowing your body to do what it knows how to do.

Now is a good time to experiment with using more of your hand to touch yourself, in order to facilitate spreading the sensation. See what happens if you expand the contact area. I suggest using a curved dildo, so that at some point you begin stimulating inside. A good time to do this is when you feel challenged holding all the energy you're generating through self-stimulation. This is where you wonder if you are going to go over the edge or perhaps even feel a bit agitated. The more you build the energy, the higher you will take yourself, so if you are not ready to go over the edge yet, expand. Imagine a pyramid: the broader the base the higher the structure can reach.

Imagine your sensations spreading like ripples in a pond, or the growing area heated by a fire. Now is a good time to add the word *expand* to your erotic lexicon: *relax, surrender, feel, enjoy, breathe, expand…*and you can suggest to yourself that you expand without limit.

Expanded vs. Regular Orgasms

When I am both giver and receiver, I find it more challenging to surrender single-mindedly to my experience. Alone, I don't have the luxury of pure expansion, that state of letting go and falling backwards into that soft magic carpet that lifts me effortlessly into clouds higher than the tiniest wisps visible to the eye. Alone, I also deliver that rhythm, that uncompromising and relentless (even when gentle) steady forward march of sensation that says, from me to me, "You will surrender...and I will overcome your resistance...I will find a way to unlock the secrets to your temple, and take you where more than anything you long to go...I will not fail you, I will persist, until you melt, or explode, or shoot up like an immense balloon to heaven...don't worry, I won't stop until you...and I...are both lying surrendered, satisfied in an endorphin-soaked bliss of complete gratification."

Meanwhile, I am also saying, surrender, feel, enjoy, breathe, and expand...

How can I expand when operating in such a dualistic mode?

Quite simply, I have learned to "toggle," or dance, between giving and receiving. I give, I receive, I give, I receive. Every now and then I both give and receive at once.

I like to focus on each and every moment. I can surrender as deeply as I want, knowing only I am present to this experience. And, I can be as playful, sexy, macho, or innocent as I wish, alone there, just me, with my fantasies and my focus on feelings.

Outcomes vary tremendously. I have come to see my own patterns of turn-on, even with myself. Every day is different. I might want a "10" every time, but my body somehow responds uniquely each time. Sometimes I go high and others I only make it into a streaming state without even going over the edge. Even I stand in some final mysterious awe of myself. Why does that happen? My own mystery about myself continues on.

Ultimately, of course, expanded orgasm is about process, not the end goal or result. The "goal" is to maximize pleasure. I love all my experiences individually just for being whatever they are. A few are regular orgasms; most are expanded ones.

If your solo pleasuring sessions have been marked by an intense focus on the orgasm(s) at the end, it is probably just a regular (or multiple regular) orgasm.

If in getting to the goal, you do what's suggested here, letting the feeling spread throughout your body, then you'll begin having expanded orgasms—in addition to regular or multiple orgasms.

Noticing—and Going Over—the Edge(s)

Perhaps no woman has fully engaged in an exploration of her sexuality without having at least some questions as to what constitutes "going over the edge." The standard Masters and Johnson definition is this: "Ten to twelve contractions, spaced eight-tenths of a second apart, at the climax of an orgasm."

Until deeply into my expanded orgasm training, this was not a meaningful answer. First, women very often cannot directly feel contractions, especially weak ones. All they feel is a sensation of pleasure. Then, even if you could feel those contractions, they are happening quite rapidly. Is that what you want to be focusing on during your climax?

And then what about those times when your climax doesn't fit the textbook definition? For example:

You climb higher and higher and higher, and then at some rounded top, seem to come down the other side of the orgasm, without a sharply defined climax.

You feel increasing amounts of pleasure but no top of any kind—just a steady stream of building pleasure.

Your pleasure builds in successive waves with ever-higher plateaus interspersed.

You have increasing series of contractions but don't feel much pleasure.

Women are in great mystery about what constitutes a "real" climax (as opposed to the one they actually had, which they often doubt was real). They have a great range of orgasms and climaxes. They look for a standard but there is none. I don't have any "standard" orgasms. Each one is different. Even the word "standard" smells suspiciously like a male benchmark. How ironic, since men too have this potential for a range of orgasms (but that is the subject of another conversation).

Here are just a few examples of people's descriptions of going over the edge:

"Going over the edge happens when the clitoris leads the way up into extreme pleasure. It is higher than any other part of the body and reaching for the clouds."

"Going over the edge, a woman surrenders to a force that is larger than herself. She is being 'comed,' not coming. She does nothing anymore but enjoy the ride she is being taken on."

"Going over the edge can feel like I am this pipe that expands from a straw to maybe a quarter-size in diameter. Then there is so much energy that the pipe can't hold it any more and it bursts. Then it's like Niagara Falls. That's going over the edge."

"Going over the edge can be like being on an inner tube, floating downstream. Suddenly, you hit rapids. You have this incredible thrill. When it's all done, you are on the other side, saying, 'Wow, when can I have the next one?'"

"Going over the edge is like riding up in an elevator. I pass higher and higher floors. Suddenly there is no ceiling and no elevator and I am in the stars."

"Going over the edge should be undeniable. Whatever happens, it is your call whether you did or didn't go. If you're not sure, then you didn't. It can be as subtle as a feeling of pure light and expansion, or as obvious as a freight trail rolling down a mountain without brakes."

"There are two sides to the experience. You'll know you've done it if you felt a certain way building up to the edge. You are hungry for more sensation. You reach for pleasure. Then, 'it' happens. A time lapse occurs. Then, as you start to come down the other side, you are smiling and feeling refreshed. There has been a release and your whole body is relaxed. You've gone over."

These descriptions share some common features: effortless expansion, rapidly mounting compelling pleasure, and a strong sense of wanting more. It's a place of self-generated momentum.

Remember how Linda felt hindered in her erotic self-development because she believed she couldn't feel much? After continued and determined erotic practice (and with Sam's attention on her success), she had a major breakthrough.

Leading up to this, Linda chronicled all of her erotic adventures:

It's still hard for me to have a date with myself. I feel it's impossible to predict how the session will turn out. Sometimes, I am immediately responsive to the slightest first touch. I can just press my middle right finger lightly on my favorite spot, which is just to the lower left of the top of my clit. One moment of contact, and I feel strong, pleasurable sensations that beg for more. A few strokes and I will be climbing. In a few minutes, I can take myself over the edge. Then I think, "Wow, I really am orgasmic!" It's such a source of pride, just to feel like that. I feel young, like a teenager, attractive and alive. The very next time, I might touch myself in the exact same way, and feel very little. Sometimes it takes two or three minutes just to feel as much as I felt on the first stroke the day before.

The last time this happened, I just kept going. I had to experiment quite a bit. Big circles, little circles, higher, lower. I was like a search device looking for that sexual heat inside me. During this process, I kept remembering to feel, to relax, and to enjoy the process. This focus helped me relax and enjoy every stroke, and not get overly focused on the goal of getting myself off. I kept going, longer than I ever would have before. I felt my pleasure container expand, and that was so pleasurable, I lost sight of the time. My focus was on feeling every stroke with intense appreciation.

Still, at some point, all the stimulation added up to a significant, irresistibly delicious force, because suddenly, a tsunami of sensation welled up inside me. I'd never felt anything like this before. The feelings were 100 percent compelling, and there was no way I wanted to stop now for anything. Moments later, I exploded into a powerful wavelike series of sequential climaxes, firing like pistons, one right after another. I was holding on to the sheets at one point so I wouldn't just fly right off the bed! Even during this, I said to myself, relax…relax…relax. I didn't want to go into my normal pattern of tensing, which is how I believe I curtail a longer orgasm prematurely. I wanted my orgasms to flow through me like an earthquake through silt—rolling, waving, and not meeting any resistance. I remembered you saying that the better I could permit my body to allow the waves to flow, the longer they would flow. And it worked!

For as fun as this is, there have been other days when I've started to get bored easily and watch the clock. I wonder how long I have to do this before it counts as a session. What turns a session like this into a success is if I can accept the little rivulets of streaming energy that intermittently do flow through. If I just continue for as long as I have in the session, I am always happy, no matter what happened during the session.

It's an ecstatic, and yet also, sobering experience. I think about my dates with Sam, and how, in the past, I've expected him to know exactly what to do. He and

I could both win or lose if I did not respond to him in a very short time. But, after these sessions, I realize that even I cannot give myself explosive orgasms many times. And I see that sometimes I too have to hunt around for the winning formula. I have much more empathy for Sam now. I can also give him better feedback because of this.

I hope to figure out why I am so shy about doing all of this. That really is still the hardest part for me. Once I get started, I am always glad I did.

Kelly had her own revelation:

What is surprising me is how rapidly I am developing my orgasmic capacities. It seems like every week, I catapult into a whole new level. I knew I was a highly sexual being when I started, and that this was important to me. I was secretly afraid I would lose that sexual, animal turn-on as I grew older. The opposite seems to be happening. I find I am getting turned on more easily. I can feel warm heat flooding my body, and I know I am getting flushed. I purposely encourage myself to respond to life this way. I have never felt so alive!

When I began this program, I was doing a session three times a week. Now I am up to every other day. I am doing something natural in jump-starting my body and getting all those hormones and endorphins running freely. I feel like I am twenty-one again, except I never looked this beautiful and attractive then! I know my erotic pleasure container is expanding rapidly at this point, and that I alone determine its size. I am increasingly focusing on expanding my orgasms. I have been very goal-oriented in the past. I've missed out on a lot of nice scenery along the way. My new attitude is to focus on feeling every stroke, and let the end come simply as the final stroke…even if it does turn out to be a glorious ending.

I focus on feeling and surrendering and relaxing. I then feel the sensations and spread them through my body just by allowing them to do so. The sensations would bring me over the edge if I just left them in my genitals, but by spreading them out, they rise into my abdomen and into my chest. Next, they travel down my legs, into my neck and head, even out my arms. Soon my entire body is vibrating from head to toe. I am specifically touching my clit, and often my G-area with my favorite dildo. But after I have spread the sensation, the touch is touching all of me.

Jason is listening to me say this and I can't tell quite yet how he feels about my increasing level of turn on. I am doing my best to bring it all to him on our dates. I guess I would love it if he would powerfully celebrate with me rather than make nice, calm, supportive statements. I want my animal to meet his animal. It's so much fun and I feel much more comfortable with Jason, no matter what we learn in this course, since increasingly, I know I can generate so much pleasure for myself.

Staying Over the Edge

OK. You've created time for your erotic explorations, taken yourself up, explored the edge, and gone over the edge. What's left? Is it time to just get up and get on with your day? Or are there other delights to savor? Let's talk a bit about the space of staying over the edge, and of coming down and reentry into your daily world. We'll just taste these topics here, and explore them more fully in later lessons. But it's appropriate to play with these phases of erotic development now, because they are such a part of the juice of the expanded orgasm experience. Most women who haven't trained in expanded orgasm tend to assume that the orgasm ends once she goes over the edge. Nonsense. Now the fun can really begin!

I've heard every excuse in the book, and invented a few myself, for why to stop stimulating yourself right after the climax: "I'm too sensitive now…that's all the sensation I want…I can't even bear the thought of another stroke…I can relax now that it's over and I've reached my goal." Well, would you rather have these excuses or a whole new world of pleasure?

Decide that you will not stop once you go over the edge. Decide to make as your goal an exploration of how long you can continue giving yourself pleasure. Decide as your plan that you will continue for an extra five minutes (or more) just to see what happens on the other side of the edge.

Often, I will take myself up and over an even higher edge. Or, I will simply extend the edge I just went over. I have found that, once over, remaining over the edge becomes effortless. It was a much taller order to transition from a busy day, relax, and wake up my nerve endings than to remain in a state of expanded, or multiple expanded, orgasm!

Whether alone or with a partner, use some of your exploratory sessions to discover what is in the realm of remaining over the edge for varying lengths of time.

Coming Down and Reentering the World

So you've had a blowout orgasm, or a dreamy sensual adventure, or combinations of both. Are you just going to get up now? If you do, you will miss yet another rich source of pleasure. And why make the transition so abrupt? After all, you've just spent a fair amount of time bringing yourself into a very special mood and set of bodily feelings. The downside is that period in which you are reentering your body, and reorienting to everyday reality. Why not enjoy the downside just as much as the climb up?

Keep a clean, folded hand towel nearby. When you have had that very last taste of expanded orgasm pleasure that you can truly enjoy in one session, gently place the towel over your genitals and blot up any remaining lubricant. Let the broad, soft contact carry you back into physical awareness. Then press the towel firmly into your pubic bone, again, relishing the pleasure of the added pressure. Notice how your attention focuses increasingly on the sensations of your hand and towel, and then on your body (and other concrete things). Become more aware of the music, and allow the room to come into focus. Feel yourself breathing in a calm, relaxed manner. Take a few moments more to savor the memories of your most present experience by alternating between the present and the memories. Gradually segue into awareness of the rest of your world. Feel your toes wiggling, face smiling, eyes sparkling, and sheets still snuggling. You are ready to face the day with grace.

If you are going to go to sleep, still use the towel and apply pressure to your genitals. Now in a meditative state, float from here into sleep seamlessly, the way dusk falls into night.

What We've Explored

I shared a lot of stories—mine and others'—with this lesson because I want to let you in on a secret. The secret is that if you want to enjoy *far* more pleasure—more connection with yourself and with your partner than you dared even hope for—then developing your erotic self is the yellow brick road.

Fortunately, your body is marvelously constructed to know what to do. All you have to learn is a little bit of technique and then surrender—release—into your body's inner wisdom. Isn't it nice to know you already have everything you need to launch yourself into a program of *dramatically* enlarging your capacity for pleasure.

With the building blocks of self-knowledge, setting the stage for a greater experience with your partner, and erotic development in place, you're ready to learn specific skills and techniques to experience expanded orgasm with your partner.

5

Step Five: The Opening Strokes

Men, imagine for a moment that you have received a message. You are to meet a mysterious stranger today at seven o'clock. This meeting will determine your course for the rest of your life. If the meeting is successful, and you suitably impress this stranger, your life will flow with wine, honey, and song. A failure to impress will result in dire consequences. You will spend your days and nights endlessly digging a hole, and then desperately trying to fill it.

The message reveals nothing of the character of this person...if indeed, it is even a person. For the next few hours, you prepare for this meeting. You review your manners; you make sure you are well fed, well rested, and well tempered. You center yourself, and tell yourself that you will handle any problem that arises. If it is a beast, you will subdue it and tame it with your charms. If it is a lovely maiden, you will bestow courtesies that would make King Arthur's knights green with envy.

Surprise! The stranger is your significant other. You agreed to have a date at seven o'clock. Prepare to ride a whirlwind of mysteries, emotions, and irrationalities that will shock and defy the greatest male mind. Are you ready?

Let's think about what may lie ahead. Assume you can figure out her mood. She will either be uncharacteristically sleepy (seeming to save near-comatose behavior for exactly moments like this), or frantic (from fending off rush hour road rage, coaxing a clutch of clambering kids, or losing her favorite earring). Perhaps she will be spiraling downhill emotionally (because a friend didn't call her exactly at 2:00 P.M. today), or absolutely flat (speaking with about as much excitement as a CIA agent passing over a secret code in a public bathroom).

Alternately, she may be thrilled to see you (and flinging herself into your arms with the excitement of a castaway being rescued). She may have decided that tonight is "Sex Kitten Night" (and as a surprise, she has lit candles, put on romantic music, and donned a provocative teddy). She may even demonstrate a surge of empathy for your hard day, and be waiting to give you a massage.

You just never know who you're going to meet until you open that door. All you can know is what you'll do once you find out. You will stay in present time. Her moods won't faze you a bit, since you already know to expect them. You will accept her the way you find her. You will help her land softly if she is overly excited, and take her energy up if this is what is required. You will do whatever it takes to turn the situation around. In doing this (and more), you know you will create the best expanded orgasm experience you possibly can for the two of you this evening.

After this brief pause, you enter the room, glowing with inner confidence, a sympathetic heart, and an expectation of the wonderful time you will create together. Even though the "date" has not even yet begun, you have already demonstrated the three principles that will get you everything and everywhere in expanded orgasm: *attention, intention,* and *control.* We will examine these principles separately, but you can see from the vignette that all three were woven together and not sequential. Let's review them one by one and then examine the tapestry more closely.

Attention: This is where your mind is focusing at any point in time. In expanded orgasm, you want to have all your attention on your partner when you are the giver. In order to do this, you will begin a process of no longer thinking of yourself and solely thinking about your partner (yes, yes, easier said than done, but, oh, so necessary). This is one of those things you will find becomes easier as the date progresses. In the beginning of an expanded orgasm date, just solely focus on your partner as an experiment. Trust me, it will lead you down the road to riches.

The giver always puts all of his attention on the receiver. When it's the giver's turn to receive expanded orgasm, the rules remain the same.

Intention: This is what you decide or plan you are going to do in a given situation. Some intentions are very broad-based—as in the vignette, where you intend to have a great time, no matter where you find yourself at the beginning of the date. Or an intention can have a narrower focus, such as to bring her up and onto a high plateau.

As the giver, you'll want to start the expanded orgasm date intending to bring your partner into the room of expanded orgasm that you have already entered. This presupposes the important step of having entered the expanded orgasm room yourself. You'll also intend to do whatever is necessary along the way to fulfill that overarching pleasure-creating intention.

The receiver does not have the same responsibility. Her part right now in the expanded orgasm dance is to prepare to increasingly surrender to pleasure. The receiver is depending on the giver to overwhelm her with his intentions so pleasurably that surrender continuously appears as the most joyful, pleasurable option.

And yes, men, when you are the receiver, surrender will be your only "job," too.

Control: These are the actions you take to implement your intentions. They will be physical, mental, and emotional actions that continuously unfold over time.

Expanded orgasm is a process, not a goal. Each moment is the best moment there is. In entering the room of expanded orgasm, you have already made the transition from goal to process. In expanded orgasm, then, control is not over the final outcome; your intentions are handling that issue. Your control is serving your intentions. Control is you steering your adventure ever closer to the intentions you have set, one action at a time.

In true control, you decide when to hold her, where to hug her, how long to listen to her, and when to lay her gently down and get her to relax. You have divorced yourself from the misleading myth that there will ever be a formula for what to do. You are in present time, responding to her every desire by creating ever more relaxation, bonding, love, connection, and, of course, physical pleasure.

As the giver, it is your job to take control. The receiver wants more than anything for you to do this, so she will have something and someone to surrender to. Even when the choice is hers and hers alone whether to surrender, she desires a strong, confident, knowing, responsive, intent-full, attentive man to surrender to. That, quite simply, is going to be your job.

In the story above, the heroic man wove attention, intention, and control into a tapestry of process. Attention on the situation (going to meet the stranger, finding out who it was, and determining her mood) generated new information over time. With each new bit of information, his intention remained constant (to create a winning situation, stay in present time, and do whatever it took to do so without getting knocked off course). What he did to take control shifted considerably (he did not give in to fears of performance; he stayed focused on the tasks at hand, and mentally created action plans at each step of the way). This ongoing attention, intention, and control mental feedback loop will continue cycling throughout the remainder of this date, and throughout all successful expanded orgasm dates.

A Special Message for Men

Pssst…men! Is that you? Are we alone now? Your partner—and definitely you—will be very happy you arrived here. You do want to give your partner exquisite pleasure, right? And you want to thoroughly enjoy it, right? In fact, do you want to enjoy giving her exquisite pleasure so much you can hardly wait to do it? You are about to open new horizons, ways of thinking, and new patterns of behavior. If you made it here, I am confident that you are already a caring, competent lover. In our practice, those who come to learn expanded orgasm tend to be skilled lovers. So right away you can relax. This lesson is not about fixing your sexual performance. It is for men who are looking for new approaches to add in to their already existing repertoire. This is an excellent and powerful attitude for entering expanded orgasm training. Just keep an open mind. Try out what we present here. Be a researcher. If what you learn about expanded orgasm works, great! Then add it to what already works for you. This is about going from good to better.

I want to clue you in on something straight off. Some hobbies or disciplines start out easy and then seem to become progressively more difficult. Expanded orgasm does just the opposite. It is hardest to learn in the beginning; the more you progress, the easier expanded orgasm becomes. This is because early on, there is much to learn, and less to show in terms of outcome. As you progress to a certain point, where you and your partner are experiencing whole new worlds of pleasure, you can add on new information incrementally, while enjoying all you've learned up to now. It's the principle of "a little bit of sugar makes the medicine go down." Right now we are in that place of fetching some sugar.

As you learn expanded orgasm, consider yourself learning the ways or customs of a strange, new, exotic land. This will help make an open-minded transition into the "expanded orgasm room" we talked about earlier. And it will help you find the sugar that can propel you through that initial learning. All right, then, let's begin to make that transition out of "life as we know it" and into expanded orgasm.

Activity #16: Arrange the Date with Your Partner

All right, women, back to you! The "date" is the time you and your partner set aside to relate intimately. It starts the moment you mutually agree on having it. The more time you have to prepare for the date, the more you increase your chances of having it be spectacular.

Everyone loves those spontaneous times when you walk through the door, see your wife at the stove, say, "Honey, let's do it...now!" and she drops everything. You take her, right then and there, up into the furthest reaches of ecstasy. I've counted the number of times that has spontaneously happened to me, and guess what? I don't need a calculator to do the math.

Fortunately, I have lost count of the number of dates that I have deliberately arranged with Allen. We arrange dates almost all the time. We don't want to leave our opportunities for intimacy and connection to mere chance!

Making a date is not the same as promising how you are going to feel when you start the date, or even promising how the date is going to progress. A date is simply an agreement to get together for purposes of exploring and enjoying love and connection. This is an ideal time for expanded orgasm to occur. About 80 percent of our dates result in an expanded orgasm session.

Here is what we ask couples to agree to bring to their date:

- Their intentions to get present with one another.
- Their desires to create intimacy together.
- Their willingness to do whatever it takes to arrive in the best shape possible.
- Their promise to accept each other as they find each other.
- Their agreement that they will drop any expectations of how the date has to turn out.

Activity #17: Create a Sensual Environment

Until you generate your own spontaneous surge of enthusiastic agreement, please, take my word for it: making the transition from everyday existence into the expanded orgasm space is more important, and often more challenging, than you may have ever realized. Please, don't rush right into expanded orgasm. Always make an elegant, thoughtful transition.

One day, this concept will come to live in you forever. You will always have that inner barometer that tells you where on the transition-meter you currently are.

(My expanded orgasm transition meter runs from totally stressed and a million miles away from expanded orgasm to Ahhhhhh, Yes! I'm here now, and does it ever feel great!)

Setting up the space can be a great and effective way to transition. It can include talking with your partner in advance about the fun and romance you plan to create. Many couples plan some expanded orgasm dates extensively, and barely manage to put other expanded orgasm dates in their Palm Pilots before running off to the rest of their day.

Men, as the givers, when you arrive for the expanded orgasm date, set your intention on creating *transition*. This is a time to begin shifting your attention toward pleasure. Ask: What can I do now to go in the direction of more pleasure? Can I make the space more sensually appealing? Does the bed look attractive? Get clean folded towels. Adjust the sound and lighting to the woman's favorite levels. Consciously go through the mental exercise of slowing down your breathing, softening your voice, and relaxing your body.

Women, as the receivers, prepare to surrender to pleasure. You, too, will want to find ways to expand your sensual awareness. You might visualize yourself connecting with your partner, or asking for—and receiving—a massage. You might imagine how soft the bed will feel once you are lying down. You might even change into something more inviting and sensual, just for the change in atmosphere this will create.

What do you think of something recent clients did? We had asked Cliff to set up the expanded orgasm session space for Janine. He agreeably said, "Sure," and tossed a towel to her, saying, "Here hon. Would you put the towel down?" The towel promptly landed in her face. Neither one noticed any problem. Janine promptly began straightening out the towel on the slightly messy bed. Cliff, meanwhile, looked around the room, slightly confused as to what to do next. Both of them would have been more excited watching a paint-drying contest.

We interjected (mustering all diplomacy as we could). This time we asked Cliff to approach Janine, give her a hug, and whisper some sweet nothings in her ear. As we directed his every move, he took specific, room-enhancing actions while Janine watched. He made the bed look beautiful. He took several moments to straighten out the sheets and to lay a towel down in the center. He adjusted the lighting, selected music that Janine loved, and put on a handsome robe. He then put all his attention on Janine, complimenting her on how attractive she looked right then. He held her in his arms and asked her softly what she wanted next. This time, she turned up the heat, eagerly begging him to continue their expanded orgasm date.

Find a way to do the "little" things that make a room look nice. Observe how your partner responds to your fussing and attention to detail. Fuss until you definitely notice the increase in your partner's turn-on.

Understand Resistance

Just because you have set the date and both of you have arrived on time to a wonderfully prepared space, doesn't mean the date can now begin.

Biologically, men are wired to "sow their seed" everywhere, as often as women will permit. Women, on the other hand, are wired to select one sexual partner out of a line of applicants. Choosiness is an asset to women and, a woman can exercise her ability to choose any time she contemplates having intimate relations with a man. This biological instinct applies even in cases of long-term relationships.

Translation: men, expect your female partner to resist pleasure. She will resist even when she had moved heaven and earth to arrive at the date on time. Resistance can be handled easily, if understood. Most women are just acting on their biological instincts. Their inner self might revert back to primal instructions, saying loud and clear, "Find out if this is 'the one' for you. Find out if he will love you and protect you against bears. Find out if he will bring you a mastodon when he goes hunting. Make sure he still thinks you are the best woman alive."

Now, men are rational, so they can't always comprehend this simple female line of inquiry. After all (as the gag implies), they married you, didn't they? Why do they need to prove to you that they love you?

So men, here is one of those moments when you can really score points. Understand you are dealing with a woman's wiring…not something you will easily win out over. See her resistance as a series of little tests that women like to give a man right before they have sex.

"Open the window. Check to see that the door is locked. Raise the heat. Change the volume on the music. Get me a glass of water." These tests are often quite small. If you (the man) hear these tests as opportunities to be her hero and pass "Go" quickly, you will respond to them with delight and enthusiasm. If you begin to question the tests ("Close the window? I just opened it five minutes ago!"), you will delay the expanded orgasm session unnecessarily. All too often, a woman wants you to pass a test before she can fully surrender. Enjoy these little tests for what they are, and allow them to add to your dance of surrendering to pleasure.

Frank is exemplary when it comes to tests. When Marcia asks him to do something little right before a date (like get her some juice), he always checks to see what else she wants. He'll always study Marcia's face, and even look around to see if he can offer other help. If she looks worried, he'll check that with her. If she looks happy, he'll comment on her pretty smile. He'll always compliment her on some aspect of her appearance. According to Marcia, on their last date, he brought a little chocolate truffle home for her. If that wasn't enough, as she was getting comfortable, he reached over and handed her some extra pillows before she reached for them herself. He then straightened up the new little wrinkles on the bed, so that it was completely wrinkle-free. With her juice, he also brought her a little flower. Marcia was practically in a state of expanded orgasm by the time he climbed into bed, long before he ever touched her.

Does this sound excessive? Not according to Frank. Frank will tell you himself: "This is the smartest thing I have ever learned. Marcia used to give me all kinds of little tests, which I would pass, or fail, with great irregularity, since I wasn't hip to her testing me. It would often take a half hour to get us both relaxed and in the mood for pleasure. If I give Marcia even five minutes of this attention proactively, she'll be cooing like a baby dove. This is as much fun for me as it is for her. I'm never going back to my old ways."

Give Pleasure without Obligation

Many couples would not make dates if they felt that the date obligated them to a certain type of behavior. Sometimes, even with their best efforts, one or the other is tired or upset, or otherwise challenged to go directly for pleasure. Often, by demonstrating compassion, listening skills, and overall tenderness, the other partner can be the hero. What greater intimacy could one ask for?

Obligations can be a real turn-off to expanded orgasm. We ask our clients to view each expanded orgasm session as a gift to their partner. If the man is giving to the woman, we ask that he give it with no strings attached. A gift given with expectations is not really a gift. Many women decline an expanded orgasm date, fearing that there is a tab running up that she'll have to pay later. As if it weren't hard enough already to transition from our everyday, fast-paced world, into one of pleasure and letting go! No one wants to feel that they owe someone else for the attention they've been given.

And, what greater gift could she give you than her luscious enjoyment?

Do you give to your partner with expectations of something in return? Does your partner do this to you? Discuss your answers openly. Can you find ways in which you can commit to giving each other even more loving pleasure just for the joy of giving, with no strings attached? Is that what you would want?

Many times, I have arrived at a date with no desire to have an expanded orgasm. Allen has accepted this completely. I feel so loved that as a result, I let my heart open and our love and enjoyment for each other expands regardless of what happens during the date.

Activity #18: Give and Receive without Obligation

Many women report that they have never had the experience of giving without a deep sense of obligation to give back. This attitude is ingrained in them from early childhood. I am sure many men feel this way, too.

Take time now to experience giving (and receiving) without obligation. Arrange two dates to spend time in a sandbox together. Women, in the first sandbox session, generate a list of what you would like your partner to do for you and to you in the session. The list can contain various forms of massage, non-genital and genital if you desire. By agreement, only you will receive physical attention during this session; there will be no reciprocation until another day.

How does it feel to enjoy attention with no strings attached? How did your response to this situation compare with that at other times, when you did feel the obligation (not just the desire) to respond?

Men, notice how it feels to give, knowing that you will not be a recipient later.

For the second sandbox session, the man will be receiver, and the woman will be giver. Now it is the man's turn to notice how it feels to receive without any expectation of giving, and women can enjoy just how much fun it is to give, without expectation of receiving.

Glenn and Wanda found this exercise very helpful. Wanda was a powerful executive, but she had to admit she felt insecure about Glenn giving her pleasure without wanting anything in return. "Even if he says he doesn't want anything, and that giving is pleasure in itself, I don't believe him. I am certain that somewhere, deep down, Glenn will be disappointed if I don't give back."

After the exercises, Wanda had the first-hand experience of unconditional giving and receiving. Wanda told us:

I don't think I really got the point of the exercise until I had a sandbox session of just giving to Glenn. I was nervous in advance. I thought I would be bored. I thought I would be resentful, too, of him getting all the pleasure.

Glenn and I discussed what he wanted in some detail; this by itself was new and fun. When I started giving to him, his body opened up, relaxed, and reached for every last drop of sensation I could create and pass on to him. I felt so powerful, creating his pleasure like that! Imagine my surprise to realize just what a fantastic time I had just giving to him. I could understand how Glenn could enjoy giving to me without expecting anything in return. Giving now became its own reward.

Glenn added:

I too was a little nervous about this exercise. I was afraid that I was really just another selfish male. I had never thought about what I did or didn't expect from Wanda. When I gave to her, I was in ecstasy. Every sparkle in her eye, every whispered purr, and especially those moments when her body reached for more sensation from me—nonverbally pulling me deeper in to her—was magic. Wow!

The Two-Minute Rule

This is so important that it deserves to be italicized:

I may not be in the mood right now for expanded orgasm or other physical pleasure. However, I realize that sometimes I need (and even enjoy) a jump-start. I will give two minutes to starting an expanded orgasm session. If I am not in the mood to continue after two minutes, we will cheerfully stop and do something else. You will give me 100 percent credit for having given this jump-start a chance to work.

We bring in the Two-Minute Rule early in expanded orgasm training. It is an effective way to respect the other person, avoid putting pressure on him or her, and yet, give each partner the opportunity to overcome any resistance to making the transitions from everyday survival to pleasure.

Use it when one partner, but not the other, would like to transition from intimate connect time into an expanded orgasm session. The hesitant partner can agree to continue, but using the Two-Minute Rule. If in two minutes, this partner wants to end things, he or she can simply make the request, no questions asked, and getting major credit for having given the idea a chance. We think you will fall in love with this little rule. I know I am usually glad I proceeded.

Sam seemed overwhelmed by all we had asked of him. "This may sound silly to you," he explained, "but the only way I have ever gotten Linda to enjoy sex is through my repeated encouragement and motivation. I'll admit it: without my nudging, I am afraid that Linda will give up being sexual forever. Sure, she'll want to cuddle, and who knows, maybe once in a blue moon, go for more, but what about me? You are expecting me to have a complete personality change. I am just not sure I can do that. I still want to have sex with Linda. And I would love to give her more expanded orgasm than she or I have ever dreamed of. I am just not willing to give up on my expectations of having a sex life, and I need to make sure it happens since she won't."

"Sam, we aren't in the personality change business," I reminded him. "We specifically do not do therapy. Fortunately, we don't think you have a fundamental 'problem' with your relationship. You love and cherish each other and only want that to increase. But you are paying us to show you ways to have even more pleasure than you are currently having with Linda. Are you with me so far?"

Sam nodded. "But what you're asking of me sure feels like I would need a head transplant to achieve. And, one for Linda, too, while we're at it."

"Sam, if you are willing to have more with Linda, then I am suggesting you use something different than your current strategy. There is a lot of history and some unresolved emotions in your dynamics. These factors keep you two out of present time. This strategy will never get you to where you want to go."

At this point Linda added a comment, "I don't think Sam heard the part about making a transition. Would that include making a shift away from the way we normally communicate, as well as a shift into the room of expanded orgasm?"

"Yes, Linda, the shift is away from your everyday mode of being, and into present time. Sam, do you think that for ten minutes, you could take all your expectations, judgments, and 'knowledge' about Linda, and put them into a paper bag to leave outside the door to the room where you are going to practice expanded orgasm? Just once? If you could do this, it would be a very powerful exercise for you to try."

Sam smiled. "I guess as long as I could get the bag back at the end of the session, I could do it."

That night, Sam and Linda had an expanded orgasm session. Beforehand, each had a little ritual in which they left all of their issues about each other "outside the door." Linda assured me that her bag was easily as brim-full as Sam's. Inside both bags were the reasons both had to be fearful and angry at one another. The anger tended to focus on unmet expectations from the past, while the fears stemmed from expectations that future needs and wants would go unmet as well. Both of them silently wrote down their expectations, fears, and angry thoughts on slips of paper and put them in the bags. They then spent about ten minutes enhancing the sensual atmosphere of their bedroom. When they finally sat down together on the bed, they looked at each other with anticipation. Now what? What was left when all the expectations were gone? Who was there now that the filters of hurt and anger had been temporarily stripped away?

Linda and Sam stared into each other's eyes for a long while, asking one question after another. Then even the questions died away. The space in the room seemed to grow larger and larger, and the energy of their magnetic attractions to one another expanded to fill the ever-growing area. For the first time in a long time, they were ready to maximize the quality of their sensual time together.

Their questions were a little more loaded than I wanted to let on. I knew we were asking a lot of both Linda and Sam. To change patterns one has had for twenty-five years of marriage is no small request. And yet, the changes that needed to be made could take as long as a lifetime of failed attempts—or a moment. It takes only a moment to decide to leave your baggage at the door and enter the room of expanded orgasm. *This is a room in which present time is all-important.* The past, and the future, will only get in your way. Even when your past and future are fabulous, they are still not appropriate guests here. This is the space of pure present time.

Sam and Linda had taken comfort in knowing that they could leave (and later retrieve) their "baggage" outside the door. That's a small, emotionally safe step.

Sam and Linda's initial experience of true transition created a benchmark experience to which they would know they could now return. In the future, we knew their entire experience of expanded orgasm was now going to be much deeper and way more fun, too.

Ironically, Sam would find he was confronting more of his own and Linda's "stuff" than ever. Each time he found things to let go of, he had to make the choice. Would he rather be "right" or happy? For him, he had to let go of his preconceived notions of who Linda was, what her appetite was, and how she might (or might not) act in the absence of his manipulation. Fortunately, he was discovering a Linda newer (and far more wonderful) than the woman he had carried in his fears. Ultimately, each time he let go of some more, he was powerfully and pleasurably rewarded with what he discovered. The expanded orgasm process was starting to work its magic!

Use Ample Lubrication

Women vary greatly in their preferences for lubrication. Some like lots and some like barely any at all little. Many women, especially those past forty, may take longer to lubricate the way they did when they were younger, but, once they get going, can lubricate well. Others, like me, just love lots of lubrication all the time. Allen and I have often fantasized about marketing a new device for women like me. Men would strap this new device to their hand or other body part, where it would dispense lubrication in a continuous stream! Since we have yet to invent this device, we have done what others do—we keep lots of it handy and ready to use.

Lubrication extends and expands the pleasure, so that delicious sensations effortlessly glide everywhere the touch goes. It allows the woman to experience her lover's touch as more continual and also smoother. And, in longer sessions, it protects her from getting sore from too much friction.

Experiment with a variety of oil-based and water-based lubrications, as tremendous differences abound. A switch to a lady's "lube" of choice can make a highly significant difference in the overall pleasure she'll experience on her date.

Your Optimal Position

Let's move from the philosophical to something really practical: finding a comfortable position for giving the woman expanded orgasm pleasure. Position is something that will be difficult to adequately describe. I'll try, in detail, in the pages ahead.

With our clients, we often spend an hour or more just on positioning. We ask our clients to get into our "standard pleasuring position" as described below. Often this will be the first time in this position. If it is new, then almost always we want to adjust the way the couple fits together. Our adjustment tools are usually a posse of pillows—ten or more, that we go around and place strategically, so that every nook and cranny of both bodies is blissfully supported, and both of them can focus their attentions on the fun stuff, and not bodily discomforts, however subtle.

Positioning is so important that we are not even surprised when clients think a miracle has occurred after we have fine-tuned their positioning. One client, Juliette, said, "Wow! I feel like I am with an entire new lover," when all that we had done was to put a pillow under her partner Ben's right arm, which thereby lowered the angle at which his hand touched her genitals and reduced the strain he had been unconsciously experiencing. His touch was so mellowed without the tension that his next single stroke nearly sent her over the edge.

While this may sound like an extreme example, it isn't. We've come to expect these types of breakthroughs when positioning is adjusted. Imagine how you'd feel if you were always in slightly the wrong-sized shoes, and then one day, a shoemaker came to town and designed a pair especially for you. What words would you use at that new moment of truth? Heaven on earth? Sheer, unadulterated joy? I want to run a thousand miles now? These are the kinds of great results that good positions give.

If you can get your position right after even one session, consider yourselves ready to proceed with the next steps. If you can't, I strongly suggest you continue working on getting the right position until you succeed. If you are not comfortable, you will not be able to relax (and hence expand) sufficiently to support the kind of expanded orgasm pleasure you are seeking to optimize.

For our training conversations, we use a standard pleasuring position which we'll describe shortly. It's advantages are this: it allows easy access to the woman's clitoris for the man, it is easy to see the woman's genital landscape clearly, the man's hand can rest comfortably on her abdomen and give him a secure anchor, and the man can use his body to cradle her with his knees and arms and create a very secure feeling.

Standard Pleasuring Position

You will need at least five and preferably ten pillows of varying sizes. Have at least four pillows of standard size or larger. We recommend getting a variety of pillows, all of which have washable slipcovers. We have round pillows, squishy pillows, big pillows, fat pillows, bendable pillows, and so on. There is always a pillow perfect for our needs.

You will also want to have a bed with a backrest that a man can lean back on. Or, consider purchasing a back jack. In a good position, men, you will have good visual contact with both her face and genitals.

The man should be sitting with his back supported by a bed-rest, pillows, or back jack. He should then bend his knees, so that the woman can slide the lower part of her body underneath his knees. They are now lying perpendicular to each other. If her knees remain bent, one of the man's knees will go under her two knees; and the other knee can go over her abdomen. If he cannot easily clear her body, he can place the foot of the over-reaching knee on a pillow.

As the woman sidles up to the man, her hip or thigh should be directly against his genitals. Men, if she is too far from you to reach her genitals comfortably, ask her to move closer to you. That ought to get her snuggling up to you. It will feel good to her for her body to be encompassed by your legs, arms, and trunk. Just be careful not to place any more pressure on her body than she likes. Take the time to get it just right.

Other accessories to the pleasure, like lubricants and water, should be readily available and easy to reach.

Is the picture clear? Let's paint it out for the right-handed man. (Left-handed men, please make the appropriate mental picture fit by reversing right and left commands here.) The right-handed man will have the woman's head to his right. She will have scooted her body under his right knee. Her knees will then go over his left knee. Then her knees naturally fall somewhat to her sides. She may want to place additional pillows under her knees for support.

Now the heel of his palm should be flat against her mons pubis. He can rest his wrist and lower arm on her abdomen. At some point, he places his left hand under her legs in order to gain access to her internal genital area.

The bottom hand may initially slide under her buttocks, leaving the thumb to gently rest on her introitus (and not inside of her). Men, as you awaken your partner's desires, she may ask you at a later point in time to place fingers from the bottom hand inside of her. (We cover this more fully in Step Eight.)

Both of you should ask yourselves, "Could we spend the next hour comfortably in this position without having to move?" Pillows can optionally go in the following places for additional support: under her left knee, under her right knee, under the man's body to raise him if necessary, under his right arm for extra support; under his foot; under her head and neck; and so on.

Men, you will know your position is not right if you feel your arm tensing up, your back getting tight, your neck hurting, or your mind continuing to look for another comfortable position. Sometimes, it seems no position is entirely comfortable. Do the best you can. Often, the only problem is one of unfamiliarity. Usually within two or three sessions, this position will in fact feel comfortable.

We realize that some people have hip, neck, back, and other physical limitations that require using other positions. You will still be able to follow along with our lessons, but may need to adjust to your own situation. Sometimes a man will want his lover on a bed or massage table, where he can then stand or sit in front of her, or beside her. Other times, he may want to lie on his side, with his head near her feet. These other positions may require more initial getting used to, and may be harder to train with, as the two handed access may not be as effortless. The man-in-front of the woman position, for example, doesn't work too well for training purposes, because then he can only access her clitoris with his thumb. Now, while in your chosen position, experiment in sandbox fashion. Stay in good communication about the comfort level. Notice what happens after two, five, and ten minutes of using one and then both hands.

Activity #19: Find Your Preferred Position

Women, you can do a lot to ensure that *all* your expanded orgasm dates are a success by having a policy of insisting that your partner get completely comfortable before you begin. Even if it takes twenty minutes, do not skip this.

There is no way to practice expanded orgasm reliably and develop skills of receiving pleasure for an hour or longer if your partner is not comfortable.

Allow me to be even more dramatic to make this important point. If your partner is not completely comfortable from the start, your expanded orgasm session may never get off the ground. As we shall see, in expanded orgasm, mind and body become one unit. Relaxation is essential to both giver and receiver. Tensing up, for either mental or physical reasons, will directly translate into the transmission of tense energy to the receiver. Tense energy does not feel nearly as good as relaxed energy, and you will be getting a partial experience.

Take a sandbox session together to experiment with the standard position outlined above, adapting it to your particular bodies. Women, before you agree on the perfect position, check. Are you feeling comfortably cradled? Is there any pressure on your body that is not pleasurable? You should agree that you both feel ready to melt into the bed for an hour when the position is optimal.

Relax Your Body

All the preparation can be a great turn-on to a woman. Skilled expanded orgasm lovers know this and enjoy the dance of preparation tremendously. This part of the dance takes time, but when a woman is finally ready to have you give her expanded orgasm, she wants you to do so with confidence, and without further delay. Now is the time to go straight for her favorite spot and begin the process of taking firm control of her central nervous system, her mind, her spirit, and her experience.

Up until now you have been empathetic and attentive. It's time to transition into beaming confidence. When the expanded orgasm date begins, you enter a part of the dance in which she increasingly surrenders to your control. However, she will only be able to do so if you can prove to her that you know exactly what you are doing. Gaining confidence is a mind game. And so, men, in your mind, you must already be confident.

Again, you are preparing the next step in entering the expanded orgasm space. Expanded orgasm space differs from your normal everyday life space in numerous ways, some of which we have already covered. Let us review some qualities of the expanded orgasm space, and consider yet some more ways the expanded orgasm space is different.

What's important is the process, as opposed to the outcome.

You get there simply by relaxing and letting go of all your tensions, both physical and mental. The more you can relax, the more you enter.

The present is what matters; your focus is on how you and your partner feel now, in this very moment.

You go deeply into a space of gratitude, surrender, breathing slowly and deeply, feeling every stroke, and expanding the sensations to spread throughout your body.

And now let's add some more characteristics:

Your body and mind increasingly become experienced as one unit. As you feel ecstasy, you are ecstatic, and think ecstatic thoughts. And, as you think ecstatic thoughts, you feel ecstatic.

Eventually, your body/mind system becomes one with the body/mind system of your partner. Thus the giver can take the receiver's entire ride of ecstasy. *The pleasure she feels is a gift to both of you.*

Similarly, the pleasure the giver feels in giving will be felt by the receiver and used to fuel the receiver's ride.

At some point, the giver and receiver are completely sharing the same experience.

In learning expanded orgasm, we encourage practitioners to notice when these qualities occur, and to have fun with them. When we are completely sharing the same experience, for example, it is almost like mind-reading. Then, I can mentally direct my partner to do something while I am in expanded orgasm and find him instantly complying.

The minute you begin an expanded orgasm session, prepare to become increasingly more transparent to your partner. If you are tense, your partner will feel it and know it. If you are relaxed and confident, he or she will feel and know this too.

Activity #20: Relax into Your Energy Current

Men, since you are the giver, you are the one assigned with the honor of starting off the fun. Therefore, it is essential that you relax. In your position, notice the following: feel your arm lie across your partner's belly. Allow it to become soft and pliable.

In this state, imagine the current of energy that courses throughout your body reaching all the way to your fingertips. Experiment with softening your arm. Do you feel the energy current becoming more pronounced as you do so? Now stiffen your arm so that you have two states, stiff and soft. Notice what happens to the energy flow. It should be maximized when you are at your most soft and pliable.

"Soft" does not mean limp and mushy. Remember, in the room of expanded orgasm, body and mind are one. You can conceptually send your intention through your body, and down and out through your arms, to give them power, even while you are relaxed.

Develop benchmarks of awareness for intentful softness, and its counterpart, stiff unfeelingness. Now you have two frames of reference.

Now bring your partner into the process. Ask her to feel the difference as you relax and then stiffen. You can do this at the level of mind alone to determine just how much she is already capable of knowing which state you are in. Ask her to tell you what level of relaxation you are at with each change. If your partner can also tell when you are stiffening up, you have one more feedback source. She, too, can point out when you feel tense. Invite her to remind you to relax even further whenever the thought crosses her mind.

As a third experiment, have her request that you alter the way you carry your arm energy. Experience your arm as an extension on your mind. It should be still lying on her abdomen, straight down the center. The heel of your palm should still be on her mons pubis. Allow yourself to feel every nuance about your partner. Is her skin warm? Is it getting warmer? Is she vibrating? Is she relaxed? What effect are you having on her? Notice, from moment to moment, how the two of you interact in a mind/body dance.

She can make requests of your mind/body state. The requests can be body state, mind state, or a combination of both.

"Melt your arm into me."

"Feel confident."

"Let the energy flow even more powerfully."

"Relax more deeply."

"Feel more of me."

"Notice my vibration reaching all the way to your neck."

In a more advanced session, you can ask questions like:

"What am I feeling now?"

"What do you feel inspired to give me energetically right now?"

You can also do this exercise in reverse. Tell her what you are doing and see the extent to which she experiences it directly.

We also encourage you to reverse roles. Let her be the giver and you (the man) be the receiver. It will be helpful for both of you to have a undeniable experience of the mind/body world that you create together.

With each suggestion, give her feedback on what you notice too. This ongoing feedback process is essential; it serves to reinforce the new paradigms that define expanded orgasm.

Repeating this exercise will repay you bountifully. It promotes deep bonding, deep connection, deep pleasure, and deep understanding of the underpinnings of the expanded orgasm world.

The Three Strokes

Technique does not play a large part in expanded orgasm training. After all, every woman is different, and even the same woman changes from moment to moment, day to day, week to week, and month to month. We emphasize *attention, intention,* and *control* as a primary means to mastering expanded orgasm. Men yearn for techniques, so this is a bit frustrating for them. They are seeking the magic stroke that will reliably send her over the edge, day in and day out. Such a stroke does not exist. Even if it did, the body/mind tires of repetition and craves novelty. So the stroke you used yesterday to ignite the fireworks may be a dud today and once again leave you in pure mystery. Expanded orgasm does teach process, fortunately, and this process will yield far greater success than any content-limited technique could ever deliver.

That said, there is one technique that you can use reliably, as long as you do so in the context of attention, intention, and control: the starting three strokes. Starting is different from the rest of the expanded orgasm experience because at the start, a woman most likely will not have made the complete transition into the expanded orgasm state. Starting strokes accomplish just that. The three strokes are intended to set the tone and produce pleasurable engorgement. It will be easier to locate her clit and her favorite spot.

Learn these strokes well so that you can spend most of your time soaring in the artistic paradise of pure expanded orgasm creation, rather than desperately hunting and pecking to find a way to pleasure her.

We will be increasingly training you to *ride the energy of your partner*, so that you come to track her every desire, moment by moment, without dropping her level of turn on. This is the royal path to expanded orgasm. These three starting strokes will get you started very reliably. They are not the only way to start but they are a dependable way, excellent for those learning the art.

First get into your comfortable position.

Stroke 1: Get a goodly quantity of your partner's favorite lubricant and, starting just above her anus, slowly draw your fingers along her outer lips, spreading her pubic hair, and covering it with enough lubricant to mat it down and thereby not get in your way. Remember to breathe, and feel what you are doing. Make this stroke feel good to *you.*

Stroke 2: Get some more lubricant. Now, stroking inside the space between her inner lips—her introitus—use your middle or index finger to part her outer vaginal lips. Slowly (and with feeling) draw your hand up until your fingertip meets her clitoris. Her clit may be quite unengorged at this point, but by now, you should have a good idea of where it is located, and what it feels like flaccid as well as engorged.

Stroke 3: This stroke starts out like Stroke 2. Begin at the bottom of her introitus and stroke her with your extended finger very slowly, parting her inner lips. Go with a firm, slow, feeling touch that allows the energy to pass from you to her and back again. The more you feel, the more you will nonverbally encourage her to feel. This time, allow your finger to rest on her clitoris, and begin a small, frictionless up and down (or possibly diagonal) rubbing motion. If your partner has already indicated that the two o'clock position is her favorite spot, make sure your finger is exactly there. Otherwise, go to where she has told you she is most pleasurably sensitive.

Continue rubbing slowly and gently and methodically. Ground yourself in the pleasure you feel giving her this pleasure. She may not be very responsive yet; it often takes a few minutes to sufficiently wake up the area.

This exercise may have to be repeated twenty times before you truly get the feel for the process you are in. Dialog is crucial. Ladies, if your man is not on your favorite spot, gently guide him to where it is. Alternate between verbal and direct physical guidance. Starting out, many women will pleasure themselves first, find their own sweet spot, engorge their clitorises nicely, and in so doing, give better directions to their partner.

When done properly, the man should soon be feeling a "hot spot" developing. It will actually feel different to you in the "hot" or "sweet spot" compared to other nearby locales.

The woman too will feel a certain pleasure starting to develop. It often is a sense of increased heat and electric current. This sweet spot is going to be your guide to expanding your erotic experience. You will probably need to practice several times in order to find the spot. Remember to use the sandbox approach. This is about cocreating maximum pleasure, not about egos and performance.

Once you can locate the spot, you and your partner can begin to train to stay on the spot. Careful now! The orgasmic energy can hit like a tornado. A sudden surge of its power can knock you off course. Suddenly, the man, the woman, or both, find their mind somewhere else. Of course, at this point, the man's finger has strayed from her favorite spot.

Did you ever dream of learning to ride a bucking bronco and hanging in there as the intensity climbed? What a thrilling feeling! Learning to stay on a woman's favorite spot as the energy intensifies is a similar experience. You can get knocked off if you are not prepared, via your intentions and attention to each stroke. However, once you learn to ride the energy and stay with this sensation, you will find a friend: the sweet spot energy becomes ever more pronounced, and makes it easier and easier to bring her pleasure. Once you can "lock on" to that spot, you can use that sweet energy as a homing device through a variety of strokes.

This lesson gives you the basic building block you need for all that follows. We ask our clients to practice this starting sequence of strokes at least twenty times, in a sandbox environment, with strong two-way communication.

Women, you need to have a high level of integrity. You must give your partner honest, direct, and immediate feedback if you want him to learn to do the opening strokes correctly. Be sure to let him know when he has found your spot and done the exercise to your satisfaction and delight.

Activity #21: Practice the Opening Strokes

Schedule at least five sessions in which to practice the opening strokes. Focus on these areas:

How relaxed is the man when starting out? Is he communicating confidence? (If he really is uncertain, then at a minimum, is he centered, relaxed, and intentful on calm delivery, with just the right degree of firmness or lightness and speed?)

How communicative is the woman at letting him know when he has found her spot, stayed with her energy, and taken up her level of pleasure?

How much feedback did the two of you share?

How willing are you to experiment with a wide range of different speeds and pressures, until you both find the ones that are the most pleasurable?

How much do your egos get in the way of your staying present in each moment? Do you or your partner get caught up in any frustrations, tensing up, and leaving the expanded orgasm state? Or do you bounce quickly back into an intention to stay calm, relaxed, and focused on pleasure?

Discuss these issues openly. If you are human, these issues and more will come up. Welcome these conversations as a means of developing even greater intimacy with your partner.

You will succeed at expanded orgasm when you and your partner can be best friends and allies during an ongoing process of learning and discovery. And remember: it gets easier and easier over time. We promise.

Bring Her Down with this Simple Method

Men, when you have spent all the time you want practicing your three opening strokes, begin the process of bringing your partner down. Since your intention up until now has been to take her higher and higher in feeling, energy, and pleasure, she most likely will be in a very different state of being. The more she experiences the expanded orgasm, the deeper will be her surrender and level of relaxation. She will be very present in the room of expanded orgasm, yet ready now to make the transition back to the real world. You, the giver, have also taken this ride, and this process of bringing her down will also help you re-ground in the everyday world. Most likely, if you have had a rewarding expanded orgasm session, the world you are returning to will seem nicer, warmer, and friendlier. You are about to help both of you make this transition smoothly and comfortably.

The first level of bringing her back is to slow your motion. You may even want to still your hands completely. Begin your own process, as the giver, of refocusing on the surroundings in the room. Breathe, smell, listen, and look at your partner. Concentrate on becoming increasingly grounded in the external world.

If your hand is inside your partner, remove it as slowly and gently as you possibly can. Press one hand over her mons pubis and clitoris. This comforting pressure also reduces her engorgement and should feel very pleasurable to her. Work together to discover the optimal amount of pressure. It may be more than you expected.

After awhile, take a folded, clean hand towel and blot up any remaining lubricant. Be careful to blot and not rub, as her nerve endings will be highly sensitive. She will feel every infinitesimal stroke!

The "downside" is a very special time. If you have truly experienced expanded orgasm, your partner is returning from a deep space of surrender, and will likely be peaceful, loving, and joyful. Even if you didn't get that far in a practice session, she will still most likely be in a somewhat altered and pleasurable state of mind. If you have the luxury of time, you can bring her down for as long as thirty minutes, using a variety of pressures, hugs, cuddles, and massaging strokes. This will be a delicious and luxurious gift. The bring down period should last at least five minutes, even if you have other plans to attend to. Don't skip this part! It's as much part of expanded orgasm as the rest. A woman can come down quite nicely even in five minutes. After this point, she will often be extremely lucid. I have often driven immediately after my coming down well, and felt I was the safest driver on the road. I was more centered, relaxed, and aware than anyone around me.

I had a feeling that learning the three starting strokes was going to challenge Jason, since he had already admitted that his confidence was weak. As much as he hated to admit it, he felt intimidated, first by his ex-wife and now by Kelly. A lesson like this one was going to cut deep into Jason's psyche. Yet, mastering this lesson would give him what he more than anything desired: the confidence to sweep Kelly away from the moment he first touched her.

Jason was a very bright man, a successful and well-regarded engineer. Unfortunately, these skills would not necessarily help him master the three-stroke technique, and might even hinder his progress. I feared he would cling to the instructions like an engineering formula, and forget about all we had said about feeling, sensing, and connecting energetically with Kelly. How were we ever going to get him to make the shift out of his left brain, and into the feeling state he would need to successfully master this lesson?

Jason was not going to make an overnight, eureka-type transition—at least not today. And if he was going to really acquire the skills we wanted him to learn, he was going to need Kelly's deliberate, focused help.

We told Kelly that it might take Jason some weeks before he really began understanding the feeling side of the expanded orgasm space. She could speed his learning process along by first letting him know whenever he did manage to get into a feeling state. Second, we asked her to lovingly point out whenever she felt he was going exclusively into his left-brain mode. This would be obvious at a feeling level to Kelly if she were to pay attention. It would feel like Jason was somehow following a formula, and losing his focus on feeling. As soon as Kelly noticed this, we asked her to bring Jason back by giving him direct feedback. "Jason, are you still in your feelings?" she might ask lovingly. Kelly would have to develop her own ability to read Jason's energy in order to do this. They agreed to communicate ongoingly about the success of this lesson.

Kelly and Jason found a way to get on the same side of the same goals at last. It was essential to reverse the pattern in which their own individual insecurities were driving a deeper wedge between them on every date. While their marriage was solid now, it would not withstand an ongoing series of wedges. In expanded orgasm, just as in life itself (and all other parts of relationship) the greatest gains happened when they could work together as a team.

What We've Explored

If you've been talking with your partner and doing the exercises, you've come a long way in this lesson. You learned about the "core mindset" for expanded orgasm success—attention, intention, and control. And, you've learned the very effective "starting out" technique of three starting strokes.

At this point, we wouldn't blame you if you were feeling as though your circuits were starting to fry. Not only is there a lot of information here, but also you might very well wonder how you are going to put it all together. This is why we emphasize the importance of really feeling that you both are on the same side, and with the same goal, and that you approach expanded orgasm with love and humor. We have never met a couple who didn't enjoy a dramatic increase in pleasure, turn-on, and bonding practicing expanded orgasm—as long as they had this perspective.

Now it's time to solidify and begin to integrate what you learned in this lesson. Let's discover much more about effective strokes and raising the expanded orgasm energy.

6

Step Six: Thrilling Caresses

Before I knew much about expanded orgasm (other than how good it felt and how much fun it was), I held some common misconceptions about how to create it. I assumed that there was a program, or a recipe, which if followed precisely would create that overwhelming surge of hormonal bliss-missiles and beta-endorphins as reliably as I might bake a cake. I yearned to find this recipe. More exactly, I yearned to have Allen master this recipe, so we could start consuming our biological bliss cocktails as regularly as others quaffed martinis.

The promise of "the big O" blares from the pulpits of advertisements, pulp fiction, X-rated movies, bridal magazines, and bestselling sex manuals. Just do as we do, it promises, and great big orgasms will descend upon you with the regularity of British trains. Is it any surprise, then, that we focused on questing after the orgasmic Holy Grail—that secret recipe that everyone else seemed to have, and that would soon enough, be ours, too? As we "evolved," we sought not the orgasmic Holy Grail, but the expanded orgasm Holy Grail.

It was a tricky little thing to track down. Persistent inconsistencies plagued us from the start. Allen could apply one recipe one day (say, start out light, then increase pressure for five minutes, then go suddenly heavy) that worked like a charm. The next day this very prescription appealed as much as pleasuring from a porcupine. Allen, like most men, is a deer hunter at heart, despite his otherwise modern day trappings, and so, like most men, he'd redouble his resolve to perfect the recipe one more time.

We did know that various speeds, pressures, angles, and strokes all somehow were part of creating the experience. What we didn't know then is that there really is no recipe. A great expanded orgasm session is far more like an improv session with a two person jazz band. From standing on the foundation of mastering the basics, the players soar in a creative intertwining that flows from moment to moment, weaving its musical tapestry.

The instrument to play is the woman's central nervous system, as accessed through her genitalia, and spread throughout her entire sensing being. But we can expand this metaphor one more level. The man is also an instrument. His hand and mind (ultimately any part of his body/mind continuum) are his instrument, too.

Now I see the folly in thinking that there could be just one perfect recipe for expanded orgasm pleasure. I wouldn't listen to a radio station that played one song seven days a week. And now, when it comes to my orgasms, I never expect to have one just like the last one. I want a new one, customized to the mood and moment I'm in now. I may want one that is as good as the last one (or even better), but I want it to be different. The differentness of each great orgasm is a major part of its ultimate magic. Our minds are wired to release chemical messengers when they encounter something new. This is no doubt a primitive reward system that teaches us to mark new and useful information as important. Whatever the reason, it is adding even more good stuff to my biochemical bliss.

What ingredients help create expanded orgasms you always will yearn for? They are the qualities of strokes and sets of strokes that the man can deliver in expanded orgasm. Think of them as the notes, rhythms, and timbres that can be created with a magnificent ensemble of instruments.

Improvisation is not something you learn step-by-step. In these ten lessons we first learn basics, and then address the finer points of mastery. Some may find there is a logical order to these basics; and yet others will find that until a certain point in their training, nothing is truly clicking in. Then, at some point, everything reaches a new, higher plateau of clarity.

Genie, for example, found that she was most sensitive in her "G-area," a topic we cover in Step Eight. When Michael added this particular stroke to their expanded orgasm practice, her abilities to feel more pleasure skyrocketed. Yet all the practice in advance of that breakthrough was essential.

We encourage you to view the information in the next three steps as building blocks to a great improvisation. Assume that these exercises come in no particular order. So remain patient, practice as we suggest, and master all the practices, so that your quantum leaps will start happening as soon as possible.

Stay On Her Favorite Spot

Men, by this point you have begun to develop an ability to go directly to a woman's favorite spot, and stay there, even as her current of energy is rising.

Congratulations! Certainly continue practicing that skill, even as you take on other practice assignments. Finding and tracking the energy of her sweet spot is a skill that develops over time. One year from now you will still be perfecting the art of finding, and staying, on a woman's favorite spot. The good news is that your abilities will be always getting better.

Earlier, we asked you to discover a language for the movement of strokes, so that your partner could identify when you were going higher and lower, harder and softer, and faster and slower. Soon, we'll revisit that exercise with one major addition: that the man stay "glued" to her favorite spot.

The current you should be feeling connecting with your partner's favorite spot may at first be almost imperceptible. As she becomes more engorged, this feeling will intensify. Women can help their men connect with this current by stimulating themselves before a date. Then they can easily direct the man to their favorite spot.

Your biggest barrier to locating her sweet spot easily is an overly logical mind. If you don't think you are going to feel it, you probably won't. *So, decide you are going to find it, feel it, and stay on it.* Once you have truly made this decision, you will find it. Each time you connect, you'll have more direct feedback on what it feels like.

As her favorite spot gets more pronounced, it develops into a bowl-shaped hollow. At this point it becomes easier to stay on the spot than to stray from it. It's as if there is a magnetic attraction pulling ever more fully into a woman's center of pleasure.

Activity #22: Stay Connected to Her Favorite Spot

So far, we have asked that once the man has found his partner's favorite spot, that he rub very lightly and with a minimum of friction. Rubbing completely through the surface (with no surface friction) is called "rubbing through the skin." Now let's focus on *staying connected.*

First, select whether you wish to use the index or middle finger of your writing hand. Or, you may wish to experiment with alternating. Each finger will contribute a unique flavor to the experience. Now locate your partner's favorite spot. Continue a very short, slow, light, consistent motion and observe what happens to the current.

Maintain your attention on *feeling*. Feel the current, feel it grow stronger and weaker as it flows, feel her warmth, feel her skin, feel her moistness, feel how she feels feeling you. Feel her go up as you stay on the spot, feel her go down as you stray from the spot, feel her feeling you while you are feeling her.

Learn to dialog while remaining in a feeling state. It may take some practice, like patting your head and rubbing your stomach at the same time.

Both the man and the woman should be feeling in every moment. The woman can say "pause" the moment he wanders off her favorite spot. She can say "begin" when she feels him return.

As the man stays connected longer, he can begin to vary his strokes by making wider circles or up and down motions. Also, he can begin experimenting with a greater range of speeds and pressures.

Men, develop a sense of comfort in this position. When the two of you are busy giving each other a lot of feedback, you may find yourselves paying such rapt attention to your process that you become a little tenser than you might wish. Allow your body to relax and expand, even while putting your full attention on what you are doing and feeling. It is possible to do this entire exercise in a deeply relaxed state.

While she is expanding, the woman too will have to get used to simultaneously feeling, relaxing, and giving feedback. It will take time to develop the sense of expansion while communicating.

Ladies, remember, all it takes is a moment to decide to expand and allow the sensation to begin spreading through your body. Don't wait for a full-blown, over-the-edge, bell-ringing humdinger of an orgasm to start enjoying expanded orgasm. Start now. With every expanded orgasm you potentially enlarge your container size and capacity to experience ever-greater pleasure.

Within this exercise, explore the manifold ways in which you can vary strokes: higher, lower, faster, slower, to the right, left, top, bottom; circles, up-and-down, and ellipses. Men can practice giving these strokes; women can practice asking for these strokes, and also giving themselves these strokes.

At this point, Jason seemed to be getting increasingly confused. We were not surprised; in expanded orgasm training, one often has to unlearn much of what he thinks he knows about giving pleasure. So we listened compassionately when he called us for guidance. (We encourage our clients to call when they get stuck during a practice session, since these are often the most significant moments of opportunity.) Jason and Kelly were in the middle of a practice session at this very moment.

"I guess I am having a hard time figuring out what the right thing to do is here," he said. Three words in his statement were red flags. *Figuring out* is a mental process; we wanted Jason to be feeling, feeling, and feeling yet some more. *Right* is also a mental judgment sure to distract Jason from immersing in the feeling experience. *Do* is a goal-oriented action, and not a state of *being*.

For now, I say nothing. A man's ego can be fragile. I want to give him positive feedback for his efforts. "Go on," I encourage him. "Tell me more."

"I guess I am looking for some kind of consistency of experience," he revealed. "It seems so random, what I do with Kelly. The last time we practiced, Kelly was so much fun. She engorged from the moment I touched her. I did the three strokes, and she was so responsive, I thought I had finally mastered this lesson, especially since the time before that, it had taken me fifteen minutes to find her current.

"This time, however, I am doing the exact same things as before, and nothing is happening. We tried everything we could think of. I went harder, faster, slower, lighter, to the left, the right, the top, and the bottom. Nothing seemed to work. Then Kelly got frustrated and said we should stop now. So here I am. Should we stop?"

Keep in mind that Jason is a caring, dedicated lover. He is producing a wonderful life for Kelly. He is giving her every little last bit of his loving attention but in his estimation is falling flat on his face. This is a moment calling for the greatest compassion. I don't know a man who masters expanded orgasm that hasn't confronted this kind of frustrating experience routinely.

First, women vary by the month, the day, the week, the hour, and even the minute. This is why recipes don't work. Jason was applying in this session the formula that brought him success in his last session. He needs to stick to the underlying lesson of learning to read and follow her energy. This is the yellow brick road to riches.

Second, Jason let his lack of immediate success unnerve him. Experienced expanded orgasm practitioners understand that there will be a range of outcomes each time they are with these variable female creatures. One time, a woman's current may be so strong it will jump out and suck you in like a whirlpool. The next time, you can hunt and peck for ten minutes before finding a baby spring. Experienced practitioners have learned that it's no use fighting against the reality of the situation, so they just enjoy the game called, "Let's see what it will be today." Patience (and not being invested in the outcome) rules the day—such is the mantra of the trained expanded orgasm man.

I don't want to tell all this to Jason right now. This will only focus him in his thinking even more. I want him to go back into his feelings. Everything that is happening here is all normal and of value. And here's something important: when people take a break like this, they have reached the end of their rope, and are open to trying something radically new. This can be a dramatic moment to instill the new behavior.

"Jason, what do you want to have happen now?" I asked.

"All I want is to give Kelly pleasure. I want to see her smile. I want to make a difference in her pleasure."

Good. He was going back into his feelings again. "You are both at your sandbox break point now. Be sure you thank Kelly for all her patience on this date. Then, ask if she would be willing to try practice with you one more time. Let her know that this time, you are going to focus on feeling her, 100 percent. If she says no, that's okay, unless, perhaps, you want to offer her the Two-Minute Rule. And the next time, Jason, whether it's now or later, remember, stay focused on feeling the whole time. Okay?"

As I sent him on his way, I had a feeling that things would go quite differently. The sooner they could both learn to stay present to their feelings, the more impact the remaining lessons would have. Sure enough, the next day Jason called, thanking me and raving about the unexpected major breakthrough they had. I was delighted but certainly not surprised.

Other Qualities of Strokes: How You Play Your "Instrument"

We have discussed how a woman's sexual nervous system can be played as a finely tuned instrument. The man can also be viewed as having an instrument— his hands and other body parts. Now let's consider exactly how a man can make even greater use of his hand instrument by adding in some more advanced qualities of strokes. These strokes are defined by the way in which they are delivered.

First we will review how remarkably the various surfaces of the hand and fingers can alter the nature of the experience. Then we review how much the evenness (or lack thereof) of the delivery can influence the receiver's pleasure.

For each of the following three strokes men should first find their partner's favorite spot and connect to the current. Once you are "glued in" to her spot, you are ready to explore the influence of altering the way your hand makes contact with her.

Angle of finger: Notice how your finger makes contact on your partner's clitoris. Ideally, your palm will be resting on her mons pubis with a sense of firmness—psychological as much as physical. Your partner should let you know the perfect firmness for her. Now experiment with varying the angle of your finger from almost perpendicular (straight up) to nearly flat. Most women express a preference for a nearly flat finger. This is because you will be touching her with more of the pad of your finger as opposed to the tip. The pad has fewer ridges than the tip and is therefore softer. It's also longer—you will cover a greater area. Ask your partner to rate the various angles from steep to flat so that you can begin to carry this distinction with you.

One finger vs. several fingers: Experiment with using first one finger, then two, then three. Especially if your hand is relatively flat, you will be able to cover an even greater amount of area below the surface with more fingers. Explore bringing in this multifinger stroking after she has engorged. Many women love how the larger surface area spreads the sensation, allowing her to expand her erotic energy.

Friction vs. through the skin: Friction and going through-the-skin are two extremes. With friction, the surface area is stimulated; with through the skin motions, the areas below the surface are stimulated in the absence of friction. Because people have changing preferences from moment to moment, there is no right or wrong way to deliver friction. However, it is a good idea to include this distinction in your skill set. Again, men, ask your partner how she experiences various degrees of friction at different times.

Dragging along: You can either go smoothly over the surface, or you can "drag" your fingers so as to create a sort of wave under the skin. Intention will help you master drag. Try this on your forearm: first, go lightly over an area. Next, stroke so as to create a longer lasting effect. Increasing the amount of finger surface that actually touches the skin can enhance drag. It may help to imagine that your stroking finger is a boat creating a wake.

Evenness of the experience: Men, observe how evenly you are stroking. Ideally, be as smooth as silk. Picture a finger winding around and around a crystal glass, creating that clear, whistle-like sound. If the finger goes around very evenly, the sound will stay constant and at the same pitch. Any variations in pressure or speed will result in a changed sound. Imagine you can circle the rim of a glass perfectly evenly, and now, transfer that skill to stroking your partner's clitoris. Let there be that same degree of evenness of pressure and speed in your hand.

To really do this even stroking well, it helps to center your own mind before giving to the woman. Visualize your hand as totally relaxed, perhaps weightless, effortlessly gliding on an even plane. This will translate into a perfect stroke. Ask your partner for honest feedback on the smoothness, or evenness, of your stroking.

Here are some additional explorations to deepen your mind/body connection as the giver:

Feel what she is feeling: Take a moment and concentrate completely on what the woman is feeling. If you have had any moments of self-doubt or insecurities about what you should be doing next, put them aside for a minute. Place all your attention on feeling as much pleasure as you can in this minute. Afterwards, ask your partner for feedback.

Make sure every stroke feels the best possible to you as the giver: Remember what it feels like when you pleasure yourself. You are always feeling for the next stroke that feels the best to you. Know that you can transfer this skill easily to giving to your partner. Intend from the start to have every stroke feel the best possible to you, the giver, and know that in so doing you will be creating the most pleasure for the receiver.

Listen to your intuition: Many of our clients are not sure how to fully listen to their intuition. We tell them, "If you hear something speak to you, then listen to it. You will have to listen with ears wide open, if you really want to hear it."

Normally, we recommend that, starting out, a man use all the visual cues he can as an aid in practicing. However, women's clitoral sizes can vary considerably. The size has nothing to do with the amount of pleasure a woman can feel. If a woman has a small clitoris, or one buried in many folds, the man may have to become adept at using his intuition to energetically sense where on his partner's clitoris his focus, and presence, are most intensely felt. Some women's clitorises are as small as pinheads. Clearly, in these situations, intuition is essential.

The giver's intuition reads the receiver's communication at levels too subtle for the conscious mind; and the receiver also reads communication at very subtle levels from the giver. An entire conversation is exchanged at this *superconscious* level. In order to take full advantage of this conversation, you will relax (once again), let down the guard of your rational mind, and invite in all that peripheral and subtle information. Alternatively, you also can decide to deliberately broadcast messages from your super conscious mind to your partner.

And exactly what is your *super conscious* mind? We prefer to let each person decide for themselves what that might be for them. This might be the perfect time to ask your own super conscious mind to define for you what it wants you to know about it, and how it wants to be heard.

Questions to answer in your journal:

Do you have a super conscious? Is that the name you have given it? (Some people call it their subconscious.) How does it show up for you? What do you do to become more aware of it? Can you exchange this information with your partner?

Activity #23: Give Sensual Pleasure to Yourself

For this exercise, we ask each of you to spend a few minutes pleasuring yourselves. As you apply the variables mentioned above to yourself, note your response. *Do you like being touched with fingertips, or big, broad surfaces? Do you like being touched in a series of staccato blips, like Morse code? Or do you like a smooth, even experience? Do you like one or several fingers, or a combination? Do you like the sensation of drag?*

Don't you dare skip out on this exercise! You will be a far better giver for having examined just what you like to give yourself.

Men in particular find this exploration revealing. Sometimes they find it hard to relate to a clitoris that is barely a centimeter long; it is like something from another universe. However, they can tell you what they like. So men, if you like to receive smooth, even, conscious touch, you can transfer that awareness to become an even better giver.

Answer these questions in your journal:

How eager are you to show your partner exactly what you do to bring yourself pleasure? What stops you from doing so, and what excites you about doing so?

Usually both men and women are similar in what they enjoy. However, one client, Dylan, had a very different experience. "I really enjoy speed and pressure when I give pleasure to myself, and I also like it when Judy gives me pleasure that way," he told us. "Maybe that's one reason I am having a hard time giving Judy what she wants. We really are very different in our preferences. Are you perhaps just assuming that all people want the same thing?"

Dylan's point was well taken. You never know where a couple is going to have their real challenges, and we listen carefully for clues. Suspecting some gold somewhere in this problem, I asked, "Judy, do you enjoy giving Dylan pleasure this way?"

Judy said, "Well, not really. We have different preferences. I like it soft and slow, and he likes it hard and fast. Of course, I like the *idea* of giving Dylan what he likes. Just not the implementation. My arm gets tired and my mind wanders. I wind up looking at the clock and hoping he doesn't want to go on too long." Dylan admitted that the same ideas crossed his mind, too, while pleasuring Judy. Now, there is no golden rule that says that one way of giving pleasure is better than another. If there is any rule, it is probably to go for whatever feels the best! We don't even say that expanded orgasm is better than regular orgasm. But I knew that if neither one of them was enjoying giving orgasmic pleasure to the other, the results would fall far short of what it could be.

I gave them an assignment: touch each other in such a way that it *brought rapture to the giver.* They could use the assignment above as a reason to explore various ways to create that rapture; but they were to be completely selfish about making sure that they themselves had a peak experience.

Next time we saw them, we asked for a report. According to Dylan, "We've never had any kind of sexual contact like this in our entire marriage. The whole issue of hard or soft, or fast or slow, just sort of vaporized. We found that it could feel deliciously incredible to the giver in any of these ways. For sure, when I was giving and feeling rapture, so was Judy. And she would tell you the same thing happened to her. Our sex together entered a whole new dimension."

As expanded orgasm teachers, we get used to seeing old paradigms about orgasm retired, as new ones emerge. Still we are always thrilled to watch our clients unlock the secrets to great sex, since what they learn about expanded orgasm will most certainly carry over into their lovemaking. Dylan and Judy's progress was about to rocket forward from that point forward.

The Art of Peaking

Peaking is the art of delivering deliberately timed breaks, or pauses, to the flow of sensation from giver to receiver. The key word here is *deliberate*. Peaking is a double-edged sword. Done correctly, it produces a smooth ascent to ecstasy. Incorrect peaking is an airplane with a stuttering engine that rises a bit, falls back, up, down—and never achieves much altitude.

As mentioned earlier, the mind gets easily tired of unending repetition. See for yourself. Tap on a hard surface without stopping. After a few moments your mind will wander. Now tap, but on every fifth beat, pause instead, and then resume. The timing of the pause should be no longer than a half second, about the length of the beats. Now you have a rhythm going and the mind can get absorbed in that. After doing this rhythm for a while, shift to yet another rhythm, this one perhaps changing after every three beats. The ear is pleased to hear the well-timed rhythm.

This same principle operates in giving a woman rhythmic pleasure. Her body will open to flow, and flow in unison, with a well-timed and rhythmic series of strokes. Rhythm is the beat of life; it's in heartbeats, rocking chairs, garden strolls, love songs, and a great massage. A good rhythm lulls us into the relaxation we seek to create in our expanded orgasm experience.

In one more experiment, begin to tap randomly. One, three, two, ten, short pause, nine, two, two, long pause, seven. If your taps sounded anything like mine, they were actually irritating to listen to. Instead of surrendering deeper into relaxation, I went more into a state of anxiety. I had been fairly peaceful before I tapped. And now? "Stop that random tapping!" my body commanded.

Rhythm, then, is what defines good peaking. Randomness is what creates bad peaking.

Intentional peaking might go something like this: stroking your partner, start by feeling your own rhythm of relaxation. Transmit this to her. When you have stroked her clitoris enough to feel her current, begin to hold back one stroke for every eight or ten. Do not make the pause longer than one stroke's duration.

Now, for the next four or five sets of strokes, repeat this pattern: eight strokes, and then pause one. Eight strokes and then pause one.

Your intuition will tell you when she is climbing nicely as a result of your peaking. When you feel it is time to shorten the spaces between pauses, do so. Drop down to six strokes, and a pause. Continue this pattern for as long as your intuition gives you the green light. At some point, as her energy intensifies, your intuition will direct you to decrease the number of strokes in a set.

Pauses are just one type of intentional peak. Stopping to get more lubricant is a longer type of peak. Changing the direction or pressure or tempo of a stroke from one type to another constitutes a peak. *Unintentional peaks* are pauses that were unplanned. When your mind wanders and your rhythm changes, you've delivered an unintentional peak. When the phone rings and you stop for a moment to see who it is on the answering machine, you've peaked her.

Any peak will cause her energy to drop. Done intentionally, you are creating a platform of steps that will enable her to climb, consolidate, and then climb some more. This type of peaking is going to give her expanded orgasm "loft." Think of a plane getting off the ground; it requires a certain loft to get into the air. Your intentional peaking will deliver this loft.

Unintentional peaking will destroy loft as easily as intentional peaking will create it.

Activity #24: Experiment with Peaking

In part one of this exercise, the man will locate his partner's favorite spot, and then begin to peak her. He can vary the timing and the types of strokes. The woman will identify each peak she notices by saying, simply, "Peak." This fun exercise teaches the woman to pay more attention to the peaks. She may be surprised at how subtle peaks can be when done properly!

In part two of this exercise, the man will continue stroking her. This time however, *he* will identify each time he peaks her intentionally. In addition, if he accidentally peaks her, say by having his mind wander for a moment, he should verbally note this too.

Allen will say, "Peak...peak...peak," in a practice we label, "Calling the Peaks." As he goes on with mellifluous cadence, he lulls me into a deep sense of surrender. He becomes increasingly present with me, and my turn-on invariably climbs as the identified peaking continues. Often, I will ask Allen to call the peaks, in order to focus my energy on going to the next level of feeling and sensation.

This exercise is an important one. Not only does it train you to peak, but also it helps to train your mind to stay focused. Very often, Allen will call the peaks just for fun, since it is a real turn on. It is a great exercise to use when one or both of you are a tad sleepy, as it will guarantee that your attention stays riveted to the experience.

This is not an exercise to be done once or twice, but on an ongoing basis. You can develop an ever-expanding sense of when you are—and are not—peaking your partner pleasurably.

By the way, we also call the unintentional peaks. If Allen or I space out, and "drop the ball," so to speak, the other one will say, "That was a nice peak." This is a sort of shorthand that gently informs the other, "You peaked me, though you may not be aware of it." Such a comment usually is a sign to renew a more regular cadence, with even more attention to the experience.

Build a Bigger Base from which to Go Over the Edge

You can think of the expanded orgasm session as containing movements much like a symphony. Some are slow and thoughtful, some build drama, some lead you into mystery, others, to romance. Each movement might be several minutes long. As usual, let your intuition be the guide. When it feels like the right time to switch from one movement to the next, it usually is.

Continual peaking will build a bigger base of pleasurable experience, so your orgasm's ultimate height will be much greater. Along the way, there will be times when she wants you to continue exactly what you are doing so that she can go over the edge. As soon as she is near that point, hold off: peak her and then begin bringing her up again.

Going over the edge should not be the goal. Rather, you focus on building the energy and intensity of good feelings in every moment. The better it feels to her, the better it will feel to you as the giver, and your ultimate goal in expanded orgasm really is to feel as good as possible in every moment.

Practice the following pattern of movements that nicely help build the energy and intensity:

Begin with stroking your partner, with very little peaking, until you sense that if she goes on much longer like this, she will become agitated, or possibly go over the edge. Let's call this the first movement. The focus here is on a slow, steady climb.

Then, at just the right moment, begin focusing much more intently on providing variety rather than predictability. Go eight strokes, peak her, repeat a few times, and then switch to something else. Go eight strokes, peak her again, then switch to yet another speed, pressure, or direction. Be sure to keep consistent within the eight strokes. We'll call this the second movement. *The focus is on variety.* This is yet another way to spread, and thus expand, the bowl of orgasmic energy.

Finally, when you feel that she has expanded to the point where she will go over the edge with very little extra pressure (and you feel that this is what she wants) take her over the edge by *adding intensity via your intention.* This intention will translate into more intense strokes. This added intensity might be accompanied by extra speed or pressure, but not necessarily. Let's call this the third movement.

This pattern is an arbitrary one—just one in an infinite catalogue of possibilities. There are many movements in each improvisation that you cocreate, each with its own unique flavor.

Touch So That You Really Feel

By now you should have a clear sense that both the man and the woman are the instruments, as well as the musicians. At a superficial level the man is giving and the woman is receiving. Now let's go even deeper into the process. Since body and mind intertwine, it makes no sense to separate them during a performance. There is a *flow* of give and take, of asking and receiving, verbally and nonverbally. And thus at any given moment it becomes increasingly difficult to tell who is really doing which part. The two of you reach a place of sharing one mind and one body.

Activity #25: Give Pleasure with a Taking Touch
For this exercise, secure at least a half-hour of alone time. You'll want a space where you can shut off the phones and lie down comfortably.

The partners can be dressed for this exercise. Let the woman start first lying down. She will be receiver, and the man, giver. The man sits comfortably by her side. He should place his hand on her heart and allow it to rest there. Both he and the woman should be in a position where they can be comfortable for five to ten minutes. Agree in advance on the time.

The man should allow his arm and hand to relax completely, so that his hand feels as if it is reaching down under her skin, and making contact directly with her energy. Some verbal feedback is allowable at the beginning. If the woman would prefer that her partner have more of an energetic contact, use more or less pressure, get a softer feel, relax more, or have other suggestions, she should make them now. The woman can close her eyes or keep them open and look softly at her partner. The man is to continue to look at her for the entire length of time. Silently stay in this position for the agreed-on time. Men, put all of your attention on her. Clear your mind, and just feel. In this state, remain still, calm, and relaxed, and *each of you* notice:

What are you feeling?

How does your partner feel?

What does the receiver want right now?

Can the giver send it energetically?

Is the receiver becoming softer?

Is the giver becoming softer?

Is the giver's hand making more and more of a direct contact with the receiver's being?

There is much to notice. Doing this exercise in a class, people who have never met can find that they had gone very deeply into a blended heart/mind/body/space shared by both.

After the woman has had a turn as receiver it is her turn to be giver. Now it is her turn to put all of her attention on him and notice what comes into her mind. Many couples enjoy doing this process as a way of connecting, and centering together after a busy, survival-oriented day. It gives them a profound way to tune into each other nonverbally, so that by the time they do start communicating, they are already putting their full attention on each other, and sharing deeply.

Sam was insecure that he would ever be able to master peaking. He worried that with his short attention span, he would get bored before he ever had a chance to fully develop well-timed peaks consistently. The idea of creating movements, each with its own style of peaks, seemed even more of a mountain to climb.

Sam tended to focus intently on what was most interesting in the moment, at the expense of everything else. This ability had served him well as an entrepreneur. He moved from one thing to another in rapid succession, always putting out the hottest fire first. I wanted to find a way to dispel Sam's concerns, since this type of hyper-focus can actually help, rather than hinder. The better he could make it feel to Linda, the more interesting he would find what was actually happening, and the *more* he would focus. If they could just get started and build some loft, a self-reinforcing positive feedback loop would take over and carry them both skyward.

We suggested they create a special date in which to experiment with how much attention and pleasure Sam could give Linda. A key ingredient to its success would be how much fun both of them could have in every moment. Linda was feeling as much as possible, and, at the same time, keeping a keen awareness on Sam's attention. The moment she felt his attention on her starting to wane, she was to say something like, "Ready for some more fuel here, Sam." This meant, "Take all the energy you are feeling, and refocus it on what you are doing to give me even more pleasure."

The time for the date arrived. They hugged and cuddled for a while. Then, Sam got into a relaxed and comfortable position, taking extra care to see that Linda had all the pillow support she needed. She fussed playfully, asking for several extra pillow adjustments under her left knee and her right knee, reveling in all the added attention from Sam. Both were on their best behavior.

Sam pulled Linda as close as possible to him, and laid his forearm straight down the middle of her abdomen, his wrist stopping neatly at her genitals. His palm and fingers settled across her mons pubis and outer lips. He ensured that the pad of his right middle finger reached her clitoris at exactly the very flat angle she had requested so eagerly in other sessions. Linda alternately moaned, sighed, and tittered with delight at the pleasure she felt in the first few contacts. No need for "rocket boosters" yet. Sam was setting her on fire with a slow, patient attention to every minute detail of his actions.

Sam used the three opening strokes next. Since he had practiced this a dozen times, his hand confidently made contact with Linda, present to the pleasure of the moment. Sam broadcast, in those first three strokes, his intention to take total control of her central nervous system and bring her pleasure on a level she had never felt before. Linda shuddered and relaxed yet again, flooded by a sense of warmth and security.

Her favorite spot seemed to jump out at him, primed from all the preparation. As he focused progressively more energy in a small circular movement, Linda climbed rapidly. She surprised herself with the strength of her response, and spontaneously begged him to continue.

Sam beamed, finding her appetite for pleasure most attractive. Her clitoris reached higher and higher, hoping to grab all the sensation it could. He sensed that though she would never admit it, she was eager for him to tease her, and draw out her delicious sensations ever more. He was giving her slow, even stroking to awaken her genital area. He hadn't peaked her once yet. Still, she was expanding quickly, using her breathing to spread all the sensations, into her abdomen, her thighs, and beyond.

Sam now settled into peaking, giving her a rewarding routine of ten strokes and a pause, ten strokes and a pause, with a rather slow stroke, back and forth short, and through the skin. Linda was climbing faster than ever, thrilling Sam. A few times Sam would pause, for one reason or another, and Linda would be right there, bringing him back into the experience. At times, the energy blasted out of her powerfully, knocking Sam's attention off course, and somewhere into the stratosphere. "More, now," she'd ask each time, calling Sam back from wherever his mind had started to go, and reminding him to bring even more energy into their shared experience. Back he'd come, within a fraction of a second, so as not to lose the precious momentum so essential for building loft in the initial stages.

Since Linda's favorite spot had grown from the size of a pinhead to the size of a dime, Sam was ready to get adventurous. Intuitively, he started increasing his variety, and also shortening the number of strokes between peaks. For one set of eight strokes, he gave Linda left-to-right strokes, still through the skin, and over her spot. Then he switched. Without missing a beat, on another count of eight, he went up and down in strokes, this time making them a little longer as well. For a third set he added more fingers, one on either side of his middle finger, so as to spread the energy. Then, through the skin in medium sized circles. Linda shot up the stairway of sensations.

Since Sam was changing strokes with each set, he didn't need—or want—an additional peak from pausing. Everything was working exactly as we had said it would. Linda continued to climb the staircase to the stars. Each set of strokes was another climb higher; each peak, another brief landing. Her face and neck flushed to a bright red, and her breathing grew ever deeper. Sensations radiated outwards and everywhere. Sam's confidence grew with every stroke.

He had energetically locked on to Linda. She could not lose him now. Nothing had ever so riveted his attention. Her favorite spot had grown so large that it now covered her entire clitoris, and extended all the way down to her introitus. The original two o'clock spot had become a bowl-shaped depression that his fingers naturally fell into.

He remembered once we had told him that getting started is the hardest, and at some point, expanded orgasm becomes effortless. He knew that was happening now, and his confidence grew further. His strokes became more exploratory and daring. At yet, even as the power intensified, there were times Linda felt his focus drop off. Each time, she again called out, "More fuel, now!" And so, the two of them played together, in an ever-rising loop of climbing, peaking, plateau, and sending each other the fuel to reach ever higher.

Soon this rising pattern brought Linda to the edge of a major climax. Her genitals—which now felt as if they extended to every part of her—were a whirlpool of hot melting sensations, rapidly spinning from a center ever outward. Would she be able to stop from going over? Sam suddenly shifted his style yet again, now giving her short, fast strokes, with six strokes for three sets, and then four strokes for three sets. Sam added more variety, this time going directly through the skin, with somewhat firmer pressure. His intention for her to go over the edge sent Linda flying over. He held her there for a few minutes longer.

Expanded orgasm had become truly effortless. He backed off and slowed. His most subtle motions kept Linda in an effortless, over-the-edge, orgasmic state. There they hung out together, enjoying a new sense of relaxation, appropriate to sitting on top of a mountain just climbed and enjoying the vast expanse of view in all directions. As long as he kept locked in to her enormous sweet spot—and threw in an occasional peak—she coasted.

Eventually they both knew it was time to bring her down. He stopped all motion and applied more even pressure to her genital area, deflating her inner and outer lips as much as possible. He sat both observing the process and reflecting on what had just happened. Having once feared boredom and his inability to pay attention, he had discovered instead that he was the cocreator of an earth-moving, deeply fulfilling, and highly entertaining drama. When Linda looked at the clock, she noticed they had been in an expanded orgasm state for thirty-five minutes. Sam's fear that his short attention span would never allow him to succeed at expanded orgasm was forever put to rest.

What We've Explored

Sam and Linda's story illustrates well how two people together created a moving and powerful expanded orgasm experience. The story addresses how you can blend the seemingly separate skills of stroke variety and peaking with attention, intention, and control to cocreate an effortlessly rising experience of expanded orgasm.

Practice these skills on yourself and with your partner. Allen and I never tire of weaving this practice right into our lovemaking—and we truly do experience lovemaking.

7

Step Seven: Feedback Loops

Jerry had tried everything. He'd increased the pressure; decreased the pressure; relaxed; checked in with his feelings; abandoned his ego. Ilene also thought she had done her part. Ilene wasn't saying anything, wanting to give Jerry time to wake her sleeping genitals up gently. She'd made the mistake often of trying to coach Jerry immediately, expecting the first stroke to feel as good as the ones she got ten minutes into the date. But she had learned, through trial and error, to give him a good two or three minutes to wake her up gently. Usually, she would need to transition from totally flaccid to mild feeling even if he was doing everything perfectly well. And so she sank into her feelings, and focused on all the good she could feel. Only, today, she wasn't feeling much, even after five minutes, other than a slight awkwardness, shared by Jerry, as her normal moans and coos failed to materialize.

She kept having this thought: "The angle of his hand is off. It should be more sloping, the way I slope my hand when I touch myself." Immediately, she discounted her thoughts as ridiculous. How would she even know what angle he was using? She could not see his hand, only feel it.

But by the third time she had that thought, she knew it was time to say something. Trusting her own instincts, she now knew it was time to give Jerry some relief. A year ago, she would have said too much in the beginning. She would have issued so many random guesses at what to try that Jerry always got unnerved and unglued before the date could really start to cook. Now, she was honing her own skills, and giving Jerry the kind of feedback that came from deep within her own intuition. "Change the angle of your hand," she suggested, and then demonstrated. Jerry shifted; suddenly, contact with her favorite spot was coming in loud and clear. They both knew in that moment, feeling the surge of sensation rise from deep within her, that today's date was going to be a blockbuster. Jerry and Ilene had encountered a catch. Luckily for them, they didn't fall into it permanently.

A *catch*, or trap, is a set of two rules, each of which standing on its own makes sense, but when taken together, are mutually incompatible. You can't get a job without experience. But you can't get experience without a job. What's a job seeker to do?

You can see the catch operating in all arenas of human activity—especially in relationships. People can and do figure their way out of catches all the time. Everyone who has a job once had none, and every great dancer has stepped on a thousand toes along the way. Usually, the way out requires some thinking outside the norm that overrides the opposing forces of being stuck.

Catches occur everywhere in relationship, and in expanded orgasm. Let's proceed, then, to dissect how the catch operates in expanded orgasm and how couples overcome this predictable problem.

Anatomy of the Catch in Expanded Orgasm

Here's one version of the catch in its most basic form:

Part 1: Until you (the man) have roused your partner through regular rides into rapture, knowingly navigating the innumerable nuances en route, how will you know how to rocket her out of the starting gate?

Part 2: Until you (the woman) can remember—or guess—how the mythical "perfect stroke" would feel right now, and notice you're having a slightly off-centered experience, *and* know how to request him to go a little higher (or slower, or to the left, or harder, or whatever) in order to bring you to that "perfect stroke," how—and what—can you communicate?

This theme displays multiple variations. In a typical variation, each failed communication leads to self-doubt and/or even more lack of communication.

Does this negative trap sound familiar? Allen and I have found ourselves in many such "vicious circles." Note how in a typical trap, such as the one I'll describe now, we passed the problem back and forth. We found ourselves digging a rut increasingly harder to climb out of:

Part 1: Allen is touching me somehow, some way, that didn't feel quite right.

Part 2: I can't tell what's not working, since I don't really know. All I know is that his carefully crafted stroke isn't having the intended effect of great feeling. But what should I say? Like him, I'm flying blind.

Part 3: And after a few minutes of experimentation, during which our date falters and sputters along, Allen's ego succumbs to his own internally driven pressure to succeed with me.

Part 4: And now, since I can feel him, feeling me, feeling him, both at our wit's end, we arrive at our date's unintentional end, feeling deflated.

Having played out this script scores of times, I know for sure that there is no way to win in this no-fault, default scenario. It's no-fault, in the sense that we were doing our level best to avoid the very traps we created, and default, since this is often what used to happen, unless we got lucky. We were smart enough, and loving enough, to know that both of us were somehow equally contributing to the trap in which we'd enmeshed ourselves—but not smart enough to figure out how to exit. If we were "lucky," it felt like winning the lottery—we'd climbed out somehow, this time, knowing we didn't quite know the steps to take if and when we found ourselves in the next expanded orgasm tar pit.

In retrospect, our roles in creating the problem were crystal clear. At the superficial level, I was not giving Allen helpful feedback. He was not reading my mind and body any better than I was. We somehow both hoped, or expected, that the other person would be the one to find a magic stroke, button, recipe, or idea that would deliver us from frustrations to the cocreative ecstasy we so yearned for.

And finally this is what happened. First we realized how our catch game was rigged for failure. A new, higher level of thinking would be needed to outfox this wily predator of our relating. A "Beat-the-Catch" game was the only way out. *We were going to have to help each other give ourselves a collective pleasure.* Over time, we developed communication practices such as *scanning, mapping,* and *bootstrapping.* I'll tell you all about those in this chapter. Using these and other practices, we ensured that no matter what the orgasmic outcome of the date, we would succeed in the most important thing of all: connecting with one another.

In this step, we share with you just how to put these types of practices in your expanded orgasm sessions. We are certain they will permanently change the nature of your game, too. They certainly did for our two couples—as you are about to see. You can make each expanded orgasm session one in which you know that you will truly get your goals, before you even begin!

Communicate Cocreatively in the Room of Expanded Orgasm

As with other lessons, it's important to understand that "communication" in the room of expanded orgasm is different from survival-based, everyday communication. It is *cocreative communication.*

Think of two people sailing a boat for pleasure. You might hear banter like:

"Do you feel a wind change coming on?"

"Yes. Let's go a little more into the wind."

"Jibe!"

"Wait, back off...you're going too far!"

They are naturally working together to cruise from this point to that and back again. Two sailors, one mind, multiple challenges, and hopefully, a lot of fun for everyone. We call communication like this *cooperative, collaborative,* and *cocreative.*

As the wind picks up and they jibe, an amateur mate screws up and almost capsizes the boat. His equally inexperienced partner yells out, "Hey you #$%#^%$, what are you doing?" Notice how, for some people, when the energy—and challenges—pick up, cocreative communication tends to suffer. Can't you almost hear the water pouring over the sides of the boat as the stunned mate blinks in the face of such totally useless feedback?

Here, under pressure, is where the pros keep their cool. Their senses heightened, they are even more alert and communicative. "Let the sail out!" the pro commands. "The boat's about to tip!" Pros are the ones who stay in for the long haul. Not surprisingly, many of these long-termers' fondest memories are of the decisions they made, and the behavior they maintained, when the going was toughest.

Cocreative communication, then, consists of:

- Reporting on the status of the mission "at hand."
- Staying in touch with and reporting on one's personal status.
- Listening for and responding to reports from the partner.

Ideally, this communication is accurate, immediate, and constructive. Such abilities are mostly only developed intentionally. Our society focuses more on survival-based thinking than on collaborative thinking, and so that is what we learn.

Linda and Sam are here for a lesson. I can usually tell how their sessions have been going just by the way Sam sits. Today, he is sitting close to the edge of his seat, very alert, a little fidgety. Linda sits a foot away, folded hands neatly in her lap. She is wearing a wan smile. I guessed that their last home practice session did not go as well as they had hoped for.

Sam speaks first. In his estimation, their progress seems to be uneven. When it's good, it's very, very good. But on those practice sessions where things don't click fairly quickly (like the last one), the session has wound up in a mutual stalemate.

It is usually by this point that couples have had just enough experience to venture beyond the clean confines of practicing strokes. The man has, at least once, taken his partner higher than she's ever been, and experienced considerable pride and satisfaction in the process. The woman has felt more desirable than she ever dreamed possible. Now, they know how good the good times can be, and they want more. When sessions don't work as planned, they see how far they've come, and yet, how far they have to go in order to become great. Predictably, they have encountered the expanded orgasm catch.

Sam began, "When we signed up for this course, I was hoping to revive the fireworks in the bedroom. I wanted Linda to feel what I feel from sex; I wanted to give her hours of unending pleasure, and I wanted to be wanted, desired, and loved for being the producer of all this pleasure. I wasn't expecting to have to have my ego made to fit through the eye of a needle in the process!"

Linda added, "I wish we could have expected this and known what to do in advance. We got trapped in our last date, and didn't know the way out."

So far, no surprises. Better to let them unravel as much as possible. "Sam, why don't you continue? Tell me what happened."

Sam relaxed a little, happy to have everyone's full attention (and sympathy). "There I was, giving Linda pleasure, when suddenly, I couldn't find her 'spot' any longer. It's like it vaporized into thin air! I hadn't expected that, so I redoubled my efforts to find it. Then, I noticed Linda staring at me. She had gone initially into a deep state of relaxation and pleasure, and then turned around and come all the way back to feeling slightly tense. She seemed annoyed. Naturally, every male instinct I had was activated."

"What instincts are those?"

Sam continued, "I have to look good. I can't stop and ask for directions. I can't reveal my frustrations. I must be in control. I can't feel guilty if it doesn't work out the way I want it to. I have to look happy even when I am not. I can't admit feeling puzzled, confused, or inattentive. I can't have any doubts about my abilities." He looked at me, wanting to know if he should go on describing his plight.

"Linda, what was going on for you?" I asked.

"Well, Sam is right. We were surprised by what happened, since the last session had been so much fun. Suddenly, for no reason, it seemed, I stopped feeling anything. Sam didn't seem to notice, and kept doing what he was doing. I finally stared at him, to let him know that his plan wasn't working. I guess I should have said something, but I didn't know what to say. I didn't want to be mean, and I knew I was frustrated, so I figured a little nonverbal communication would be best."

I knew all too well what she was talking about but stayed focused on the story. For now, I wanted to draw her out even further. "What were you feeling, Linda?" She thought for a few moments before responding, as if asking herself this question for the first time. "Oh, I have a long list of feelings that came up, I suppose, now that you ask. I can't appear to be demanding, needy, or bossy. I don't want to ruin his ego. I have no idea what to ask for even if I could. I am doubting my attractiveness; I don't know why I want something different from day to day. I am peri-menopausal, and worried about my libido falling. I don't know how to say stop at the right moment, and change things before I start feeling upset." She looked at me as if to ask if the list was long enough yet.

Both their lists were long enough. In expanded orgasm coaching, we never need the whole list. The list can go on indefinitely. A few minutes of deep communication from each person is enough to reveal the underlying structure of the problem. Each person is hungry most of all for the listening and compassion of their partner. They want to be seen, they want to be heard, and they want to be felt.

Facing them squarely, I said in a matter-of-fact tone, "You know, you're never going to deepen your expanded orgasm practice with the approach you are using, don't you?"

Both of them stared at me, clearly at a loss for words.

"Couples come here to learn expanded orgasm, right?" I continued. They nodded through the daze. "Well, just why do you think these couples are really taking these lessons?"

Linda volunteered, "Well, to have expanded orgasms, of course!" She could hardly believe this. Surely they had come to the right address?

"There's more. Keep going."

"Okay…I want Sam to be my red-hot lover. I want a turned-on life with him. I want to really *want* Sam. I want to spend the rest of our days together. I want what newlyweds are getting! I want to spend a lazy afternoon, curled into Sam's arms, and tell him he's the greatest hero in my life." She looked around, first at me, then at Sam. "Of course, I already do feel that about Sam…it's just that I want even more. I want it all, and I want it with Sam. I want to push our relationship beyond its limits, and explore the outer reaches of those limits. I want to be in love forever, and in ways I haven't even thought of yet!"

I probably don't have to tell you how Sam appeared at this moment.

"Good. Now, have you noticed that expanded orgasms were just one item on your list? Tell me, Linda, what would be the most important thing of all you've mentioned so far?"

"I want Sam and me to be happy together. To be honest, anything that brings us that precious quality is priceless."

Sam was looking the best yet. He was sitting back in the chair, more fully relaxed, and genuinely happy. His ego must have decided it wasn't going to have to shrink to the size of a pinhole. Quite the opposite; he had been—and felt—deeply acknowledged.

Sam ventured, "Thank you Linda, for saying everything you did. I feel the same way too. Connecting with you is the most important thing. But that raises an important question: how are we ever going to love each other more if our egos get trapped in every other expanded orgasm session?"

I jumped in. "Sam, congratulations, you've just asked the big question!" Sam was starting to like all the acknowledgment. Both of them were holding hands now, and looking toward me.

"Of course your expanded orgasm sessions will be hit and miss, if your biggest goal in every session is to have the greatest expanded orgasm of your life. Have you considered making the most important goal to connect with Linda as best as you can, in that moment? Think about it. If Linda makes that her priority too, then you won't wind up in the vicious circle you described. Instead, you'll enter every date with certainty that your date can be a masterpiece of communication and connection."

Linda was holding back tears. "This is really wonderful. Obviously, we have a lot more to learn about communication than we realized. I am just wondering one thing. How come you waited until now to tell us this? Wouldn't you have wanted us to understand this on Day One?"

I laughed to myself. I *had* been telling them this since Day One! *The goal is not as important as the moment-to-moment experience. You must enter the room of expanded orgasm, where the connection is everything. Drop the survival behavior. Get on the same side of the same team. Connect...talk...communicate...reveal...share.* I have said these things many times.

I even know that I will keep delivering this message every time I see them. I will find new ways, new words, and new reasons, to drive home this one point: connection is everything, and communication is what will be the most significant vehicle for them taking each other to the stars via their expanded orgasm practice. It is what will keep them in the game and what will make the game the best one of their lives.

For now, however, I have gotten their attention and made a central point. I am satisfied.

I still had to answer Linda's question. "Oh, I don't think people really hear this until they've been caught in this trap at least once. And now you have. Getting to where you can observe your vicious circles shows significant progress. Fortunately, today you have also already demonstrated the very cocreative communication skills you'll use to get you out of there. Shall we proceed?"

Activity #26: Communicate about Expanded Orgasm

For most couples, expanded orgasm practice is squeezed into a busy schedule. Even if expanded orgasm is a deeply important practice, it takes up only a fraction of a week's time. Still, its importance cannot be minimized. The room of expanded orgasm serves as a kind of microcosm for developing the type of relationship for which you have always yearned. What you do in this space has a way of reflecting back into the original room of your relationship.

Let's take a sort of "mid-term" inventory to see how far you have come in your practice. Use this time to give yourselves the thoughtful reflection you—and your partner—deserve. Use this exercise and develop the art of deep connection, both with yourself, and with your partner.

In Step One, you considered the kinds of experiences you would like to have in an expanded orgasm session, and the kinds of experiences you perceive to be the overall benefits of expanded orgasm. Now is a time to step back for a moment and review your progress in a deep way.

You can do the following exercise alone with a journal, or with a partner, verbally. If you choose to write in your journal, we recommend that at some later point, you communicate the results with your partner. Writing in the journal first gives you the opportunity to fully explore your own emotions and perceptions without concern for your partner's opinions, approval, and reactions. Remember to talk just about yourself, and your relationship (where appropriate) for now.

What are your current goals from an expanded orgasm session? Just list things as they occur to you.

What are your current goals from being in the expanded orgasm training program?

What are your strengths? What are the areas that could use improvement?

Have you felt "trapped" in any of your sessions? Where did you experience stuckness? How did you feel? What did you think? What did you do?

What have been the benefits that were intended (that you set out to achieve)?

Which benefits have you experienced that were unintended or unplanned?

Ken was one of those clients who had initially been quite nonverbal during dates with his wife, Melanie. They had only dated for five months, and then had a brief engagement period of a month before marriage, due to other pressing family concerns. He had always regretted not having a long engagement, during which they could have negotiated more of what was important to each of them. Now married for a little over three years, Ken and Melanie were hoping to have their first true honeymoon as a result of taking expanded orgasm lessons.

In carrying out this exercise, Ken wrote:

Current goals: "Improve my physical skill; give Melanie great sexual experiences; more connection; have her beg me for a date; more playing around."

Current strengths: "I am very good at setting up the room; I make a good beginning; I take care to transition from the rest of the day; and I am a pretty good talker. My hands are more relaxed. When she asks for a change, I do it immediately. And, I am getting much better at finding her sweet spot, and coaxing it out when I need to."

Areas for improvement: "I get unglued when things go wrong; I don't respond as quickly as I would like; I can't always tell what Melanie really wants, and I forget that I have the option of asking her. I still don't always trust the process. Somewhere in my mind, I am waiting for a little bomb to drop when I do something wrong. It doesn't, but I haven't quit thinking that it might!"

Trapped in the catch: "Actually, nearly all our recent dates wound up in traps before we started the expanded orgasm training. Maybe I am being overly optimistic, but I see this entire program as a way of climbing out of all our deeply engrained sexual traps for once and for all. And who knows, with any luck we will be able to use this skill in other areas of our lives, too."

Intended benefits: "We are connecting much more frequently about how to give and receive expanded orgasms. I feel that I can bring up issues about how to give her more pleasure—I don't have to read her mind. Our sexual conversations have become far more open. As a result, I am giving her more pleasure, and she has been far more responsive to me too when we make love."

Unintended benefits: "I find we are talking more in other areas. Topics that were never discussed are now fair game. We are more honest with each other in general. We are not playing so many games. Most important, because of our combined efforts to give each other greater pleasure, being together is sweeter.

"Our practices of expanded orgasm take up only a small amount of our time. But the learning seems to seep in to everything we say and do. Just yesterday, I barked at Melanie when she let the cat in too soon and it woke me up. At one time, I would have fumed for a while before forgiving her. Now, I look at her as my pleasure partner. I can't expect someone at whom I am barking to connect deeply with me. Within ten minutes I apologized to her for flying off, and gave her a hug. Melanie pointed this out to me no less than three times yesterday. It felt like she and I were becoming new people with each other."

After Ken shared his comments with Melanie, he added, "Just sharing with Melanie all that I've written has affected me deeply. It is hard for me to admit weakness, or even areas for improvement. I thought she would think less of me. Instead, she got really turned on to me and said she felt a lot closer. She strongly encouraged me to continue letting her know what I am feeling at this very deep level."

Melanie later wrote in her journal. "I have always hated it when men try to use sex to smooth over difficulties in the rest of our relationship. I want the difficulties removed first, and then I feel better about giving my all to the sex.

"For me, expanded orgasm practice is that common ground, or midpoint, where both of us can agree to work things out. It's not lovemaking, and it's not the kind of processing that only digs us deeper into a rut. Both of us are building out our room of expanded orgasm by sharing deeply and cocreating pleasure. Now we often make hot love after an expanded orgasm practice when we otherwise would have been trapped in another one of our standoffs. Our breakthroughs in connecting and communication somehow address issues and problems surfacing not only in sex but in many other areas of our lives."

Ken and Melanie's experiences are pretty typical. They have followed the program closely. Their areas of improvement lie in making sure that communication happens sooner, and more frequently. They experienced unanticipated growth and passion in all areas of their relationship.

Communicate with Yourself

How do you communicate with yourself? Does your ego's self-talk about whether or not you are meeting your (or your partner's) expectations get in the way? Or do you immerse in a feeling state to notice what is going on with every stroke? Your ability to make finer and finer distinctions in the feeling state will power your expanded orgasm practices forward rapidly.

Let's see how this works by listening in on an inner monologue of a woman touching herself: *I am not feeling very much right now…let me find where I do feel the most. OK, it's here. I can make very tiny circular motions and feel a lot. I enjoy how slowly I am going…mmmmmm…would diagonal strokes add anything…no, the energy went down, so back to the circles…increase in speed…slightly. I think I will stay here a while and build the energy higher…oops…my sensation is falling…try wider circles…good…even wider…perfect! Now maybe I can shift the circle a little higher.*

At a later point in the date, she might also be noticing any tensions in her pelvis…hands…face…jaw…neck…feet, etc. As climax approaches, her focus may rest almost entirely on the pushed out feeling in her pelvis. She is aware of both the expansive experience and the blissful relaxation and sense of letting go. Immersing in this feeling radiates messages of letting go to the rest of her body.

So let's make "her" *you*. You noticed what took you higher, lower, or kept you at the same level. If something didn't work, you often guessed at some next move.

If that carried you in the direction you wanted to go, you took it from there. If it didn't, you went back to what you knew felt better. The feedback and response times were instantaneous; the feedback loop was closed and potent.

What about your partner? He, too, can monitor his interior thought and feeling processes: my hand is relaxing…I feel her sweet spot…a buzz of energy…it's getting stronger…stay relaxed…the feeling is flowing right up my arm—it feels warm and tingly…oops, I am speeding up, and the energy is going down, so slow down…OK, the feeling is going up again…perhaps I can slow down even a little further…no, that didn't work…perhaps I can add more pressure…wow! She loves this!…keep going, stay relaxed…ride that energy…don't change anything now, she's really climbing!

Note how the man (the so-called "giver") is just as capable of creating a closed, intimate feedback loop with you as you are with yourself. However, he will probably have to train himself to do this, and you will help him train.

We recommend that periodically (every minute, perhaps) the man make a routine check of his own body. It is easy to pick up unwanted tension as the energy and turn-on builds. In this situation, the man may unwittingly apply so much extra pressure that he brings a woman down just as she is ready to go higher. With each scan, he can release any unwanted tension just with a simple mental decision.

The woman can also scan a man's body and point out if she notices tensions. She will find she is "intuitively" able to do this with increasing ease as she becomes more engorged and turned on. Tensions often accumulate as the energy builds. A mere mention of it is often enough to have the giver choose to "let it go" mentally.

Men enjoy a good challenge. Ken loved it when Melanie presented him with an interesting new request. She asked him to figure out how to increase the pressure he was delivering, but without increasing the tension in his hand. Ken reported, "I had to figure out a way to send pressure, with my mind, through my body, while staying alert and relaxed." Trust me, he was not looking for sympathy. He had a real sense of accomplishment when he put this all together and he wanted Melanie to be proud of him. And yes, he had figured out a perfect strategy for increasing pressure—the sense of *contact*, really—without increasing tension.

When Ken and other men start scanning, they learn how to give their partner much more (or less) pressure and contact without the unintended consequences of bringing their partner down. They can also use scanning to make sure they are immersing attentively into the overall experience. No one wants to feel stress and tension when what they really want to do is to relax into an expanded orgasm.

Activity #27: Scan Your Own Body

During your next expanded orgasm practice session, scan, that is, become aware of your own internal processes, both physical and mental. Men and women, notice when you are relaxing more; notice how this feels; notice how it feels to your partner when you relax, and so on. In other words, feel yourself, feel your partner, and feel your partner feeling you.

Take five minutes each to report to your partner everything you notice. Clients often report being powerfully aroused by hearing their partner talk to them so intimately, and with so much attention. How does it feel to be on the receiving end, hearing your partner notice his or her process in such detail? Following the practice session, share with your partner about your own experience.

Communicate with Your Partner

Now that you understand the principles of watching your own feeling level rise and fall, and of experimenting verbally with yourself and a partner about possible changes, we turn to the more complex activity of communicating with a partner.

Activity #28: Scan Your Partner's Body

This exercise has two parts to it.

Part 1: In this exercise, the woman starts out as the receiver. Men, as giver, notice how your energy feels and shifts in each moment. Scan for how relaxed you feel, and how present you are to the experience.

I'm just getting comfortable in this position…she looks very relaxed…I am going to start out with the three strokes. "Are you feeling comfortable and ready to begin? Good." *My hands feel very relaxed…her lips are still relatively unengorged. It feels so sexy to run my fingers up the sides.* "I love it when we start out and I get your lips to engorge." *She liked that comment, I can tell by the look on her face.*

At a later part of the date, notice how relaxed her body is. Is she breathing deeply? If not, you might encourage her to do so. Is she tensing up? Offer her a gentle reminder to relax. Is she clenching her fists? Let her know that she might find it more pleasurable to reach for more sensation by opening her hands rather than clenching them.

Ladies, notice it's as if your partner, in this exercise, is a voice-controlled vibrator. What might you be saying to both him and to yourself?

If you are experienced at communication, it might go something like this: *Okay, breathe...relax.* "That was a nice first stroke." *I can feel how relaxed his hand is...I'm just settling down...don't feel too much...let the feeling develop...would faster feel better right now?* "That feels great, could you go a little faster?" *No, that didn't help.* "Try slower, please." *Ooohhh, that worked.* "Yes, that was nice."

In this example, the only difference is that you are talking out loud to a partner. There is an echo effect; first you think it, then you say it, whereas before, when just being with yourself, you simply carried out your every whim.

In a more advanced session, you could notice what sets of strokes, and peaks, brought you higher.

He just switched from circles to this diagonal stroke...that worked. I am climbing. I wish he would slow down..."I love the switch, and now could you slow down?" Ooohhh, yes. "Mmmmmm, that's great" *Oh, there's the phone...my energy is dropping fast now...he is pausing, that is the right thing to do.* "Thanks for pausing until the ringing stopped." *Okay, interruption over...good, he's starting off really slowly again, like when we first started.* "That was a fun break! I am glad you are starting off again slowly and that you kept contact during the interruption."

At a later point in the date, you might want to check and see that you are both still comfortable. Positions shift; what started out as comfortable may no longer be. Is your partner leaning on you with too much weight? Is his arm unsupported and therefore tiring? When possible, look out for each other's comfort as well as your own. Since comfort changes often creep in over time, scan periodically.

Part 2: Switch Roles. It is quite helpful for men and women to experience both giving and receiving while communicating and scanning. Now the man will be the receiver, and the woman, the giver.

In this exercise, not only did you offer gentle and sure-to-be-appreciated guidance to a partner; you confirmed what went well, and offered suggestions on how to make the experience even better. Rather than appearing needy and demanding, you made your requests nicely. Probably you racked up major points with your beloved, and an offer for another training date soon!

Your ability to notice distinctions allows you to be creative about what to try next. And, if you are worried that you are going to have to become overly verbal to succeed in cocreating expanded orgasm, don't worry. You will use verbal methods to learn how to immerse in the energy of the delightful and intimate feedback loops we promised earlier.

Still, until you communicate with yourself, and notice which strokes and peaks work, and which don't, you can't communicate fully with a partner. The attention required to notice subtle distinctions is significant. Some of our clients have objected, "I just want to be in the flow." Actually, when you are at the level of attention where you are noticing, in every moment, both the feeling in that moment, and whether the feeling is going up or down, you are more in the flow than at any other time possible.

It is a discipline. Clients often resist the intimacy that accompanies so powerful a tool for focusing attention because it feels so unlike what they are used to doing and feeling in relationship. This is an intimacy born from the vulnerability to express deep desire, and the willingness and ability to respond to that desire. With practice, such intimacy becomes less unfamiliar and more rewarding—an intimacy brimming with powerful and immediate richness.

This *call-and-response form of communication* is a learned skill. The power behind acquiring this skill is the intention to connect powerfully and intimately and to cocreate outrageously pleasurable experiences.

Activity #29: A or B?

In this playful exercise, the man lets the woman know he is going to give her two different strokes, and then ask her to pick the one she likes better. After each question, deliver several of the same strokes so she can enjoy and evaluate them, before offering her the next set.

Here are some examples from Ken and Melanie's exercise. Each time, Ken offered Melanie a choice, to which she responded either "A" or "B."

"Which do you like better, A or B?" (Ken applied slightly firmer, then slightly softer pressure.)

"Which do you like better, A or B?" (Ken made circles, then he changed to elliptical strokes.)

"Which do you like better, A or B?" (Ken's finger traveled more to the left, then more to the right.)

"Which do you like better, A or B?" (Ken's speed increased, then his speed decreased.)

A few times, Ken offered the same choice more than once. He suspected that Melanie would reveal differing preferences each time. He was right. The first time he asked, Melanie wanted him to slow down. A few sets later, when Ken asked the same set of questions, Melanie preferred the faster stroke. This is an important point: when you find something your partner really likes, do not assume he or she will always want that.

With each response, see if you can tell energetically, before she responds, what her answer will be. You are learning to "read" your partner.

This exercise is a good one to open up lines of communication during expanded orgasm. Occasionally, Allen still asks me "A or B"–type questions when he thinks I may be spacing out a little. The question snaps me back into my experience and reminds me to be more verbal again. Sometimes, he will also ask them playfully; and sometimes, he is a scientist doing pleasure research for the benefit of all womankind on my behalf!

Varieties of Communication

Studies have found communication to be 10 percent verbal and 90 percent non-verbal. If you smile and shake hands with someone at a business party, by the time you've said, "Hello," you probably have revealed one of more of the following bits of information: what part of the country you live in, what level of education you've had, your general level of income, and the nature of your job. How? The information is in your accent, the condition of your teeth and hands, your makeup (or lack thereof), hairstyle, clothing, posture, and attitude.

Many levels of communication weave the tapestry of expanded orgasm. Here are just some of the ways in which this can happen.

Report Facts and Feelings

The woman to the man:

"That was a great stroke."

"I love having all of your attention."

"Your hand feels so soft on me."

"I loved it when you just picked up the energy in that last move."

The man to the woman:

"Your clitoris just doubled in size."

"Your abdomen is starting to contract."

"I felt the energy go up with this change in stroke."

"Your face looks so beautiful right now."

Ask for Changes

The woman to the man:

"Could you go a little to the left, now, please?"

"Could you relax a bit further in your left hand?"

"Could you go back to giving me shorter peaks, please?"

"I preferred the shorter strokes to the longer ones."

The man to the woman:

"Would you like me to go a little higher?"

"Would you like me to drag my strokes even more?"

"Did you like it when I made that extra long stroke as a peak?"

"Would you like me to call the peaks for you right now?"

Have Fun with Dialogue

Between the woman and the man:

"I just went up a lot! Did you feel that too?"

"Yes, the energy surged up my arm and even into my chest."

"How did you know I was hoping you would do just that?"

"Your energy was broadcasting that request powerfully just then."

Show Your Intentions

(Note the emphasis on "wanting" to create a certain effect):

The man to the woman:

"I want to make this next stroke the best one yet for you."

"I am going to take you into the stars."

"I want you to feel totally loved and cared for right now."

"I want this to feel the best possible for you."

The woman to the man:

"I want to fly higher and higher as you pleasure me."

"I want to feel every stroke you give me."

"I want to have a great time here with you today."

"I want this to be a great date together."

Tease

Between the woman and the man:

"Whatever you do, don't tease me!"

"I would never do a thing like tease you…well, maybe, maybe not."

"I am not going to bring you down until I am good and ready."

"If you don't stop resisting so much I am going to have to bring out a surprise move I have been saving for just such an occasion."

"Oooh, I'm really nervous now! What could that be?"

Promises, Promises

(These are certain and should only be given when you know you can deliver the goods):

The man to the woman:

"I am going to make this date a memorable experience for you."

"You are going to experience first hand my lust for your touch."

"I will take you even higher than you are hoping for."

"This next stroke will send you into orbit."

The woman to the man:

"I am going to go over the edge if you do that stroke one more time."

"I am going to make your attention pay off big time as soon as our date is over."

"I am going to send all this energy I'm feeling right back into you, right now!"

"I am going to go much higher if you just keep doing that very same stroke."

(Note: Confidence is a real turn-on! Be sure, however, that you can deliver on your promise before making it. If you are not sure, stick to intentions, as they are the safer bet. A failed promise can lead to negative consequences like disappointment and a loss of confidence.)

Listen for Semi-verbal Sounds

Sounds of all kinds: moans, mmmmms, coos, sighs, purring. In general, pleasant sounds indicate relaxation; shrill, unpleasant sounds indicate a tightening up.

Communication through Your Body

Is the body becoming more relaxed? Are the muscles of the abdomen and pelvis releasing? Are the throat and jaw relaxed? Are the hands and toes spread wide? Is she lying relatively still? All these are signs of relaxation.

If you see your partner stiffening up, then you may wish to help relax your partner. You might take her hand and open it up if it's clenched, for example. Or, you might spread the energy up her abdomen if she looks as though she is tensing up there.

Notice Altered Breathing

The breath can be getting deeper, or more intense—or rapid and more shallow. Sometimes, when a woman is pushing out, she will stop breathing for a short time. Some women find this intensifies their experience.

Nonverbal communication communicates to the giver information about the effects of his actions. For example, if breathing shifts from being intense to normal, you can deduce that the feeling intensity has dropped off. If this is intentional, that is good to know. If it is unintentional, take that as a cue to change what you are doing.

You can also remind your receiving partner to breathe more deeply, or start doing so yourself in a way that she can hear and feel clearly.

Communications Tips

Keep comments focused on the here and now: on how you feel, how your partner feels, on the physical changes taking place. Once the date has begun, it's best to avoid general or negative talk or past-time comments like, "I had a really hard time getting present earlier." First, you are not talking about present time. Second, you are taking the energy down, not up.

If your partner makes a comment like that, you might say something to bring him or her into the here and now: "Well, I am glad you made it, because you look so sexy right now."

Does this sound like another silly rule? Why can't people be negative during a date? Try it sometime. I have found that until I can bring myself fully and positively into the present it is difficult to feel and magnify pleasure. Thus, I do whatever I need to do in order to feel positive and be present when I do begin the date.

Try touching yourself pleasurably when you are in a bad mood. Notice the results. Try touching yourself pleasurably when you are in a good mood. Notice the results. Based on the results of this experience, ask yourself, would you ever want to start a date when you are in a bad mood? Most people would immediately say no!

Let's take this idea one step further. How are you feeling right now? Look for items in your environment or present circumstances about which it is easy for you to feel negative. Continue to do this until you feel down or a little blue. If you can, touch yourself pleasurably now (or at least think about doing so). Now, wipe your mental slate clean. Look for items in your environment or in your present circumstances about which it is easy for you to feel positive. Continue to do this until you feel good. Again, touch yourself or think about doing so. Do you notice how by directing your attention you can rapidly change your internal feeling-state? What effect does your internal state have on your ability to feel sensual pleasure?

Activity #30: Write Your Own Lines!

Most people are not born with a library of lines to use during sex. They learn them—from movies or books, or from their friends or partners. Sadly, there are not many opportunities we have to learn expanded orgasm from each other. How can we share our great lines when we never have a chance to watch the masters in action?

While we personally can't transport ten or twenty clients to your house for an evening of sharing lines, in this exercise we invite you to create several lines from each category listed above. They don't have to be eloquent poetry. "That feels good" and "I am really glad to be here with you today" are fine. Believe me, almost any positive verbalization (if authentic) will sound like celestial music.

Don't hesitate to practice a small list of lines until you feel comfortable improvising more. Many of today's greatest expanded orgasm practitioners started out using a limited list of lines and playing with them for a year or more. Their partners never minded, since they were so overwhelmingly grateful for this playful and turned-on banter.

Rules, Patterns, and Formulas

Now that we've told you it's OK to use the same lines over and over again, especially if you are just developing your hot, juicy expanded orgasm vocabulary, we are going to switch gears. It's OK to use the same banter over and over, especially when the alternative is silence! However, we don't want you to use the same routine for physically delivering pleasure, even in the same ten minutes.

A mistake some men make (but certainly not you, I'm sure), when receiving directive feedback is to rely on it exclusively. Say your partner asks you to go higher now, and to the left. Some men might go higher and to the left, and if this works, breathe a sigh of relief and stay there for hours! The more a man relies strictly on directions, the less of a chance he has to practice and learn other forms of communication. Men tend to love roadmaps and formulas for success, so when they think they might be getting one, they try to memorize it on the spot.

While directive feedback does often point the giver in the direction of knowing what their partner likes in general, it can be quite misleading if used inappropriately. Slavishly applying a "pleasure formula" drains the juice from the connection. Perhaps she only wanted you to stroke her like that for a few moments!

It is more empowering to view verbal, directive feedback as a way for you to learn how to determine when you are on course. You can do this when you know clearly what "being on course" feels like!

To see this, let's distinguish between *rules, patterns,* and *formulas* for purposes of learning expanded orgasm.

Rules are short sayings that apply forever.

"Always stop giving her pleasure when the doorbell rings."

"Never take your hand away suddenly from a woman when you have been touching her genitals."

"Always make some verbal contact at the beginning."

"Never resume at the intensity you were at when you started a break; always start a little slower."

Rules are fine, if and only if you and your partner agree on them. Check them out with your partner.

Patterns are sequences of actions taken together.

"She usually likes it when I move my right and left hands in unison, going up and down, at exactly the same speed."

"When she gets to a certain level of engorgement, I can put often three or four fingers over her clitoral area. She doesn't tend to like this early on, but later in a session, she loves it."

Patterns should be viewed as the results of experiments and are very often—but definitely not always—useful. They're like "rules of thumb." Notice the emphasis on words like "usually," "tends to," and "often."

Formulas are recipes for producing pleasure.

"Go slow and then gradually start building the pressure until she goes over the edge."

"Try covering a broader surface area, and start dragging two or three fingers very slowly."

Men love formulas, since at first they appear to promise that a man will not have to figure things out a second time. The problem with formulas is that many of them contradict one another.

"Go slow, and on occasion, slow down even further, to tease her even higher. Sometimes if you go lightly enough, she'll go over the edge."

"Start out slowly, increase the speed, and then slow down again, making sure not to go faster than a certain amount, if you want to take her over the edge."

Suddenly, what once was a library of useful hints is a cacophony of contradictions.

"Go faster if you can't find her spot."

"Slow down when you don't know what to do next."

"Admit you don't know what to do next and ask her what she would like next."

Trying to use reason to determine which formula to apply is certain to shatter a man's attention! The problem with formulas is that most women change what they want from month to month, day to day, and even minute to minute (men do too, but, in our experience, to a far lesser extent than women).

Mechanical adherence to formulas will gradually cause even a very verbal woman to stop talking. Here's why: as a man makes increasing use of formulas, rather than "dancing with her energy," he restricts his range of pleasure-giving. Women and men vary considerably in their preferences and responses over time. What they really want is to feel met—connected with—not treated like their desires are part of a formula.

What are your rules, patterns, and formulas? What are your partner's? You might want to compare notes to see where you agree and disagree.

Map Your Partner's Preferences

Mapping is a royal road to bringing your partner increasing pleasure. You gather information (biofeedback) about your partner, and use this information to help determine what to do next. You can do this because you know how to "read" how and where and to what extent your partner feels pleasure. You do this reading with all your senses. Mapping draws upon the skills of communication to oneself, and one's partner. Another term for mapping is *reading the energy*.

Men, you can learn how to read a woman's energy the way you read other kinds of maps! Think of going down a river in a raft. Even if you have been down this river before, each time is a new experience. The changing water levels alter how the currents flow, and determine which rocks will be the challenges. You must learn how to navigate rushing rivers so that you can be prepared for whatever you might encounter. This same type of preparation works with giving women expanded orgasm.

Mapping conveys to you the effects of your last decision, and guides you into what your next move could be. In mapping while rafting down a river, you would always be looking for the smoothest flow of water. Any time you run into rocks, you risk tipping over, and possibly damaging the raft. Any time you stray too far from the current, you risk finding yourself in boring, brackish backwaters, having to paddle back. At your best, you ride the current, always looking out just a bit ahead, and ready to change in a moment, dancing with the terrain, and utterly focused on where you are in relation to where you could be. As the speed slows, you check the current. Are you moving away from it? Paddle back. As you speed up, are there rapids ahead? Is the present course safe or are you too close to an edge you are not ready to go over?

Moment by moment, your mapping is telling you to move closer, or further, from the current. Mapping is at the heart of expanded orgasm. In so doing, you are reading the current in the river, one moment to the next. This is the surest way to stay with the energy and to direct it as you wish.

Men, make sure you know how to lock yourself into your partner's sweet spot, her current. You will be thrown off for all manner of reasons. Don't try to analyze why—thinking will get in your way! Rather, see yourself as a sophisticated and sensitive communication and biofeedback device. Perhaps you are a bionic human with an ultra-advanced radar device implanted in your brain. With it, you can detect communication at every level of subtlety.

Your "device" might register as follows:

Moved my finger left—her current went a little higher.

She's smiling; her face is getting a little flushed.

She stayed put—holding steady with the same stroke.

Her body became a little more tense—peaked her after the tenth stroke.

She seems to be getting restless—visualized more energy streaming through my own body.

Her energy up yet again—added a little more speed.

Her eyes closed again, and her breathing got deeper—stayed where I was with her.

Energy still climbing, her hands are spreading apart now—changed from circles to diagonals to peak her again.

Energy dropped a little—slowed down a touch, starting to build again.

I used words and measurement-like concepts here, but remember that most of this "chatter" is happening deep in the innards of the detector; your experience is more like dancing or surfing—being in the flow. The basic pattern is this: watch/feel/intuit her; do something (or keep on the same course); watch/feel/intuit her response; do something (or keep on course); and so on, in an ongoing cycle, with occasional scanning of your own body and mind thrown in every so often.

This is one of those points where men panic. *I can't do all those things at once!* But stop for a moment—didn't you say that at least once while learning to drive a car? Did you want to learn how to drive? Where there is the desire, you will find the way. Believe me, one day, your abilities to surf the current of ecstasy will be as thrilling and natural for you as it is for master racecar drivers and champion surfers. There will come a day when you do these things without even thinking; all you will feel is the ride on the current, and how it makes you feel as it goes into the higher reaches of pure pleasure, and as your connection with your partner becomes so seamless that you no longer can remember (or care) who is giving, and who is receiving.

Some people feel love is expressed by the words they say; others by their actions. In expanded orgasm, you are weaving for your partner a tapestry of words and action, communication (both verbal and nonverbal) and attention. You are telling your partner you care deeply about her in every moment, as you watch her, feel her, talk to her, play with her, and give her the kind of pleasure you (as a man) have always found easily available. No wonder so many expanded orgasm practitioners use the excuse of an anniversary to start their practice! This year, they want more than just roses and love letters. They want the full-on experience of the deepest possible engagement with each other.

Activity #31: Flowing Communication

Men and women: take turns at this! Do this exercise during a sandbox date.

First, men, begin a verbal dialogue. Notice factual items about her; notice how you feel when you deliver a particular stroke; tell her loving things, such as how happy you are to be with her right now. Even tease her a little. Try to keep an ongoing monologue in play. Notice what happens to her "energy," and yours, as you do this. Just stay focused on the present moment. For example, don't compliment her cooking! Compliment the rosy blush on her cheeks *right now.* Don't talk about how excited you felt this afternoon, in advance of the date. Tell her how happy you are *right now.* Then it is the woman's turn. Each of you should talk for at least five minutes.

Women, notice and communicate how each stroke feels. Stay positive in your comments; if the previous stroke felt better than the current one, tell your partner you'd like another one of the strokes like the last one; when you allow your pelvis to relax, mention that you are opening to feeling greater sensation. Tell him how much you enjoyed it when he said he was excited to be here with you; and let him know you are basking in the warm glow of all this attention. Again, keep your monologue centered on experiences happening right now.

If this exercise is challenging, bear in mind that you have likely shut down your ability to verbalize and feel genital sensations simultaneously. Most people can easily carry on about how great a massage feels. "Oooh, keep going, the pressure is great…no, go a little lower, right into that muscle! That's perfect. Now stay there! Don't stop. More pressure! Ahhhhhh, I'm feeling so good right now. You're a genius, you make me feel so good."

Why is it we can be so vocal during a massage, then, and not when our genitals are being touched? It is our conditioning—and nothing else—that has led us to believe that this is how our minds and bodies work. Body—OK to discuss. Genitals—ssshh! If you do these exercises a few times, you will most likely be able to surprise yourself with how much practice can improve your abilities to talk.

If the talking is just too difficult starting out, try this exercise on non-genital parts of the body first. Get used to maintaining a steady stream of verbal feedback, and then slowly shift over to talking during genital foreplay, then genital stimulation. Melanie and Ken had never experienced all the honeymoon fireworks she'd seen in the movies, and she had to admit, she wanted those fireworks. She was starting to realize, however, that trying to remain in silence whenever she could get away with it was not the best path. For one thing, she had already experienced the value of talking more. Still, she wanted Ken to take full control over her, so that she could relax on her expanded orgasm dates, not "strain her mind." But every time she had talked to Ken, it seemed Ken had turned her request into a formula. Now it didn't feel safe or easy for her to talk. Was there going to be a happy medium between talking and being swept away by Ken? She couldn't reconcile the two states at once.

These conflicts had created the following pattern. Ken would "get Melanie going." She would enter a nice, expanded state of streaming. But, they didn't seem to go any higher. She yearned for Ken to take her explosively over the edge. After some heavy resisting, I finally persuaded her to practice some further communication, if only to humor me. Her fears of Ken's formulizing and her going out of her state of relaxation were pronounced.

The two of them were in a communications trap. If she didn't try to break out of their catches, how far could she ever get? Even more communication would be the only solution. Since she had practiced communicating, she knew how to do it, and even that she could do it rather well. She just didn't really want to. Still, she agreed to follow our recommendation—once!

This was to be a highly cocreative session. We got Ken to agree to focus on reading Melanie's energy moment to moment and stay focused on her feelings at all times. He was not to create formulas from Melanie's feedback. For her part, she was to maintain good levels of verbal and nonverbal communication.

On their designated date, Ken brought her into an expanded orgasm state and into the streaming. "This is where we always stop," she thought. "Now is the time I need to pay attention." She noticed that in order to bring up the intensity, Ken was adding in more speed and more pressure. However, that was not her favorite method for bringing herself greater amounts of pleasure.

She was an expert on bringing herself to climax. She liked to tease herself higher; she would add a little speed, and then back off, creating a hunger in her clitoris for more sensation. Then she would slow down a little, ever so subtly increasing the pressure to make up for the slowing down. As soon as she was ready for more sensation, she would actually lighten the pressure, and then speed up a little. She would do this many times until she could barely contain any more pleasurable energy—then she would increase the pressure a little more, keeping the speed relatively constant. At that point, she'd slingshot over the edge.

Noticing now that Ken didn't have a handle on her pattern, she started walking him through the motions. "Ken, you've done a great job getting me started. I feel lots of energy streaming through me."

"I feel it too."

"Did you notice the point where the energy dropped off? That happens to me too. When it does, I slow down a little, and reconnect with my favorite spot."

Ken slowed down. "I have found it again."

"Good. Now this time, try circles instead of up and down strokes. It's easier to go slow with circles."

"Okay…hey, you're right."

"That's good, and you could still be going slower. Here, count: one, one thousand, two, one thousand…."

"Wow, I never knew that's what you meant by *slow*. And wow, circles let me go much slower than up and down strokes! This is great."

"It is feeling really good. Now, relax a little more. Good. Mmmmmmmm, I feel the energy building really nicely now."

"Me too! This is great!"

"OK, now, I am getting more engorged and turned on, and my genitals are starting to melt like hot wax. My face and neck are flushing..."

"I was just about to tell you that!" They both laughed.

"Now, ever so subtly, can you increase the intensity just by feeling how good you feel right now?"

"Yes, your energy is getting hot; your lips are getting even fuller. Ooohhh, this is fun, taking you into such high places. And as I tease you, it's like your clitoris is standing up and begging for more! I feel you starting to contract even more now. I just sped up, but I noticed it and stopped. You want to be teased mercilessly, don't you? Well, I want to hold you here until I am ready to do the slightest thing differently."

The date went so well that Melanie felt more experimentation was possible. This time, she let Ken know she wanted him to start mapping her more actively. She asked him to start verbalizing his mapping.

For Ken, it was as if a switch flipped in that session. From that point on, he looked to speak, not the *language of rules*, but the *language of change*. Every time he felt a change, he pointed it out to Melanie. And so, the trap of not communicating was broken.

Once the vicious circles that blocked this ongoing dialog were broken, the floodgates open to all the other things that had remained unsaid, but which are yearning for a voice. Melanie began to verbalize how much she wanted to have that honeymoon they'd never quite had. And Ken began, for the first time ever, to feel confident that he could provide her with a first class honeymoon far better than the one they would have had when they first married. Shortly after this breakthrough session, Ken took Melanie explosively over the edge. To Melanie's surprise, he took her over longer and deeper than she had ever taken herself!

Ken and Melanie finally took the plunge, and went on a cruise around the world. It was to be the honeymoon they'd always yearned for, and because of their openness it exceeded their expectations. Here, for sure, their thawed communication led quickly from the bedroom to the stateroom!

Bootstrap to Go Higher in Pleasure

Bootstrapping is the art of starting with nothing and winding up with something through a process of iterative building. The term often is used in reference to those "bootstrappers" who seek to make something of themselves in life, while starting with very little. Bootstrapping begins with tiny momentum, but immense desire. The momentum arises in the building.

In the world of computers, bootstrapping refers to the process by which the machine goes from being an inert object to a useful workhorse. When powered up, certain instructions are loaded. These lines of code contain other sets of instructions, which, when activated, initiate other actions. Soon the inert machine has transformed itself into a powerful processor.

In expanded orgasm, bootstrapping is the solution to a situation where there is *desire but no momentum*. The two persons gathered together for an expanded orgasm session work collaboratively to take themselves from some initial state to the expanded reaches of orgasmic ecstasy. Bootstrapping is what creates the trajectory. The couple starts out with:

- a certain amount of *desire*, and hoped-for outcomes such as orgasms, pleasure, connection, fun, and relaxation.
- a certain level of turn-on (or *momentum*). One person may be flat (not turned on at all), while the other may be very juiced, or vice versa.
  Both may be juiced, or both may be flat.

No matter where the starting point, each person feeds the other useful information and energy that enables them to keep adding more desire and momentum to the experience.

Candace, a mother and professional tax preparer, came to us with a problem. With her outrageously busy schedule, she and her partner Carl could only plan dates when her kids were away for the evening and Carl (an attorney with a growing practice) could also clear the time. From experience, they knew how easy it was for the good intentions when setting up the date to crumble upon arriving tired and feeling "spent." In advance of their date they did much to fan the flames of their initial motivation and desire by sending each other little love notes, making sexy phone calls, even flirting outrageously right before their date.

Still, once the date began, one or both of them lost focus. In time, they found themselves letting go of the goal of a deep, intimate connection on dates.

Candace even joked, "We keep threatening to both take up drinking coffee so we are awake enough to enjoy our dates!"

Do you suppose they are just "tired"? Or do you suspect that something else might be getting in the way? I asked Candace if she normally became exhausted so readily just from being a mom. She then noticed that her exhaustion seemed particularly problematic with Carl right at those times when they were about to share intimacy. At other times, say, when they were going to dinner party, both their energies seemed fine.

Exhaustion is one way people have of giving up. They love their partner but feel at the end of their rope for what to say or do to energize their time together. Both are desperately hoping the other has better ideas how to do this! They find themselves at a loss. Another evening drifts by, a silence made to look like comfortable security but covering up a hunger for hot passion. Progressive unexplained and persistent exhaustion is a way of saying, "I give up."

Carl is also unclear about the slowdown in their sexual life. "I don't think I am doing anything wrong. It's as if the newness of our relationship was what was fueling the passion, and the newness can't last forever. Sooner or later the bubble bursts. Candace has kids, I have a career, and these things take up time and energy. Unfortunately, it seems that she and I wind up with the leftovers from the rest of our life. And often it seems there is little left even of the leftovers."

Candace and Carl are excellent candidates to benefit from bootstrapping. Bootstrapping can take you to much higher levels of pleasure, no matter where you start.

Bootstrapping utilizes all the communication techniques we have already discussed. Both parties to the date have at their disposal the ability to scan their own bodies, communicate to their partners about either their own experience or what they are noticing about their partner. Either person can offer a piece of needed information at just the right moment to avert losing altitude. Either person can laugh at just the right moment to keep the energy feeling warm and loving. Either person can be the one to take the next step to carrying the date to a yet higher level of feeling.

In bootstrapping, no one is keeping score. Some days you may be the one doing more of the talking; other days, it may be your partner taking the lead. Both of you benefit from the magic of cocreation.

Candace and Carl are in the bedroom, holding each other. They have practiced the communication exercises to their satisfaction, and are now ready to try bootstrapping. Their goal is to generate an entire pleasurable experience, starting from wherever they find themselves.

Candace is clearly nervous. Her body is a little tense, and she has looked at the clock three times in ten minutes, even though they have the entire evening together. Carl points out, "You look tense. Is there something I can do for you? A massage? Talk? Just let me know. I am here for you."

"For the first time in seventy-nine hours, someone has put an ounce of their attention on me," thought Candace. "I had no idea how desperately I am craving attention." Her eyes brimmed with tears.

"Your eyes are teary. Does that mean you want to talk?" asked Carl.

"Actually, I think those are tears of joy. I have never, ever, wanted you to hold me as much as I do right now. Please, hug me, hold me, and whatever you do, keep noticing me...tell me something, anything. Especially something nice!"

"I've missed holding you closely like this, Candace," Carl revealed. "I don't know what happened, how it stopped feeling special, since right now, I'm the happiest man alive, just to be here with you."

Carl spent the whole evening holding Candace in his arms. They talked more about their sensual lives then they ever had before. They looked at all the constraints before them, and problem-solved ways to have pleasure anyway. They never made it around to having expanded orgasm, but the two of them ended the evening feeling that they had asked for everything they had really wanted from each other in every area of their lives. Both of them knew that in the future, they had a much greater chance of helping each other get to a place where the expanded orgasm did occur.

A new pattern was born that evening. When either wanted something, they asked for it. The requests ranged from physical to emotional, from playful to loving and deep. Before then, it had not seemed OK to ask for what was wanted. In the new pattern, either could notice what they wanted or what their partner seemed to want, and could offer to fulfill the request. Their bootstrapping quickly escalated from hugging into red-hot passion, as each tendered increasingly pleasurable offers.

Keep in mind about bootstrapping:

183

The most important goal of an expanded orgasm session is pleasure. There are many ways that pleasure can be cocreated. You can connect well, feel more than usual, communicate better than ever, open your heart deeply, and so on.

You and your partner train each other to give each other increasing amounts of pleasure. You are the perfect person to train your partner to your desires—no one can do it better than you.

Repeated bootstrapping is important. In so doing, you both vastly enhance your expanded orgasm library of "what works." Old rules are updated and/or discarded; new patterns are added to the library.

Each session has value. Look and celebrate. Did your partner do something that felt especially good? Did you learn something new? Was your connection especially deep? In almost every date, there is an opportunity for some bootstrapping to occur. Seize these moments!

Activity #32: What Are Your "Catch" Patterns?

The need for bootstrapping comes in many forms. At the core, the couple could be doing an even better job of cocreating their relationship. We have looked at a few variations so far. In other variations, people feel a deep sense of upset that the other partner has stopped doing his or her part to make the romance hot and juicy—and they find plenty of evidence. These same people feel unclear about their own part in cocreating the current situation. Any time one of you feels the other partner is carrying a disproportionately small share of the responsibility, stop—and think again.

Here are yet some other patterns:

One is not bringing enough turn-on and/or enthusiasm to the date; the other is not putting enough attention and acknowledgment on what the other person has been bringing to the date.

One is not asking for what they want and need; the other is in mystery as to what they can do to give the other person what they want.

One is angry at something that happened in the past, and unwilling to get into present time; the other is feeling hurt, misunderstood, and "up against the wall," with no idea how to create fun from here.

See if you can identify what your cocreated patterns are with a partner, both in and out of the bedroom, and especially during expanded orgasm sessions. The more specific you can be, the more useful this exercise will be. Are you willing to take full responsibility for your half of the cocreated patterns? Are you willing to share with a partner your observations, and to hear what patterns your partner finds?

The solution is always the same: start building out the room of expanded orgasm. There is nowhere to go in a stuck pattern, unless it is back into communication and pleasure. In your expanded orgasm dates with your partner, see how much fun you can cocreate by actively helping each other through the tough spots, as they come up.

After doing this exercise, Linda and Sam described their experience:

Linda worried, "I find I don't speak up soon enough when I am ready for Sam to change what he is doing. I could be noticing my own responses much more accurately, and asking for changes sooner. Also, Sam tends to go very quickly when he gets excited. I wish he would slow down about 20 percent in general."

Sam listened, and then responded, "I do go fast when I get excited, and would love to be reminded if I do this without noticing it. Also, Linda tends not to talk very much, but it's such a turn-on when she does talk. I'd like to talk to her and remind her to talk as well."

Linda, getting aroused by the depth of the conversation, responded with increasing passion. "Yes, when you talk to me and especially when you ask me 'yes' and 'no' questions, that reminds me to talk. If I am too quiet, do talk! I think if you tease me, that will get me to tease you back."

Sam was thrilled to hear what Linda wanted! With glee, he told her, "OK. Also, I would like to see you breathe more deeply sometimes. How would you feel if I pointed that out?"

Linda was almost getting dizzy with the level of intimacy she felt. Why was it so unusual to be talking like this? All would be revealed. "Funny, I was thinking the same thing about you. Sometimes you look tense, and I think I would breathe easier if *you* were!"

Both laughed, and made a deal to take deep, loud, long breaths that might inspire and motivate the other, while at the same time, setting a good example.

The most interesting thing about this exchange is that neither of them revealed much—if any—new information. Sam tends to speed up; Linda tends to be quiet, and not to let Sam know about changes she would like; both of them tend not to breathe deeply, and so on. What is new is their agreement to help one another by communicating, in the moment, what they really want.

Communicate All the Time

You are communicating all the time, whether you know it or not, and whether you want to or not. Approval and enthusiasm—and the lack thereof—are communicated nonverbally and verbally in a continuous stream. Don't take comfort in supposing your true thoughts and feelings about your partner are well hidden! Quite the opposite; generally, your partner can tell very accurately just how highly (or poorly) they are held in your esteem, without ever having to ask. Assume, therefore, that your true feelings are evident at all times.

If you are doubting that your partner has the ability or interest to practice expanded orgasm with you, or to share pleasure with you, or take you over the edge, or love you even if you do not want to go over the edge, your partner will know and feel this.

If you feel that your partner is the best person alive, has made your life ten times better than you ever dreamed possible, and that he will take you on the best ride of your life, your partner will know and feel this too.

If you have a range of feelings, that vary from day to day, understand that your partner will know and sense all these feelings too.

What can you do? You feel what you feel, right? That is your truth.

The truth however, is quite a flexible thing. Monday's "truth" may not be Tuesday's "truth," once the "truth" is filtered through our labyrinth of emotional realities. On the one hand, we can be driven by our emotions to see life through vastly different sets of lenses. On the other, we have the power to decide what the truths in life are for us now.

We can choose to complain about what our partner brings to the relationship, or be in gratitude about what we have. Whichever way we choose, expect that this choice will be communicated clearly to your partner.

Remember that communication is 90 percent nonverbal and only 10 percent verbal. What you are bringing to an expanded orgasm practice session will be in your touch, your hair, your clothes, your skin, and your eyes. It will be in the fact that you changed out of your cotton underwear to your satin panties, just because you want him to know he—and your date together—are special. It is the fact that he shaved extra close, even though he'd shaved four hours earlier, too—just in case you ask him for a long, lingering kiss.

Experience Intentional Communication

Are there times when you do want to communicate on every level of your being? When your heart, mind, body, and spirit all line up, this communication gets through loud and clear, without your having to think of what to do or say. We call this type of communication "intentional."

Kelly and Jason had a profound experience of intentional communication. Kelly called to tell us:

The other day, Jason lost an account that he was counting on to get a promotion. His review is up any day now. It was really unfair the way it happened and Jason was feeling down and so had gotten up unusually early. Now we both were up—as in awake—but down, in spirit. I thought I heard him sniff, and I wondered if he was crying. That upset me even more. Suddenly I began to realize how I could have been much more loving to him, knowing the past few days had been stressful. I began thinking about how selfish I am, and unsupportive.

Then I blinked, and realized Jason was just rubbing some sleep out of his eyes. He wasn't falling down a rat hole of despair. Nonetheless, I had had a moment to reflect on my priorities. I was so happy to see Jason smile, that I determined to make this one of the best days of his life, and show him how much I loved him by giving him my love, approval, and turn-on.

I asked Jason to have a date before breakfast. He was thrilled, since normally I don't do anything sensual before lunchtime, and that's on weekends! I prepared Jason for the date by having him make me a cup of coffee and raving about how good it was. Jason, unaware of my scheme, was thoroughly taken by surprise. He just allowed me to pour my approval and turn-on into him.

As we started the date, Jason was unusually relaxed and confident. Sometimes, after a hard day, he will be tense. Usually, the minute he touches me, I can pretty much tell exactly what kind of mood he has been in, and how far he has come in shifting into his sensuality. This day, he was already flowing, alert, and confident. He joked around with me, and gave me even more attention than usual.

It was one of those effortless experiences. He touched me and my entire skin bristled with electricity. His warmth flooded me, and I was quivering with delight before his first stroke ended. I cooed and purred, so joyous in this moment to be creating fun with him...to be giving Jason my turn-on, my juice, and my deeply sexual self. As if time had slowed down, his every stroke seemed rendered into the stretch-limo version—each one wobbled deliciously while traversing from one point to another. As I was feeling so much pleasure, it was easy to verbalize, and I acknowledged Jason effortlessly, without having to search for words. My energy climbed steadily. I asked for changes the moment I thought of them, and he implemented them with unerring accuracy. His confidence reached new highs, as he teased me, said yummy things he'd never said before, and stayed calm and relaxed, while intensifying the speed and pressure.

Before long, he was down to peaking me every three or four strokes. I hadn't had to ask for much on this date, but now I begged him, "Don't stop...please...just keep doing that...don't change anything." It got so that I couldn't say another word. He kept going at the same steady rate until I exploded like a nova star. The room shook for a while, and it took him maybe fifteen minutes to bring me down, while I thoroughly delighted in the slow and gentle descent. By now I was fairly "post-verbal" but the connections between us were so strong, we just sent energy back and forth. I had soared on a magic carpet ride, and now, was drifting in for a landing, with Jason's expert guidance.

He was so happy the rest of the morning before work, given the great fun we'd had on our date. We had truly cocreated happiness. I promised myself any number of times that from now on, I'd do this every so often, without letting him know why he was being showered with approval. I loved him, that was my reason, and that's all I wanted him to know.

I was unprepared for what happened the rest of the day. He went to work, enthusiastically hugging me good-bye. He practically leaped into his car, full of energy. He called around midday, announcing he had just closed a new account. This is big news.

I reflected on the chain of events that had occurred since this morning, when I had decided to shower him with love and approval. I couldn't help but feel that his success that day was a continued outpouring of the good energy and momentum that we had generated that morning. When he came home, bearing flowers for me, I knew that something major had happened to my awareness of how relationships worked. I had far more power to make mine just as great as I wanted it to be!

When I awoke the next morning to Jason handing me a fresh cup of coffee inspired by my praise of yesterday's cup, I remember then how much power I had. I knew in that moment that I could make our relationship even more immensely passionate and nourishing. As he stood there, beaming (in memory of yesterday's coffee praise) I took a sip. Of course, it was just as delicious if not even better! The new "me" leapt upon this opportunity to make another day start out right.

What We've Explored

We have explored communication and its relationship to connection. Communication is an essential part of expanded orgasm. Without good communication, your expanded orgasm practice will be at serious risk of running into insurmountable obstacles. The greatest obstacles are often catches, or traps, in which both partners feel stumped in finding a way out of a black hole of communication. Explanations of these catches, and exit strategies, just won't seem to work. It will either look to you like the other person's fault or you will blame yourself or otherwise stop trying to reach through the apparent barriers.

In this step, we have provided types of communications strategies that will get you where you want to go—out of these traps, and into a place of deep connection and maximum pleasure. Often, people find it easy to talk; and much harder to actually hear what is being said. The hardest part is taking action, and communicating despite the fact that past attempts at communication may have failed. People need a place to go that does not merely recreate the rut they are already stuck in. The room of expanded orgasm serves as just such a place. In the room of expanded orgasm, couples focus on self-disclosure, and equal responsibility for cocreating the session. If couples can leave their stuck patterns in the old room, and enter the expanded orgasm room, they can begin building new patterns of communication around the present time of their practice. The effects of such *connective communication* can spread far beyond the practice itself. Often couples find that after using communication, inspiration, and motivation successfully in their expanded orgasm practice, they are using these skills to melt patterns of stuckness in other areas of their life together.

8

Step Eight: Spreading the Sweet Spot

Claudia found herself beginning to deliciously expand. It was not the kind where her mind was carefully directing; if anything, the expansion crept over her, taking territory, inch by inch. Her mind could not focus everywhere at once; and like a fire fighter directing attention to the fire on the left while the fire on the right seemed contained, for the moment, she was doing her best to resist the onset of extreme pleasure. Fiery fingers of delight would dart through her clitoris, and travel up her abdomen into her chest and neck.

As soon as her attention would rivet to her clitoris, new waves of sensation would flood into her vaginally. Her G-spot area was growing rapidly. First it was the size of a dime, then a grapefruit. It was poised to enlarge to the size of her entire pelvic region and to overcome her entire body next.

Part of her wanted to resist this onrushing pleasure; it was happening much too quickly for her. That part hoped that *she* would set the pace for how and where the pleasure spread. Yet as she continued to taste how *good* it was, as it melted her inner sense of solidity, she now found herself surrendering to a compellingly intense delight. She didn't want it to stop, even if she would lose control of the process. And so, caught between the double pleasures emanating from her clitoris and her G-area, she let go completely of trying to contain them, allowing herself to being swept away on a magic carpet.

A Journey into a Woman's Interior Spaces

Welcome. You are about to enter a sacred place, full of mysteries and secrets. Please remove all preconceptions and leave them at the door.

Up until now, our main focus of pleasure has been the clitoris. Most men find a way to make some sort of peace with it. It is, after all, a miniature version of their own sexual equipment. It gets sleepy, it gets hard, it reaches for pleasure, it rewards the seeker with compelling, direct, and immediate gratification. Who wouldn't want their partner to be an expert on its deft handling?

With this lesson, our course turns in a new direction. We finally enter a woman's interior genital space, the vagina. For men, a woman's vagina is just that:

a mysterious, interior place, a cavern, perhaps, a territory filled with those essences that make a woman different. To most men, and far too many women, the vagina remains a foreboding, dark *terra incognita*.

If your instincts tell you to proceed with caution, take heed. The interior is full of meaning as well as feeling. It is, after all, a woman's sexual center. It is her strength, as well as her vulnerability. It is her pride and her mystery, both.

It is her world. Surrounded by space, it is not the concrete object kind of world. It is the world of possibility, of desire, of potential manifestation. Touch this inner world with great feeling and connection, and you arouse planet-sized thoughts, memories, and sensations.

Explore the nooks and crannies, the textures and the open spaces, the way you might travel to and respectfully savor foreign lands, open to learning about new scents, flavors, landscapes, and customs. In each area you visit, be careful not to offend, and be eager to model your own kind's most laudable standards of conduct.

With this attitude of respect, curiosity, and sensitivity, you are now ready to begin to explore this very special place.

Increased Expansion of a Woman's Focus

As we noticed in Claudia's experience, when a woman's attention is solely focused on her clitoris, she can easily go in and out of present time. She can space out and return, in a sense modulating her involvement with her degree or lack of, focused presence.

Once the man touches both her clitoris and vaginal area in the feeling and coordinated way I will show you, there is just so much more to occupy her attention. Mental and emotional expansion can continue as before, and with the additional physical stimulation, she can switch focus between the underside of her G-area and her clitoris. She now has the option to take a break from continual concentration on her clitoris, and yet to stay very present to the experience by simply focusing on the simultaneous pleasurable feelings of vaginal stimulation.

Follow the Path of a Woman's Physical Expansion

Ladies, as your clitoris is stimulated, and your erotic energy rises, your "hot spot" area expands roughly in concentric circles from its original few-millimeter size on the clitoris. Thus, the most pleasure-sensitive zone expands in all directions. However, since the body's largest concentrations of nerve endings are first, in the clitoris, then the introitus, and then the anus, the "hottest spots" may be perceived as traveling down the body.

Let's follow this path of pleasure-sensitivity in more detail. What started out on your clitoris as a small fraction of a centimeter in size will expand to cover two centimeters, then more. With training (of both giver and receiver) your sensual hot spot can easily expand to fit every touchable part of your pelvis.

Expanding beyond your clitoris, your sweet spot first reaches your introitus—that area of your vagina perimetered by your labia minora, or inner lips, and leading to the opening to the vaginal canal. It's what you can see in a mirror without having to spread the labia apart (in some women it may be necessary to gently separate the skin-covered labia majora or outer lips to reveal the inner ones). The introitus is the part of your vagina most sensitive to touch. The slightest stroke there will usually send you into shivers of delight and a hunger for even more contact.

As you become even more erotically aroused, your expanding pleasure center will reach to include your *G-area*. Commonly (and perhaps, misleadingly) called the G-spot, it covers a wide area of your anterior (front) vaginal canal. As the G-area lights up in response to touch, the lights can begin to come on almost anywhere within this area. As soon as one part of the G-area illuminates, another contiguous area can turn on, or perhaps a different area. No doubt you and your partner will enjoy discovering how your G-area comes to life in each session! Eventually, your sweet spot has grown to include the entire G-area.

There's no magic formula to predict the trajectory the "underside" hot spot will make. One time, the hot spot may first catch fire to the left, the next time right, and the third time, straight to the anterior wall. It's also convenient to think of the G-area as having an inner, a middle, and an outer third. It takes sensitivity, training, and a real sense of playfulness to connect where she wants you to connect, men—but it's oh so worth it!

Eventually, the hot spot grows to cover the entire area. As this occurs, the range of motions and territory that the giver can pleasurably cover will expand so that pretty much any stimulation delivered to you with feeling and attention will send you into paroxysms of ecstasy.

The next stop along the way to whole-body sweet-spot heaven is usually the back or posterior of the vaginal canal. This is the area leading to and then encompassing the area behind your cervix. At a stage of vastly heightened sensitivity, when the expanded pool of orgasmic bliss has spread this far, the merest entrance to this deep secret can lure you into wave after wave of whole-body orgasmic delight.

Next, the area of pleasurable sensation spreads to the anus. After the genitals, the anus has the most pleasure-oriented nerve endings of anywhere in the body. Even a finger lightly brushing the hairs in the area surrounding your anus (when you have been aroused to this level) will often leave you quivering with massive pleasure.

As the intensity of sensation builds, its volume expands to include the abdomen and thighs.

Imagine how a light brush stroke, perfectly timed and placed, can cause intense pleasurable contractions all the way through the body.

Activity #33: Understand Her Inner Anatomy

Since our nerve pathways are so intimately linked with our minds, our memories, and our emotions, expect to find that there is a great amount of variation amongst women in how they respond to touch. You will learn to "map" what it looks, sounds, and feels like as various places light up, as sensation spreads through her clitoris, introitus, G-area, pelvis, and body.

Some women who are touched there before they feel "ready" may not feel any sensation, or may tap into a host of other feelings. Memories, whether real or imagined, may arise relating to times when they have been touched before they issued the invitation. A woman touched in these circumstances will go in the direction of contraction, not expansion.

Some women—not the majority, but more than a few—prefer being touched vaginally before anywhere else, even clitorally. These women view the clitoris as an add-on to the central, vaginally inspired expanded orgasm.

Some women thrive on all sorts of touch, almost anywhere. And most women vary in their preferences from one time to another.

Women, share in your journal and also with your partner, your feelings and experiences about being touched vaginally. You might discover you need to set limits to exploration in order to feel secure about really letting go inside those limits. Explore your patterns of stimulation, paths of rising desire, and what you would like to find out more about.

Claire, a client of ours, wanted to share with her husband Joseph that she had never quite recovered from an experience she had giving birth to her child two years previously. During the delivery, the doctor had to perform a routine episiotomy (wherein the tissues around the lower tip of her introitus had been snipped in order to make more room for the child's head to pass). She had experienced discomfort during and after this surgery. While there was no discomfort now, just the touch in that area brought back conflicting memories. She was thrilled to have given birth to a beautiful boy, but she was afraid, perhaps illogically, that the pain might resurface.

Joseph was of course aware of the surgery and her issue surrounding this area of her body. However, for this exercise, he gently asked permission to explore how much of her discomfort was due to fear, and how much due to actual risk of feeling anything uncomfortable. She agreed to explore this. During the exploration, Joseph was careful to get her clitoris engorged first, insuring that the initial contact with her introitus was pleasurable. The engorgement gave the entire area a sense of cushioned comfort, setting up a condition in which she would feel more pleasure.

She experienced a certain amount of fear reaction, but without feeling physical discomfort. Joseph continued going very slowly and gently. Still, Claire felt no discomfort whatsoever. If anything, she was aroused by all the loving attention this area was receiving!

She concluded that she was willing to spend a little time in each expanded orgasm session putting attention on the healed episiotomy area, so that she could build up a new set of experiences about it. In the meantime, she assured herself anew that Joseph would not give her more stimulation there than she had indicated would be safe. Having discussed this issue, both felt free to proceed with the rest of the lesson.

Increased Expansion of the Man's Pleasure-Giving Abilities

Men, as you light up your partner's body with increased erotic sensation, know that she is becoming ever more engorged. If it were your own member, imagine that on the first round, your fine specimen became erect. Now, in round two, because you are engorged, the sensation in your penis and testicles has tripled. You know how at this stage you reach and hunger for more! This is truly how pleasurable it is for a woman to feel so fully engorged. Now imagine that engorged, reaching hot feeling enveloping your groin, your anus, your abdomen, your thighs.

As you spread the sweet spot, men, you are doing two things: You are enlarging the area of most-pleasurable sensation. You are spreading the sensation over a wider area, and making it possible, therefore, for your partner to take in even more sensation (by creating a bigger container for it).

By now, it should come as no surprise to learn that if you are going to provide this increased pleasure, then you, too, must expand both your physical repertoire and your focus. The addition of your second hand in manual stimulation doesn't double the potential amount of available sensation—*it expands it exponentially.* The clitoris is only a few millimeters in size; so there is only so much you can do with your top hand (use your regular writing hand as the top hand). But while adding the other hand gives you a whole new dimension of pleasure-creating opportunity, it also adds lots of variables to take into account at once. You might at first feel that you have to walk, chew gum, and play the violin all at once.

Some men worry how they will ever keep track of so much going on at once. Worry, however well justified, is counterproductive. It takes you in the wrong direction, into your mind, and away from your attention to pleasure. Let's say, for example, that you are at a lively party, worriedly coping with mutually conflicting calculations about what to do next. Should you stay put with present company? Attract a crowd by looking great and laughing it up? Mingle? With whom? To maximize what aspect of your life? Other people there will feel you worrying, even from a distance. If you were there to have fun, your anxiety certainly has kept you from it!

Expanding expanded orgasm is not really about learning how to do many separate tasks at once. It's more about creating a whole and coherent symphony from many different instruments, each with its own characteristic timbre.

Training, obtainable through the exercises we outline in this chapter, is essential and does take time and perseverance. However, once you have mastered these exercises, you can increasingly put your mind on automatic, leave it running in the background, and center on having a really good time. Let your *inner sense* of feeling be your guide. Suddenly, *voila!* You'll discover that you can do just fine without too much thinking. You'll be moving, as you need to, where you need to, at just the perfect moments. You will be "in the flow," connected with her, with yourself, with your dance together.

Men, I will guide you step by step into making this critical shift: from thinking in terms of one hand to the experience of feeling and interacting with two hands, and one body, and then from one body to one body-mind-heart unit. This is what it takes to give your partner ever-expanding pleasurable stimulation.

Look at this lesson like learning how to drive a car. One by one, you cover the various rules and the individual activities of driving. Then, you get in the car and somehow put them all together. Doesn't it seem hard at first to simultaneously master a brake, clutch, gas pedal, and steering wheel? Still, in time, you hop in your car, crank up the music, and enjoy getting around.

You master all these driving skills by driving around enough that these skills integrate naturally, freeing your attention to the most important thing in any one moment. Your body-mind as an integrated unit knows how to do this and can also become an integrated giver of expanded orgasm pleasure.

Develop the Man's Second Hand

I will first lay out several exercises for you to practice individually. Do these exercises on an ongoing basis. You may combine as many of these in the same session as you wish. Sometimes, just pick one exercise to focus on. Pay attention to and respect your natural learning rate, pushing a bit into any frustration, going with it as a sign of learning. Sometimes you may find it best to include only one of these activities in a session; at other times two or three will feel like the right number.

The next series of exercises are divided into four sections: entering, exploring, rhythm, and riding the wave over the crest. Each section contains multiple specific exercises.

Suite of Exercises: The Art of Entering

In the first series of exercises we will focus on ways in which a man can pleasurably approach and enter a woman's vaginal area. We call this an art, since done properly, the two partners create an exquisite dance between her desires for more contact and his abilities to sense just how much contact she wants in each moment. Entering is a process that could be part of a much longer date, but is so special that it could also be an activity to spend hours examining and enjoying fully on its own.

Activity #34: Track Her Hot Spot

We have covered this already, but will review here again, since this top hand will form a significant part of the experience. Men, keep your top hand firmly glued to your partner's favorite spot. While you may vary in your tracking precision, for now, allow your top hand to take its place as the lead in the expanded orgasm symphony you are about to create. Without this hand glued to her favorite spot, what is the point of giving her added things to focus on? Give her a great top hand, so that as you add more, you permit her to include in her focus more than one very pleasurable experience.

Women, don't hesitate to give your partner honest feedback. Your willingness and ability to give clear, honest, and compassionate feedback is a foundation for all that is to come.

Practice this now. Be sure you can confidently anchor onto her favorite spot securely—and stay there, even as it moves around—before proceeding. Spend an entire session or more if needed. Anchor in your perception what it feels like to you when you are tracking her favorite spot.

Sam remembered initially feeling impatient about having to do this exercise. How much more fun it would be to go on! But Linda insisted they follow our instructions to the letter.

Since his last exercise on finding and staying on Linda's hot spot, Sam had had many practice sessions and also some wonderful lovemaking with Linda. He was sure this exercise would be over in five minutes. He was therefore surprised to discover that staying on her sweet spot was more difficult than he had realized. Linda noticed it before Sam did.

"Sam, I'm really enjoying our session, but I'm noticing that you keep going away from my hot spot. You're there for about a minute, then you drift off."

Sam admitted noticing the same thing happening but it took many seconds before he was willing to acknowledge it. Slightly perturbed by this, he called us for advice.

We assured him, "Yes, that's exactly what you should find. You see, you are getting Linda to go far higher than before. So now, her energy is that much stronger. Consider this a whole new level of the same practice. It's a sign of real progress. This time, ask for even more of Linda's feedback."

Sam reframed his experience. He was a hero for bringing her that much higher than before! He returned to Linda and the exercise. Indeed, as he now focused, minus the negative editorial comments, he was feeling her energy so powerfully that it almost clouded his ability to fully concentrate on what he was giving her. At times he felt as if more current was "pouring through his circuits" than he was able to contain. He shared this with Linda and asked for her support in doing this exercise in the best possible way. Linda loved Sam's request. After all, if they were going to train to have him ride her current at those more powerful levels, then they needed to teach each other what to do.

"Scan," she told him, before he even started. "About every fifteen seconds, just check to see one thing: are you still right on my spot? You should be able to feel it energetically as well as physically."

Sam agreed to do this, and even gently said the word "scan" when he did, much to Linda's delight. With this new strategy, Sam found himself staying right there. He kept scanning, and kept taking Linda higher. He had locked onto her at a whole new level.

Sam reported Linda's comment on the outcome of the training session. "Gee," she told us later, "I planned on doing all this verbal coaching. But, suddenly, Sam was doing everything perfectly and all I could do was to keep saying, 'Yes!'"

Activity #35: Awaken Her Introitus

Men, starting out, you will most likely find that even a small portion of one finger, brushing lightly against her introitus, will generate a tsunami of sensations. This is where the majority of vaginal nerve endings live.

Feeling builds in the vaginal area just as it does with the clitoral area. The first stroke feels very different from the twentieth, even if they are the same stroke. Thus, your only way to proceed is going to be from "reading her energy" with each stroke. Did it take her higher or lower?

Too often, men think more is better. More fingers, more volume, deeper, harder, and so on. But "more" depends on the appetite of the woman. If "more" means more intensity, it does not necessarily mean harder. Going lighter, and thereby giving her more sensation to reach for, for example, can create more intensity. Just having the man send a blast of new sexual energy through his own body, without consciously altering the stroke at all, can also create a feeling of "more."

A woman's taste can change dramatically over the course of a single expanded orgasm session. Intensity may mean "increasingly heavy pressure" in one part of a session. In another part, the same request for "more intensity" may mean more nuance, and light sensations that make her dizzy with desire.

A man can get a woman very turned on, and engorged, by gently stimulating the nerve-rich introitus. This is especially true if he really feels her while doing so. Allen says that he feels me by "feeling me feeling him feeling me"—another way of acknowledging our intimate biofeedback dance.

This feels so good to some women that they may prefer a man put attention on her introitus almost exclusively for quite some time. Don't go deeper yet, even if you are invited in. Take the time for a full, luscious exploration.

Men gently stimulate your partner's introitus with great feeling—make her feel really good to yourself. You may apply a variety of strokes, speeds, and pressures. Explore the extent to which she can become engorged simply by focusing on this area.

Linda had been looking forward to this practice session for a long time. She has been married to the same man for over twenty-five years and here they are, ready to explore her in a whole new way. She thrilled at the thought of getting this much of his focused attention. Was this the man she used to think she knew inside and out?

Like Sam, she had never thought much about her own vagina. It had remained a hidden zone, something that men went into and children came out of. Tonight, she was going to encounter herself at a whole new level, with Sam, and discover layer upon layer of new sensation, feeling, and ways of being together.

She reflected on the training and chuckled to herself. They took this course to learn expanded orgasm together, hoping that it would draw them closer. And now, she realized how silly it had been to hope. What else could one expect when two people play together at this level of intimacy? So much had changed for the better. They had whole new patterns of touching each other during the most routine conversations, talking frankly and yet lovingly about problems, and fantasizing with real juice about their future plans for pleasure.

Sure, there were still lots of areas of their relationship that needed working on. But since they were having so much fun, those areas seem to grow less important over time. The connection was growing ever more important.

"Linda?" Sam was looking into her eyes.

Startled, she came back to present time. "Oh Sam, that one stroke you just gave me on my inner lips, it was so light, yet with so much *feeling*. I've never felt anything like that before. Do me a favor: keep talking. I am going deeply into some feelings here, and I want to stay present, too."

Sam continued experimenting with various strokes on her introitus. Linda very nearly went over the edge several times. Sam held back just as her energy felt ready to enter that final lunge to explosion, because he wanted to take her higher first. Her inner lips now looked and felt like two plump cushions, and her introitus was quivering in delighted response to his every subtle touch. He went lighter, and lighter still, escalating the effects, until he lost contact. Then he turned around and gradually increased the pressure until he found a limit at the other end of the pressure spectrum.

He then experimented with speed. Linda loved it slow, she loved it fast. She loved it in between. Sam wondered briefly if he was ever going to remember all of this. And then he scanned his body, noticed he was just beginning to veer from her favorite spot, and returned to this ever so pleasurable task of cataloging all the results of his experimentation.

Activity #36: Enter, with Permission

You will usually begin by very gently stroking her introitus. Can you feel her quiver with sensation? Is she asking you for more with each stroke? If so, at some point, she will invite you to enter her, either verbally or nonverbally. Let her tell you what her preference is. By showing her this respect in asking, you are allowing her to invite you in and feel fully in control. This makes an enormous difference in the total amount of pleasure she feels in the expanded orgasm date.

The same woman may differ from time to time. One time, when you will find her already moist, and waiting eagerly, she will want you to enter almost immediately. Yet another time, she will want you to linger, to take your time, and go nowhere except around and around her inner lips, eliciting waves of new delight. There may even be times when she wants nothing more. For practicing energy-reading and nonverbal communication, there is ample opportunity for both parties to participate noticing what is the next best action.

When she is ready to invite you in, you will know. Her vaginal muscles may be contracting, in which case they will almost literally suck your fingers in. Not all women contract, and so, you may get this signal only on a more "energetic" or feeling level.

Stay observant for the woman's invitation for you to enter her more deeply. If and when you receive this signal, proceed slowly, using only one finger (either your middle or ring finger, and go up to the first knuckle. Allow her to experience how full she feels being entered in a state of high engorgement.

As he and Linda carried out this assignment, Sam wondered. How many times had he entered Linda during the twenty plus years of their marriage? Out of those times, how many had he entered, asking her permission first? Something powerful was happening. Linda was not the woman he thought he knew. As he felt her at this new level, he met her as a whole new person. He really didn't know what she would say when he requested permission.

Finally Linda asked him, in a polite but husky tone of voice, "Would you like to come in soon? I want to feel you at the next deepest level."

Her words brought back their first sexual experience. They were on their honeymoon. But how much better it was now than then, with all the conscious awareness added in! This is how it should be. Always the first time. Always new. Always present to the mystery of this moment and the next.

With a glint in his eye, he responded, "Any moment now," and proceeded to give her that delicious moment of entry that she so craved.

Activity #37: Add Fingers to Fill Her Even More

When you first are invited to enter her, her vaginal area already will be engorged. Her lips should look full, puffy, and moist. They should feel soft and cushiony. You have started by inserting just one finger, up to the first knuckle. It might feel—to her—like you are going in with more volume, and greater distance than you in fact are. This is because she has supplied much of the "filling" with her engorgement.

The nerves serving her vaginal wall, G-area, and introitus can spread apart, creating a spacious feeling. Their threshold for pleasurable stimulation has been lowered—it has become much easier for her to respond to pleasurable touch. If her sexual nervous system is well tuned, it will be eager for you to deliver more pleasure. Know that every tiny motion you offer will be multiplied when experienced by her increasingly well-tuned nerves and muscles. Be slow and gentle in starting out to give her every opportunity to savor this exquisite experience and the pleasure you offer her.

Are you savoring this as well, sir? She will feel what you are feeling. She will feel you feeling—or not feeling—her. Your experience and enjoyment of this will express itself in your every touch. Your pleasure will circle back around through you to her and only add to her feelings. Men, imagine how it would feel if you were her, receiving this experience right now. Tell her, "I can feel you reaching for every millimeter of sensation."

Each finger you add is a new universe of experience. Do not rush the process of adding on the additional volume. Feel your way from one to the next. Again, different women vary considerably in their preferences, and even the same woman will want different sensations of volume, from one date to the next, or even within a date.

Women, don't be afraid to ask your partner for changes, and to let him know what you are enjoying most. Make sure you know exactly how he is touching you so that you know what to ask for. Sometimes I will ask Allen how many fingers he is using because I can't tell! Sometimes I will ask him to decrease or increase the volume by changing the number of fingers he is using. Oftentimes I will tell him that I want him to *feel me* more (he may decide to change the number of fingers or their depth to do this, but he navigates by feeling, not by thinking about what would feel better). Don't ask me how I know to ask: let's just say, if I have the thought to ask, then I ask.

Men, experiment with giving a woman clitoral pleasure with your top hand, while slowly adding in additional fingers on your lower hand.

Start with one finger (usually the middle one). Go up inside only to the first knuckle. Explore. Explore some more. Get some verbal and nonverbal feedback. Explore some more. Then try adding a second (most likely the index finger). Then see how three fingers feel, then four.

Don't go in further than the first knuckle. Remember, every movement is magnified significantly at these higher, more expanded states of erotic awareness. Go slower than you think you should (try counting one, one thousand, two, one thousand, three, one thousand, and move a fraction of an inch on each whole number).

Watch her carefully, and take full satisfaction, as the pleasure washes over her!

Linda wrote in her journal:

I love the feeling of being filled sexually. I never thought much about it before recently. It seems that when I am really engorged, the way Sam typically gets me, every sensation is greatly magnified. One finger, up to the first knuckle, felt like two fingers all the way in. I was amazed to learn how different the sensation was from what I expected. But the best part was when I was already aroused and Sam had all four fingers inside me. My vaginal canal is loose from having had two children, so the entire volume of his hands touched me almost everywhere inside. It felt like he was inside my whole being, not just my vaginal canal.

Sam told me he could feel the ridges inside my canal for the first time ever. I felt them too! I loved the way his hand lingered on these ridges. I could feel him taking great pleasure from the whole experience, and of our making a loop of feelings, from him to me and back again to him.

It's different than I thought it would be. My connection with Sam comes through most of all. It's like Sam and I are really together, sharing one same space—or like two people feeling one feeling from different viewpoints—how romantic!

There's something about feeling so filled that relaxes me deeply. Perhaps that is my beloved answering some ancient biological imperative. Who knows? I look forward to when he does it again.

Once you have completed these exercises, share your experiences verbally with your partner. Men and women should both reveal what went on for them physically, emotionally, mentally, and spiritually during these processes.

Suite of Exercises: Explore the Interiors

We are now ready to engage in the second suite of exercises. Here the focus is on exploration of the variety of experiences a man can provide a woman using his hands to explore her inner vaginal areas.

Activity #38: Discover Different Strokes

When you consider every square millimeter of a woman's vagina as a pleasure goldmine, with untold possibilities for delight, then your hand becomes a pleasure-giving giant, thousands of millimeters large. Look at your hand now and see it as I have described. Keep that image with you always, especially when you touch a woman inside.

With the hand, just as with the fingers, you have many strokes to give pleasure:

You can rub back and forth with finger pad(s), in small or wide strokes, with fast or slow motions.

You can move your hand (or a finger or more) sideways, in what I call "windshield wiper" strokes. This is a very popular stroke, and one that can be alternated with up and down strokes to create lots of variety. This stroke works especially well toward the beginning of a session, as it sweeps the area from side to side, and stimulates engorgement over a wide area.

You can create almost no superficial, above-skin motion, instead simply pressing into her.

You can press "through the skin," and also create a sense of motion without friction, by vibrating your hand, either quickly or slowly.

You can move your hand in the direction of up and down her vaginal canal.

You can put your fingers inside so that they are straight, or curved, into the "come hither" position, where the fingers are slightly bent upwards from the first knuckle.

As you experiment with different strokes, take care to notice the effect on your partner. You don't have to memorize; just notice. As you pay attention, you will effortlessly develop a databank of little patterns that your partner loves! Then, in the dance of the moment, you'll possess a vast repertoire of possibilities.

Experiment with all the above types of strokes. Men, let your partner know which ones you are doing, and when you make changes. Women, pay attention to how each variation feels, and give feedback.

Activity #39: Press against the Four Sides of Her Interior

Is there a normal for anything sexual? But I'll go out on a limb to say that most of the women I've known say their anterior wall (the front of the vaginal canal) is their favorite area for contact and stroking. But the canal has far more area than that. Let's say that the vaginal canal has four directions: top, left side, bottom, and right side. All four sides respond very favorably to stimulation at the right time.

Since you are now inside, rather than at the nerve-rich opening, your partner will be much more responsive to pressure rather than the nuances of touch—just the opposite condition to what we noticed at the introitus. She may not feel much touch at all now other than what comes to her via pressure.

Let the journey be the reward. The following maneuvers promise to bring her great joy and a sense of your uncompromised devotion to giving her an experience of total indulgence.

Take "a trip around the world." Still with your fingers (one to four, as she prefers) in up to the first knuckle, apply pressure, first to the top, then one side, then the bottom, then the other side, then return to the top.

Don't rub much; just give pressure, coupled with your focus on transmitting your own energy to her via your touch. Feel her deeply as you press.

Move slightly as you press, if you wish. Allow her to take in the delights. You will be yet again waking her vaginal area up even more, and increasing the engorgement.

Activity #40: Notice the Variety of Locations

Continuing our theme of increasing engorgement, a woman's pleasure-hungry area expands as you feel your way deeper into her. Here are some landmarks along the way to help you develop a sense of location. (Guys love maps, right?)

You have entered in to the first knuckle, anterior (front) wall, and you can sense an engorged button of tissue—her developing G-area. Now, s…l…o…w…l…y, millimeter by millimeter, keeping in mind that every millimeter is a universe of pleasure unto itself, work your way up to the second knuckle. I say "slowly" because since everything is magnified in sensation, every little motion can feel like a comet gliding through space.

Men typically have some hair on the backsides of their fingers that may provide more abrasion than a woman was expecting. It's best to check in with her, especially initially, about how quickly or slowly she feels is her preference.

To manage the friction to her delight, men, check frequently with your partner to see that she has just the right amount of lubrication.

An engorged G-area is especially sensitive. Women thrill to have it caressed. Try a variety of speeds and motions, a variety of fingers. And, of course, keep trying these variations. Just remember the mantra: feel…feel…feel.

Try a variety of strokes at each location. Come back to ones she didn't especially like the next time. You may find she has changed her preferences dramatically.

Once up to the second knuckle, and you are deeper inside, the pressure aspect becomes even more pronounced. As your hand fills her, the feeling of fullness can be a delight. It will feel grounding, and give her a place (your hand) to send her excess energy. It will give her something marvelous to focus on if you are still massaging her clitoris at the same time.

Extend your hands even further back, up in all the way. You will encounter her cervix.

Most women do not like the feeling of anything entering or pressing on their cervix. However, when she is sufficiently engorged, and desires all of your fingers inside her, you may find a way to place your fingers under (posterior to) her cervix. This creates a feeling of being totally filled. Women properly prepared for this experience will find it gives them yet another reason to let go completely of any resistance to pleasure.

Again, let your partner direct you about adding more fingers, and more pressure. Two-way communication is essential to insuring that you cocreate a thoroughly enjoyable experience and explore the full range of pleasure.

Claudia revealed her own path of discovery:

I used to think that I didn't have any G-spot responsiveness at all. We had read a book that told my husband Jake to stimulate the G-spot right away. His stroking on me, when I was not properly engorged, felt almost irritating. I felt very inferior, after all this raving about how great the G-spot is.

When we learned that the "problem" might be not be that I didn't feel much, but that I was just insufficiently engorged, Jake and I immediately experimented to see if that was the case with me. As usual, I shrank when he touched me, unengorged. But after about ten minutes of playing with my clitoris, my whole vaginal area seemed to wake up, swell, and unfold like a rose. It was throbbing with desire. Imagine my relief to find out after all these years how alive I really was, once touched properly!

Suite of Exercises: Get into the Rhythm

Are you ready for a more advanced topic? Since you may at times wish to be creative, you will want to master the art of knowing just what each hand is doing, and when. To do this well is indeed an art. To master the principles of rhythm the fastest to the extent that you view your arms as one part of the same artistic expression, you will feel the rhythm also flowing through her.

Activity #41: Bottom Hand Rhythm

When the man is using both hands, he is magnifying the sensations dramatically for the woman. If you are reliably going to take your partner over the edge, it's essential to master rhythm. Done right, it is a catapult. Done without full consciousness, it can take her down, rather than up.

A still bottom hand can be pleasurable when your thumb is simply resting on her introitus, not yet inside her. Her sensitive nerve endings reach for pleasure and find this external contact yet another delight.

However, once a man's hand is inside, the dynamics change. The pleasure comes now from pressure, not just contact. If there is too little pressure, it can actually feel somewhat aggravating, like an itch that is not being fully scratched. If there is too much pressure, it may be aggravating, bringing her down in the process. If you are moving your top hand, she will want to feel some coordination between your top and bottom hand. Too little coordination will be disorienting to her.

Most women, then, prefer some motion inside to a feeling of a man's hand just "sitting there doing nothing." If the pressure is not quite right, often some motion will lend just enough excitement to compensate without your having to change what you are doing. You have lowered the risk of bringing her down, or upsetting her unintentionally. (Remember, in these high states of being, a woman and her partner are both quite vulnerable, and moods can potentially swing from joy to upset in a flash.)

Since the man has one rhythm going with his top hand, how will he create an entirely different one with his bottom? Initially, do your best to coordinate both hands with a similar motion. Next, get yourself into a sufficiently feeling state. With practice, in a feeling state, you will be able develop your abilities to vary the rhythm of the bottom hand.

There are two generalities:

The bottom hand should move at the same speed, or slower than, the top hand. Generally, women are not aroused by the inner hand going faster (but there may be times when this is not true—especially when she is close to her orgasmic edge).

Allow the top hand to be the lead, and the bottom to be the base. A woman also has her own rhythm. As you increasingly deliver higher levels of pleasure, her contractions will be stronger and stronger. At some point, her rhythm may take yours in tow and become the lead for the whole experience. When this happens, get ready for a great ride! Experiment with using both hands to create pleasure for your partner. Experiment with using variations, and take note of the effects this has on your partner's pleasure.

Activity #42: Use Your Bottom Hand as the Lead

There will be times when the woman desires more focus on her G-area than on her clitoris. Each woman will vary in terms of this preference. Most women will tell you that as she goes higher, especially in a long date, she'll yearn for increasing variety. At some point, she may want her partner to put his top hand on "automatic" and then have his bottom hand be the main attraction. This is easy to do when the woman's clitoris is quite engorged. Either she wants her clitoris to take a break from being the main focus of attention, or she'll simply want you to place more of your attention on exploring her G-area. When she feels a desire for a switch, then she should immediately communicate it to you. This switching into greater variety provides the momentum that takes expanded orgasm to ever-higher levels.

Once a woman has requested that the main focus be her G-area, the man is now free to focus on giving her far more attention there without having to coordinate as carefully. His top hand is simply glued to her favorite spot, and making minimal strokes. He can therefore become even more exploratory and creative with his bottom hand.

This is an excellent technique to add in longer dates, when there is often great appetite for variety. The clitoris doesn't have quite as much room for variety as the vaginal area, due primarily to its small size. With the bottom hand taking the lead, you can explore many new edges, upon which to string out your willing partner.

Switch your main lead hand from the top to the bottom hand. Do this once she has become quite engorged. Observe the effects on her level of pleasure.

Activity #43: Coordinate Your Focus

There are several ways for men to view the issue of where to put their focus. We have discussed centering it on your top hand, and also centering it on your bottom hand. Then there is the option of focusing on yourself. You are a whole person, and just as if you would drive a car, or play the piano, there is only one *you* directing the entire scene.

Here is something that often delights women. Get her "going" with both hands, so that she is in a state of expanding into more and more pleasure. When you feel that you have her in a somewhat steady state of expansion, start switching your focus from the top hand to the bottom one; from the clitoris to the vaginal area, every five or ten seconds. This is not a physical switch, but purely one of attention. Done properly, it will cause her to start switching her own focus.

There is something magical about the shifting of focus back and forth; it opens a door into lowering a woman's overall resistance to pleasure. And, the lower the resistance, the higher the chances you men will have of taking your partners powerfully into a climax.

Why would people resist pleasure? Perhaps it's biological. Pleasure-seeking is not necessarily the surest route to survival. Even more, pleasure–resistance is cultural. From an early age, we trained ourselves to hold in our feelings, to bring our minds into sharp purposeful focus, even at the expense of our feeling pleasure. Over time, pleasure-resistance goes on automatic (remember what we said about unconscious competence?). Expanded orgasm is about finding ever more creative ways to reverse the processes of constriction and holding-in so that we can let go; but to train ourselves to let go, we need to let go, then feel how good that felt, so that we train our nervous systems to do this yet again—to learn to navigate by desire rather than by survival.

This is an iterative process of which the results accrue over time. Each time of letting go marks yet another victory. We long then to be cajoled, somehow, into that let go, even if in a sense, it is against what our conditioning and some of our biological imperative demand. We yearn to be overcome with pleasure, and to melt away our resistance, as our mind's order-keeper throws up its hands and says,

"I'm out of my league now. She's going to be swept away, for sure. Yes, I am trying to hang on, it's just getting harder and…." And off you go, over the edge.

Switching focus is one way then to fool the control system a little bit, in the most pleasurable of ways. Focus here, focus there. It's like trying to watch two movies at once, and then, having your partner ask you a serious question. You are distracted to the point that you cannot possibly give a rational answer. Your body succumbs to the impossibility of focusing on so many pleasurable inputs in a linear fashion simultaneously.

After you have brought your partner into an expanded orgasmic state using both hands, let your partner know that you are going to start switching focus. Observe the results.

In a second experiment, simply begin switching mental focus, without informing your partner of your plans. Observe the results.

Once again, you will benefit greatly from sharing your observations with your partner.

Activity #44: Ride the Wave Over the Crest

Let's continue on with the theme we've been developing. There comes a point when increased stimulation causes the muscles surrounding a woman's vagina to begin to contract at higher and higher intensity. Earlier, clitoral stimulation caused fine contractions through the vaginal and clitoral area. Often a woman can't feel these as contractions very well or at all. Once the vaginal area has become engaged, uterine contractions come into play. They are heavier, more intense contractions that a woman can definitely feel. As these more powerful and coordinated contractions get rolling, the woman beings to experience herself as being in a *pushed-out state.*

The pushed-out state has physical and mental components. Physically, she's engorged, especially in her pelvis and face; her pelvic floor muscles are also literally pushing down and out. And, she is pushing out from her mind, reaching, reaching for every bit of sensation. Whereas when she began to climb, the pushing-out-and-reaching sensation was a voluntary expression of her desire to move toward and feel more pleasure, at some point, the reaching outwards becomes automatic. Now she is "reached out," and need do nothing other than to enjoy just being there.

Pushed-out and contracting heavily, she is riding the orgasmic edge. Now, men, you can play with this edge. Take her very close to going over, by subtly adding more sensation, either physically or by mental intention; then, drop her slightly away from the edge, even as she begs you to take her over. The longer you can prolong her stay her at the edge, the higher a platform you will create for that moment when she finally does go over.

To take her over…it's amazing how little I can tell you here. That's because it is such a unique experience each and every time. I've been catapulted to the far reaches of the Milky Way when a man has lightened up—just when I was ready to go over; and I have been whisked away on the express ride to Andromeda by having an intense increase in pressure applied at just the right moment.

Now is a good moment, women, for that communication. If you're ready to fly, leap, melt, explode, or dissolve over that edge, go ahead. Ask for that perfect pressure, or that speed, or that extra motion with the bottom hand. Men, now is the time for your intuition to be in full control. Like an orchestra conductor bringing the movement to a crescendo, allow your whole self to be so fully involved that you no longer think; you are one with the object of your delight, and deliver the next step of the dance.

This is a moment when everything seems clearer, more effortless, and more obvious. Men, having brought their partner to this point and beyond, often remember it for days. They remember the sense of power, of control, of being beyond themselves, and with their partner, in that place beyond time. They replay memories of her face and neck, so red and flushed as to be an incandescent vermilion. They remember the heightened sense of smell, of sound, of orgasmic energy pouring through their own bodies, as she goes over. They can remember forgetting whose orgasm it was and whose pleasure was felt.

She will want to remain "over the edge" for some time, and then when she's ready, staying in close verbal and nonverbal communication, bring her down slowly. Most women desire steady, firm internal and external pressure for coming down. If you manage the dance on the way down as you did on the way up, she will continue to find it extremely pleasurable.

Men, at the end of the experience, remove your hands slowly. Remember that to her, your every motion feels dramatically multiplied. Take special care in removing your bottom hand. Stay in communication and connection.

Experiment with building up her level of turn on to the point where you can use both hands reliably, and then take her over the edge. Do not remain especially focused on the goal, even if this is the goal of the exercise. Just have the intention to do so, and also the ability to fully enjoy whatever outcome you achieve together.

Be sure to remove your hands and your physical presence very slowly and deliberately.

For some unknown reason, Jason was feeling unusually confident today. It was a feeling in his body. He got into his favorite position while retaining a peaceful calm. He was already present to his own body, and even feeling Kelly as she did her best to "make a landing" into the space of the session. "Kelly, I want to give you a very special experience today," he informed her, with a confidence that surprised even him.

Kelly shivered. Who was this man who was taking control of her like this? Fiery juices began to surge within her, even as she struggled to shed the memories of the moments leading up to the date. The freeway, the traffic, the parking, the out-of-breath feelings she had carried with her all day...and now, it seemed that she was going to be rewarded in a very major way for all her efforts to arrive.

Jason felt her shiver and placed his hands on her. One over her heart, one on her abdomen. He just held his hands there, gently, sending her more love and attention. Kelly, once jittering, quickly grew calm and quiet to match him. His hands seemed to sink in inches below the surface. They felt simply very present, making exquisite contact with her being.

Slowly, he began caressing her. From the first moment, his hands electrified her. She smiled and cooed at this delightfully surprising pleasure. Her clitoris grew quickly in engorgement, enabling him to lock on to her favorite spot within three strokes. "I've got you now," he teased, "and I'm not leaving you either, so relax and get used to having pleasure continually sweep you away as you enjoy all of my love and attention." She just smiled, immersing herself deeper into a fantasy of what this promise might mean. The day slipped away, the stress melting out of her. She felt Jason's grounded calm. It was a new experience, but very palpable. He was a different person; in some ways, a stranger. This excited her. She dived into the calm herself; focusing fully on the warm, steady rhythm of Jason's touch.

Within moments, Kelly invited Jason to give her attention with his bottom hand. Slowly, surely, he circled her introitus, watching for any feedback that would steer him toward delivering ever more pleasure. As Jason perfectly synchronized his top and bottom hands, she found herself contracting more powerfully. The regular strong rhythm of these autonomous contractions rocked her into an even greater sense of peace and openness to pleasure. She found herself surrendering, reaching for sensation, pushing and bearing down with her pelvic muscles, yearning to soak up every infinitesimal amount of touch.

Her rocking was gentle, more like a wave rippling through her as she lay in relative stillness. She found herself letting go, into the rippling, her energy now flowing, and this rippling motion enabled her to take in ever more sensation. At some point, her focus, which had been ever more turned to this amazing feeling of waves, returned to her clitoris. Jason was pouring in sensations there, and to her G-area, simultaneously.

With one especially delicious stroke on her G-area, Kelly was catapulted to yet another level of sensation. Suddenly, there was nowhere to turn with her focus, except back to the rhythm of her rocking, and she surrendered to the rhythm once again, letting go of yet another layer of holding on. She was melting and moving at the same time. Jason, noticing her rhythm building, stopped generating his own. Now he could just dance to her timing. As she waved forward he met her perfectly by going in ever so slightly, and as she pulled away, again ever so subtly, he pulled out, exaggerating the impact of her waving. He continued stringing her out in this way, building her energy ever so slowly, taking her higher by adding increasing variety to his strokes.

This was truly an effortless occasion. She experienced every stroke in slow motion, and he could feel her feeling each one carry her to a new level of sensation. His peaking was happening naturally, too, without thinking much anymore. He too was caught up in the grander rhythm, an oceanic wave, riding with Kelly, spiraling ever higher, without knowing how high or how long or even how he was going to create the next pleasurable moment for her. It didn't matter anymore, climax or not, they were already there, relishing the compelling and inevitable climb upwards, both knowing a point of inevitability lay in wait.

What did surprise him was the strength of the energy flooding into his body. He had always been a little afraid of this energy; it had seemed so much larger than he was. But now, he knew it was his friend. He had locked into this energy and it was guiding them both. He had his first true experience of harnessing her energy, through him, so that he could multiply it and send it back to her.

As Kelly approached the edge, her rocking grew subtler, as if she were letting go of even the resistances hiding inside her contractions. Her body became almost still. Suddenly, it was as if she were being vaulted into space, she felt weightless. Then, like a giant new wave washing out from the shore back into the mighty sea, she glided into the ocean of bliss, over the edge, sailing on beyond anything she'd ever dreamed possible. Her whole being expanded to the point where she could not find any end. She had merged with the ocean itself.

"Hold me here," she told Jason. "Ease up. Go slower. That's it." She felt that she could stay there in the bliss indefinitely, with Jason's help.

Jason had gone over the edge with her, but that only seemed to have increased his already calm and collected sense of being. "I'll keep you here as long as you like, baby. Just take as much pleasure as you can."

As he held her there, the slightest motion extended her orgasm. "This is the easiest thing I've ever done," he thought, immersed in the joy of sharing this moment so fully together.

At some point, Kelly jerked in a certain way that told him she was starting to lose her total expansion and relaxation. He checked, and she agreed, that she was ready to come down. Somehow, he knew just what to do, despite never having been there. The state of being itself imparted all the information he needed to take his time and to feel what her energy wanted most in every moment.

Slowly, ever so slowly, in fact, he began applying more pressure. Time had slowed profoundly.

It took many minutes to bring her down. She focused on her contractions once again, and she was rocking rhythmically again, enjoying each one. "The ride down is as much fun as the ride up," he noted. "The performance pressure is completely over. I'm thoroughly relaxed, and yet the sensations are still powerfully coursing throughout her body. What a special moment this is!"

At some point, Jason slowly removed his bottom hand, and then slid his upper hand, first up the sides of her abdomen, and then, followed an energetic straight line over her stomach and up to the level of her heart. He then gave her heart area a light, high-contact circular massage.

Jason knew in this moment he would never fear Kelly's sexual energy again. Fear was unnecessary, especially as he now knew that her energy was so available to serve both of them in creating such exquisite pleasure. He saw that from this moment, he could give her a universe of pleasure to explore. He gazed into Kelly's eyes and knew that Kelly was right there with him.

Bring Her Entire Body into the Experience

The expansion of sensation doesn't end with the innermost reaches of the vaginal canal. It continues to spread ever outwards, until a woman's entire body is one ever-expanding mass of pleasurable sensations, reaching for yet more, and savoring every bit. Let's explore some additional erogenous areas that can awaken.

Anal Stimulation

Generally, the anus will be aroused when the clitoral and vaginal areas have been engorged. You can tell when this occurs. Allow your little finger to brush ever so lightly against the little hairs or skin that surround her anus. If she responds with delight, you know she is ready for more attention there.

Just as with the vaginal area, a woman will verbally or nonverbally invite your finger in. Until she does, be patient, and continue teasing her higher.

If the man already has one finger inside his partner's vagina, and one finger on her clitoris, then he will have to use one finger, most likely his little finger, to engage her anus, while the rest of his bottom hand is still providing stimulation to the G-area.

This additional stimulation will add even more for her to focus on, and thus potentially allow her to take in even higher levels of sensation before climaxing. As with the G-area, there are many variables to consider. How deeply does she want your finger in? How fast or slow does she want you to go? How does she want your pressure to vary over time?

While we won't cover anal stimulation in detail here, suffice it to say that once again, communication and dialog will be essential to determining your most winning strategy. Many women may display more variability about anal play than about contact to the G-area. One day they may enjoy it; on another, not. As long as there is plenty of communication (and liberal lubrication), your partner may be thrilled that you give her the chance to "vote" regularly on what her preference of the day might be.

Discuss with your partner how each of you feels about anal play. If you have never tried it, you may wish to set up some sandboxes in which to experiment with it. Remember, the more engorged she is, the more she will be open to enjoying this experience.

Caress Her Thighs and Abdomen

As she becomes aroused and engorged, her thighs will increasingly come alive with erotic feeling and sensation. A good way to spread sensation during an expanded orgasm session is to periodically use your second hand to draw energy away from the genitals by making a sweeping motion downward on the upper thighs. This stroke should only take a few seconds on either thigh, and be just long enough to register as a long peak; too long a stroke, you run the risk of bringing her down.

Simultaneously, her abdomen is also lighting up its ability to register and spread pleasurable sensations. Instead of stroking her thighs, a man might wish to spread the sensation by stroking her abdomen. Try stroking up both outer sides of the pair of muscles running the length of the central abdomen, on either side of her belly button. There is often a natural groove delineating the outer margins of these muscles.

Even something as simple as a stroke down the thighs or up the abdomen can be the topic of a sandbox. We have spent an entire hour coaching clients on the right kind of stroke. It should be a slow stroke, with maximum surface area of the hand contacting her body. Most of all, the man should feel her energy, and his hand acting as grounding.

A "draggy" stroke, the kind that would make ripples as it crossed a pond, demonstrates the giver's intentions of spreading out the energy. The man should be able to feel the energy he is moving out; and to do so, he must remain extremely conscious as his hand traverses every fraction of an inch.

She will want the energy to be spread out when the sexual intensity feels like it is getting to be "too much." Similarly, men, when you feel like taking a slightly longer pause, here is a way to take that pause that adds to her turn on.

Tell her exactly what you are doing: "I'm spreading the energy here to prolong your pleasure and expand your sensations." Note: spreading the energy is also a great thing to do when you feel the need to pause for any reason whatsoever.

Often, Allen pauses when he simply doesn't get a clear "read" on what to do next. A pause, and spreading of energy, is often just what I wanted.

Make a point of including her thighs and abdomen on as many expanded orgasm sessions as possible. This is a great way to spread the expanded orgasm energy. Again, you can profitably devote one or more sandboxes to this topic.

Extend Sensations to Her Feet and Hands

As expanded orgasm intensifies, the woman's hands and feet will reflect the increase in energy pumping through her body. They will be splayed—spread wide—to allow energy to outflow.

But you might see the opposite reaction. Since expanded orgasm is a process of tension and relaxation that builds to successively higher levels, the tension aspect of the experience will sometimes try to predominate, thus short-circuiting the goal of expanded orgasm, which depends on opening, releasing, and expansion. If you notice your partner cramping rather than spreading, you might remind her to relax, or even gently open her hands to trigger the relaxation portion of the expanded orgasm.

Pleasure Her Breasts

Many women can orgasm through the touching and manipulation of their breasts and nipples. Some women like to have nipple play precede any other orgasmic contact, and nipple stimulation could, in turn, stimulate clitoral and vaginal contractions. Other women may not have such sensitive breasts, and yet find that sufficiently stimulated elsewhere, will come to enjoy stimulation there as well.

As with other body areas, different women will desire differing amounts of pressure, and one woman may prefer variation over the course of an expanded orgasm session. Men, encourage her to stimulate herself to examine and report the degree of stimulation during the experience.

A good use of breast and nipple stimulation in expanded orgasm is to add yet another diversion of focus. As the intensity of the expanded orgasm builds, this diversion is like another "escape hatch" that allows some of the buildup in energy to relocate, thus enabling more energy to enter her nervous system without overwhelming her (which can cause her to go over the edge unintentionally, or to resist by tensing up). With enough resisting, the expanded orgasm session may come to an end. At a minimum, it will cause the woman to drop down to a lower level of energy, and require her to be built back up once again.

Sometimes, the woman will discover that, at a point when the expanded orgasm intensity is high enough, she can squeeze her own nipples to divert her focus and thus add more pleasure to the experience.

Discuss with your partner how you might include some breast and nipple stimulation in your expanded orgasm session.

Spread the Energy into Her Heart

Because a woman in expanded orgasm is in a very expanded state—emotionally, physically, mentally, and even spiritually—every action can seem magnified. This is an excellent time to give a woman additional emotional input. At the end of the expanded orgasm session, draw your hands up along her abdomen; at about the navel, make a straight line up her center, over her heart, at the center of her chest. Now, with slow, steady strokes, massage the area with circular strokes, and send her love as you do so. You can tell her you love her in any number of creative and endearing ways. Watch her thrill and delight with this energetic expansion!

Connect with Her Eyes

Each woman will have her own preferences for degree of eye contact. Some like almost continual contact; others prefer intermittent contact. Try several degrees of contact to see what you both like best.

Extend Feelings Over Her Skin

During expanded orgasm, her skin becomes exceptionally responsive to additional touch. In an extremely expanded state, you should be able to touch her softly anywhere and watch her whole body ripple with delight. Remember to keep communicating about such touches since she will be sensitive to *every* touch you give.

Spread Sensations to Her Teeth

If the climax is powerful enough, she will even feel her heart beat forcefully in her teeth. Talk about *expanded* orgasm!

Women: Expand Your Intuition

Women, you will benefit from developing an expanded sense of what your partner is doing to you. It may not be easy at first, so ask. You could say, "I love what you're doing right now! What is it, exactly, that you are doing?" Your partner might do the same thing a dozen times so that you really get the kinesthetic awareness locked in. Once you do, you will be able to request this type of stroking when you desire.

A beginning expanded orgasm practitioner will be able to say, "Honey, try those windshield wiper strokes." A more advanced student like Claudia, who has been practicing expanded orgasm for some time, might request far more detail. She'll tell Jake, "I'm really turned on! I'm ready for a little more variety right now." (Remember, the moment you have the thought, notice it, and if he doesn't seem to respond nonverbally, then verbalize the request ASAP.)

"I'd love it if you tried those windshield wiper strokes right now." Don't stop there, if your intuition tells you there is more you can experience. "Your finger feels great, can we try adding another one? I'd like a little more volume."

Claudia will keep the feedback going. "Yes, that volume is great, now I'd like a little more contact on my upper wall. You're feeling better and better." Jake will be climbing with her, and she knows that her feedback is giving him the chance to win even more with her. "Those strokes are great! They are giving me just the variety I was wanting. My whole vaginal area is really waking up now. I can feel the sensation spreading and it feels really hot and sexy. I think I'd like a little more of a curve to your finger. Can we try that?"

She confessed, "I don't know what made me ask him to curve his finger. I've never asked for that before. At first Jake was going to respond back that he was already doing that, since he was. But, he knew we were just experimenting with our performance envelope. He went along with my request. We discovered that, for me, there was much more curvature than we had realized. That's the really fun part of experimentation—there's always something new to be discovered."

Claudia has become increasingly confident about what she will ask for. She may desire his hand stroking down her thigh, or for him to gaze deep into her eyes, or for him to dig his nails in the soles of her feet—a favorite she developed years before. Nothing is off the menu for this couple. And she'll just ask for these things, confident that every request is really another opportunity for Jake to give her more pleasure.

Claudia loves to relay the following illustration of this point. She felt like she was wanting to climax but falling short. "Jake," she begged, "take me by surprise. Do something, anything, I want to be surprised."

Jake didn't have a clue what to do, so he asked her what a surprise might look like.

"Oh, I don't know, you could lighten up here, or maybe change what you are doing to go in slightly higher circles…"

Suddenly, Jake switched from the slow, thoughtful, draggy strokes he was giving her to very fast, light strokes—steady velvet tap-like strokes punctuated by short, almost imperceptible peaks. She had never felt these strokes before from Jake—and he admits, he had never thought of these strokes either, before this very moment. Within seconds, she was hurling over the orgasmic edge.

Expanded orgasm practitioners like Claudia and Jake experiment liberally. In just the little harmless boasting she did with me, I noticed several things she's done with style:

- She's asked for what she wanted.
- She's let Jake know his responses were giving her pleasure.
- She's asked to try new things, and in so doing, truly participated in the creative process.

For some expanded orgasm students, the transition from a beginning level to a more advanced one comes right about here. The man and the woman are elevating their dialog to a level that includes creative experimentation in addition to the simple requests and feedback loops.

This can be a powerful leap forward for women especially. Recall that many women say their greatest barrier is not knowing what to ask for from a man. We have asked the man to read her energy, and increasingly, we will ask the woman to read her intuition. Women, like men, remember: there is not always a map or formula to guide you. Your intuition can be a key source of inspiration to what strokes might be pleasurable to try next. Thus, you don't have to know what to do next any more than the man does. All you have to do is have a little fun, and share whatever fun thought comes in to your mind. Practices like these are essential in building up your request vocabulary. From that point on, you can let your intuition do the asking.

This is the food for those sky-high breakthroughs that make expanded orgasm practitioners such lifelong enthusiasts. Often, one request, with enough clarity, makes the difference between a ho-hum date and the kind of date that you'll be passionately remembering and re-savoring for months to come.

Men: Touch Her Whole Body with Your Whole Body

Men, once you have understood how to touch a woman with two hands, you are well prepared to expand your own sense of touch to include the rest of your body. You have already learned how to let her energy merge with yours, and how to feel everything she feels. You have learned that every place you touch is a possibility for great sensation.

Feel everything about her, everywhere. Is your arm on her abdomen? Feel your mind pour through your arm. Is she starting to relax under the skillful guidance and intention that you are providing right now? Feel her relaxation warm your own body and invite you to relax, too. Is your leg resting on hers in a way that is connected but not too heavy? Enjoy those two patches of skin touching. Be pleasurably aware of every part of your body touching hers.

Claudia shared with us the following. "Since we have started our expanded orgasm training, Jake and I have both learned that to touch from heart to heart, *vis-à-vis* our bodies. Jake touches me with his loving intention to give me pleasure, even before he makes contact. He moves me with the simplest act. Light a candle and I lubricate. Compliment me for some small thing, and I flush with delight."

Expand Her Orgasm with Oral Stimulation

Everything you have learned about touching a woman with your hands applies to delivering oral pleasure as well. You want to get her engorged. You want to relax, so that your mouth and tongue are soft and sensual. You want to feel her energy and let this feeling guide you in what to do next. You want to make contact with as much of her body as possible, so that she will be able to ground her own energy and spread it using yours.

In some ways, oral expanded orgasm is easier to give than manual expanded orgasm. The tongue is a larger, softer surface area capable of hitting her spot all the more easily. We are often asked why we do not start with the "easier" methods such as this, for delivering expanded orgasm.

First, not all women or men prefer receiving or giving oral sex. Second, the tongue is not as dexterous as a finger. Finally, there are so many more variations to explore with the hands. Having done those explorations, it will seem very fun to make the transition to giving exquisite oral pleasure, almost effortlessly.

The need for ongoing communication and dialog remains. Obviously, this may be a case where the woman does more of the talking, at least during the session itself!

Activity #45: Explore Oral Expanded Orgasm

There are many positions for enjoying expanded orgasm through oral pleasuring. For training purposes, we recommend that the woman place her bottom at the edge of a bed, her buttocks flush with the edge. Her legs are then free to rest on the man's shoulders, if this is comfortable. As an alternate position, she may choose to have pillows under her knees so that her feet can still rest on the edge of the bed. In either case, the woman's legs will be open and her clitoris readily accessible and easy to observe. Here are some experiences you may wish to explore orally:

Sucking motions: Your entire mouth can be used to create a pleasurable feeling of suction on a woman's outer lips, inner lips, and clitoris. Use these motions, with encouragement, to generate greater engorgement.

Changes in speed, pressure, and direction of your tongue strokes: similar to the explorations you have made manually.

Changes in the texture of your tongue: Your tongue can be made to feel hard by tensing the muscles. Also, the tip of the tongue will tend to register as a firmer surface than the broad, flat part of the tongue.

For getting her engorged, you may wish to cover a greater area and use the flat part of your tongue. For precision, you may wish to try using the tip. However, since women vary tremendously, each experiment is best done separately, with a stream of clear feedback from the woman.

Using one or both of your hands at the same time: Your ability to use one or both hands may depend on the position you choose for oral sex. It will be easier when her legs are around your shoulders. Your bottom hand is now free to enter her, with permission. You may wish to put your top hand on her leg or abdomen to create a feeling of additional pleasurable contact.

Exploring other positions: Once you have had adequate dialog and communication in the training position, feel free to try other positions. Please bring as much of your consciousness to your tongue as you have learned to bring into your hands.

Expand Her Orgasm in Intercourse

Men who have had intercourse with a fully engorged woman will rarely want this intimate contact before she is in this state.

Unengorged, a woman's lips are thinner and closer together. She is not well lubricated, and her feeling level is quite low. The man might still enjoy the feelings in his genitals (and it may feel good to be connected), but will wonder if they are sharing any pleasure at all during their mutual contact.

An engorged woman is wet and ready for your penis. Her outer and inner lips are puffed and cushiony, inviting further contact as they glisten with moist lubrication. If she is in an expanded state, she may be contracting, her pelvic muscles pulsating with involuntary squeezes in a region that men thrill to immerse in.

As it feels better to her, it feels better to you. By the time she is in an expanded state, your penis transforms from a mass of flesh into a potent pleasure-wand. Even if you remain soft, the barest contact will electrify her.

Now, when she is fully engorged, is the best time for penile stimulation. At this point, since every sensation is dramatically magnified—even, a half inch of entry into her introitus will feel like a far deeper level of penetration to many women. Even when a man's penis is soft, he can give her great stimulation and pleasure at this point.

Activity #46: Experiment with Penile Stimulation

Have an expanded orgasm session whose goal is to promote the optimum amount of engorgement. The woman can climax if possible; but it is not necessary as long as she is feeling very juiced.

Here are some experiments:
- Rubbing her clitoris with the head of your penis.
- Playing with her introitus the way you would with your hands or mouth, exploring various strokes, pressures, and directions.
- Experimenting with having a hard, and then a soft penis, touching her introitus.

Ask your partner to direct the motions of your penis to her exact liking. Many women find that they can take themselves over the edge once or more with this technique. Using your penis in conjunction with your hands to give her even greater stimulation. This can be done in a variety of positions, so experiment!

Again, ongoing communication and dialog, throughout the experience, will further your understanding of how to use this stimulation to the greatest pleasurable effect.

It's a Whole Body Experience

Men, every bit of your body counts as a potential pleasure-giving device! As your partner becomes progressively engorged, her body will increasingly be a pleasure sponge, keeping you matched in your pleasure potential.

Some other areas to include in a pleasure session are:

Your chest against hers.

Your face against her face or body.

Your hands, anywhere they can touch with awareness.

Your breath, softly into her ear.

The list is unlimited. Once you have mastered the expanded orgasm basics, you can unleash your creativity completely.

What We've Explored

This step has focused on how to expand your basic practice of expanded orgasm. Up to now, you have worked on developing a solid foundation for understanding of anatomy, broadening your scope of strokes, learning to feel for more, reading each other's energy, and communicating so that you support each other in creating the best experience possible. All this is essential as a foundation for expanding pleasure and orgasm.

Expansion for the woman occurs outward in concentric circles from the clitoris. It travels downwards to the genitals, anus, and thighs, and upwards to the abdomen, heart, and eyes.

Expansion for the man includes learning to extend his own concept of his body as a pleasure-giving device. His mind, his heart, and his body can all expand to give his partner ever more of his own total being, as he immerses playfully in the positively reinforcing biofeedback loop of feeling her feeling him feeling her.

We have asked you to practice many physical exercises in this lesson. We remind you that the exercises here can be practiced many times. Expanded orgasm practitioners will most likely be practicing these over the course of their life together. We hope to have encouraged you to practice enthusiastically, with the greatest of reverence and cooperation. In so doing, you will find the greatest of rewards both in terms of skill and bonding with your partner.

And now, let's explore the quality that makes all you've learned worth doing.

9

Step Nine: Live a Turned-on Life

Suzanne was a former professional model who had dated many men and been married twice previously. At age forty, she had met Rick and decided it was time to settle down and focus her relationship exclusively with him. They had now been together for six years.

"I don't know what happened," she began. "In the beginning, this cloud of love and lust seemed to follow us everywhere. Rick is a highly skilled lover. The sex used to be *meltdown*—you know, bombs bursting in air—it was passionate and enthusiastic. We loved our long sessions of effortlessly great sex. We could hardly wait to see each other at the end of a day, when we could reunite in each other's arms and progress into hours of deep lovemaking. The passion extended into all areas of our relationship. We dreamt of our life together. We exited the dating rat race with a lavish marriage ceremony and never looked back. Our deep and profound love has only grown, not diminished. I am certain I am with the right person and that we will stay together forever. Our problem now is that…" She hesitated, not wanting to say something hurtful to Rick.

He completed the sentence for her. "We just don't seem to have a lot of *juice* for each other any more. I'm doing all the same things she used to love so much but they don't seem to work on her anymore, or not nearly as well. Maybe I have more juice for her than she does for me and that carries me emotionally to some extent. But it's pretty hard to have a one-way love affair. I miss the passion."

Rick, too, stopped abruptly. How much more there is to say when speaking such stark truths? There was an awkward, resigned silence.

Suzanne continued. "It seems so ironic, to have come so far, to have found the man of my dreams, to have finally gotten it right for once, and go for the love, only to find that the passion has slipped away. How? Why? Rick is kind, thoughtful, and giving. He has always been there for me emotionally. And somehow, I feel guilty, like I can't do enough in return. I think maybe my ability to feel has gone numb. Maybe it's perimenopause. Mine will start soon, maybe it's started. I'm forty-six now. There are times when it's wonderful. Just not a lot of them, and fewer and fewer over time."

I let my eyes rest on Suzanne. While the model-quality beauty was still evident, it seemed more an echo of a beauty whose reigning days were rapidly passing by. A certain sadness hung over her.

"Suzanne, where in life are you turned-on? What lights your fire?" I asked.

She thought for a while, then replied, "I don't know. Rick, I suppose." Into the silence, she continued. "I guess I always thought that when I gave up modeling, I would be the happiest person alive. No more pounds of makeup every day. No more having to say no to chocolate-covered Oreos. No more worrying myself sick wondering who would love me for me, and not my looks. Too many times, I'd smiled when I wanted to cry, and when I didn't feel well, and when all I really wanted was to curl up in front of my own fireplace with a novel. And now look at me! I have it all. The great house, the great car, the great clothes, the great guy…and so what? Two years ago, I quit modeling forever. I stopped reading my trade magazines a year ago. Now, I don't even know what I care about."

Rick added, "She's not depressed. She's been to all kinds of doctors. They said it must be hormones. We tried hormone replacement therapy but that made her sick. Finally we found a doctor who took her off hormones, saying that hormones don't help much, anyway. Of course, he gave us some other kind of stuff to try. I think it was an antidepressant that didn't do much. Then we tried special vitamins. Can you imagine taking vitamins to feel passion? Suzanne did. Really! We wound up feeling silly more than anything. We've spent a lot of money to go nowhere. We were hoping that somehow you could help…though we don't know how. At least we knew that your solution would not be another pill to take! I think we've taken all the pills they make."

Life changes, hormonal imbalance, chronic illness, and depression can certainly sap passion—but Suzanne wisely had competent evaluations of these and—like most people in her situation—found them not to be major contributors.

Could we help? It depends. If Rick and Suzanne see expanded orgasm training as another fix-it in their string of attempts to buy back their turn-on, then the answer will have to be no. But if they are willing to go deep into the heart of the issues that powerfully influence their *overall* levels of turn-on, then their chances are much more promising. They will have to commit to the goal of reawakening their turn-on. This will require returning to its wellsprings and consciously bringing them back to life as methodically as they have unknowingly disabled them.

I wondered just how long it had been since Suzanne's entire face had flushed with the exuberant miracle of life.

"Tell me, Suzanne. Surely something allows you to feel turned on?"

This time, Suzanne didn't look for a ready answer. Instead, she closed her eyes, scanning her memories. She allowed herself to go deeply into a state of relaxation, a technique honed over the course of her professional life. A sweet gentle smile traced across her face. She must have been thinking of some wonderful experience. Perhaps it was a memory of walking down a favorite runway, glowing in the hue of footlights, or the thought of being the belle of a future ball. Or maybe it was just the memory of seeing Rick glow with joy the way he did when she'd thrown him a hot little kiss for no reason at all.

Whatever it was, Suzanne's own glow surfaced, and for the first time I felt her turn-on. Her deep inner beauty shone through with new intensity. Natural color flushed her cheeks. Her eyes sparkled. We all felt her energy suffuse the room in waves and our own temperatures begin to rise. Rick slid her hand in his, seeking closer contact with her radiance.

He was instinctively drawn toward seeking greater contact with her. To him, this turn-on felt like liquid rays of warm sunlight dissolving the night. He realized he had almost forgotten how magnificent this felt. And then Rick began radiating the warmth of his turn-on, too. At that point it was easy for me to feel their magnetic essence. And then Suzanne felt us feeling her. Our attention fueled her inner flame yet more brightly. I felt heat rise within my body.

When I met Suzanne, I wondered whether she had given up on her sexual turn-on completely at the same time that she stopped caring about life in general—perhaps due to anger or apathy.

Clearly, and fortunately, however, this was not the case. Her ability to access and display turn-on melted my doubts about Rick and Suzanne's potential for progress in expanded orgasm training. Both of them proved that they were able to summon their life force given the requisite context. We had some real turn-on to work with here. Enthusiasm filled the room. With this kind of turn-on, magic was sure to happen.

Shortly, you will discover just what Suzanne thought and felt to allow this magical essence to glow in her. And, we will also look at ways that you, too, can begin to unleash and grow your own turn-on whenever you wish.

In expanded orgasm, technique and turn-on weave intimately together. Consider truly superlative creations in other areas of life: great art, great cooking, great performances, great food. What makes these extraordinary?

Here, as with expanded orgasm, the most memorable occasions reflect the presence of two distinct influences: *skill* (mastery of technique), and *inspiration* (resulting from fully expressed turn-on). Either skill or inspiration, alone, is a wonderful thing to have. Together, skill and inspiration combine alchemically to create the magic that carries us beyond the ordinary. Together, skill and inspiration power artistic practice to its highest potential. If that is what you yearn for—in love, in sex, in life—you are ready for this lesson.

It is often easier to acquire skill than inspiration. Practice alone will help you sharpen and perfect your technique. But do you know that you can practice developing your turn-on as well?

In this step we discuss turn-on, and show you how to access, develop, and magnify this precious energy, so that over time it infuses and powers your expanded orgasm sessions. With a commitment to continuously growing your level of turn-on, along with your skill level, your entire expanded orgasm practice is certain to grow steadily hotter, rewarding you amply with ever-juicier sessions.

Important Note:

We are about to explore certain aspects of passion and turn-on, and to point you toward a program of accessing and increasing turn-on in your sex, relationships, and life. As I suggested above, turn-on can be influenced by life changes, circumstances, hormones, physical condition, and psychology (depression, for example).

The stories and advice that follow should help anyone expand their sense of passion from its current level, but it is *not* meant to substitute for competent medical or psychological evaluation or treatment.

If you have reason to think medical or psychological issues are impacting you, please incorporate evaluation by appropriate professionals.

The Magic of Turn-on

Have you ever made love and felt fully met, excited, yearning, and fulfilled at the same moment, compelled and stretched and your every cell was engorged and profoundly alive?

Then you have met *turn-on*, the Holy Grail of love and sex and creativity and surely the very home of the Life Force!

Have you ever had fun and pleasure on an intimate date—and known that still you are missing something? Have you made love and your lover did all the right things, made all the right moves, said all the right words—and yet you finally had to admit the experience was not as juicy as you knew it could be, that he or she was not as much at *home* as possible?

Turn-on: you know when it's there; you know when it's missing. Though we are going to make a valiant attempt, words are not fully adequate to describe it. It is the vital essence of the expanded orgasm process, what infuses every stroke with intensity, and lights up your ability to feel them, whether giver or receiver. With turn-on, whatever we do is illuminated with an undeniable energy beyond logic. We all yearn for it, for it beautifies us, makes us glow, intoxicates those around us, and brings us youthful vitality at any age. A turned-on person is young in heart, in mind, and in spirit.

Turn-on: that spirit of wonder and enthusiasm people feel naturally when something or someone excites, interests, or pleases them. It's an energy that comes from being fully alive and present to each moment.

This dazzling current simultaneously involves heart, mind, body, and spirit. A special word or mental picture, for example, whispered in the right way and right time will shiver though your body (physical), tingle your heart (emotions), and uplift your spirit.

The turn-on energy fount, springing from deep within our core being, floods us all the way to our tippy-toes. Others immerse themselves in our energy whenever we are truly delighted and enthused. Sexual turn-on is one particular form of this turn-on. In the broadest sense of the word, turn-on can extend to all there is to love about life.

Turned on, your bodily electrical and chemical systems align with your desires and goals. Turn-on can be seen as biological—wired-in—like hunger or pain. But, oh, how bountiful and gushing! As you experience turn-on, various neurological, hormonal, and biochemical systems switch on as a masterfully choreographed and multilayered dance. And what makes turn-on even better is that all of your body and mind—even your emotional being—is swept compellingly into pleasurable involvement.

Activity #47: Feel Turned-on

Take fifteen minutes just for yourself. Allow yourself to *stream*, if you have developed this ability. Search your memories to locate one juicy aspect of someone or something, past, present, or future. It can be real, such as an upcoming wedding, job success, or vacation. It can be imaginary, like a fantasy date or a move to your dream home. Observe where you feel genuine joy and turn-on.

Now notice how you respond to this turn-on. Do you express it? Do you regulate it somehow? If nothing catches your imagination, sit quietly and imagine what would turn you on. You will know when you have found something exciting when you can feel a tingling or sense of heat in your genitals.

Make a list of those items that arouse your passion. Give yourself permission to feel what it's like to long for some thing or experience. With practice, you can train yourself to notice a subtle tingling running through you when true turn-on exists. Notice how your turn-on increased just by writing the desire list!

When Suzanne ventured into her inner world to answer this question, she first felt a degree of alarm. What could she find to be turned on about? With the exception of our first meeting, no one had ever asked her this question, and she felt vaguely uncomfortable even considering the question privately. Once she talked to her "inner voices," and assured them that she wanted to explore her turn-on for healthy, positive purposes, her sense of guilt soon shifted into a sense of mild worry. Nothing came to mind.

After a few minutes, Suzanne discovered what her fear was about. *She was afraid to feel her turn-on*—afraid that if she admitted to a particular desire, then she would soon have to come back to the reality where this desire would never come true. Talk about a self-fulfilling prophecy! She didn't need anyone reining in her passion. Her own inner critic was doing an excellent job. She wrote:

In one moment, I realized that I was onto something powerful. As long as I had the fear, at least I didn't have to confront the worry that there might be no real desire. But I came to recognize that there must be a treasure on the other side of this wall of worry. I was not going to stop looking until I found something.

I recalled being warned that this might happen, and that I should write down even the tiniest thing that got me to feel energy going through my body. I thought of my cat, and how I loved holding him and petting him. Just connecting deeply into his unflinching, cat-staring eyes brought me peace and healing. I let myself remember my love for him. I felt him purring, and my responding with my own inner purr. I began streaming, so gently that no one else would have noticed. But to me, my own purring unlocked a giant door. Once I had crossed the barrier into this state of turn-on (even though I judged it as a minimally turned-on state), I opened the doorway to my feelings. Turned on, it was much easier to think about what else turned me on.

Remember that song, "My Favorite Things"? Chocolates, and ribbons, and sultry breezes, and kisses seemed to be in there. I couldn't remember most of the words, but I could hum the tune and remember its true message. As a little girl, I remembered a time when I believed in princes, fairy godmothers, and the dream of growing up to be the queen. I would be beautiful, and loved, and cherished. How I loved to imagine that day! How I loved that song!

It's funny, but turn-on begets more turn-on. Like a ball gathering momentum rolling downhill, the world of turn-on began to come in louder and clearer; so fast, in fact, that I couldn't keep up with all the images. Finally, I realized I had several distinct categories of turn-on. Experiences—Material things—Health—Spirit—and of course, Love.

Cashew nuts. I'll admit it. They're fattening, but I am wild about them! Clark Gable—I think he is the sexiest man I have ever seen. Why haven't I seen more movies with him in them? Old movies, especially from the '30s. I love the sun! I love the ocean. Just hearing the waves heals my soul, births me, and cleanses me. I love it when someone takes me out to dinner and doesn't expect anything but my company. Wow! That always turns me on. It gets my curiosity going. I love being able to make the first physical move, too. Even now that I am married, I like feeling so turned on that I seduce my partner and he has no ability to resist.

I love nature, and flowers, and walking in a garden, especially in the spring. And I love getting new classical music CDs. I love clothes that are extra soft, and stolen kisses, just enough to whisper a promise of more, but at the same time leaving me a little hungry. Oh oh! I also want to go back to work in the modeling business. Maybe do something where I didn't have to travel or be on a permanent diet. I bet I could be a great talent scout. Should I even be thinking like this? Oh well, I guess this is about turn-on, not what I am going to do in the next ten days.

The list went on and on and on.

When I had completed my desire list, I remember two things. My body was tingling from head to toe. And, I felt a strange sense of curiosity. Why had I been so afraid to write this list? And why did I not spend much more time surrounding myself in things that get me feeling so full of joy?

I don't think there is answer to why. But on the spot, I made a promise to keep this list in sight, to take a little time every week to review and add to it. I knew that by doing so, not only would I be giving myself the gift of more turn-on, but giving to those around me the gift of my turn-on, too!

Make Each Moment Special Forever

Did you ever realize that your time is a commodity for which there is a supply and a demand? Looking at time this way exposes an unfortunate, but all-too-true, situation faced by all long-term couples.

When you first meet someone, each moment together is special; you look into your new lover's eyes and find the heart of a sparkling new diamond. From a supply and demand point of view, every moment is extremely rare. Future supply is in no way guaranteed.

Long-term couples have cleared the hurdles of early dating and made a commitment to go through life together. With this commitment, the "supply" of time has changed radically. It is (or at least is experienced as) now closer to infinite. If before each moment was a special diamond, now you live in a field of diamonds. What's so special about another diamond?

Can there ever be wonder for one diamond in a field of thousands? Can one eat chocolate mousse for 365 days in a row and still thrill at its taste? Does the thrill of owning a spectacular new home lose its value with enough exposure? If you can (however reluctantly) admit that these things happen, then you can also ask, what will it take to keep your own ability to appreciate the diamond of each minute of being together, since you are now living in a diamond field known as an ongoing relationship?

If, like some couples, you focus merely on the outward sources of turn-on, like pretty things, nice experiences, and exciting new surprises (like promotions or weddings) to keep your turn-on high, you are not alone. You also know that this strategy doesn't work. The thrill is temporary and keeps you always looking for your next fix. True turn-on must come from inside as well as out. When it doesn't, even the sweetest dreams for a turned on day, vacation, and life, can fall awry. Consider Sam and Linda's experience. By this point they considered themselves reasonably experienced expanded orgasm students, and planned their first vacation in years. The person Sam had hired to oversee the day-to-day operations in his restaurant was doing a fine job. The children were gone. Sam and Linda had never gone away for more than a long weekend since their youngest was born.

Sam was expecting to have the romance of a lifetime. He eagerly looked forward to sharing this special time with Linda and showing her that he was still capable of sweeping her off her feet. He wanted to prove, more than anything, that a long-term relationship was not a life sentence for boredom. As a result, he had reserved a suite in a five star hotel, and arranged for first class tickets.

Linda and Sam arrived at their hotel, exhausted but eager to have the vacation of a lifetime. The first night, they hoped to have a honeymoon celebration, complete with fruit, champagne, and room service. However, the trip had taken a toll on Linda's energy, and so they postponed the celebration. The next day, they did some sightseeing. Sam eagerly arranged to have their plans end early in the day, so that their expanded orgasm celebration could commence. Again, Linda seemed vaguely unresponsive. She noted the time zone differences, and suggested some laid back hot-tubbing as an alternative, with a plan to "do more" tomorrow.

On the third day, Linda and Sam finally had their first expanded orgasm date. But Linda wasn't acting as if this was her second honeymoon! Sam thought, with some despair, "She's treating me—and our date—like she had to do an extra load of laundry." Something else was up. Totally bewildered, Sam pleaded with her to let him in on the secret he knew she must have been harboring.

At first, Linda seemed as much in mystery as Sam about what had derailed their finest plans. She seemed miffed at the suggestion that she was at fault for failing to live up to his expectations. They stared at each other, not knowing what to say next. It felt to Linda that Sam was pushing on her, which made her want to withdraw even more. Sam recognized he was feeling hurt and resentful, and that that attitude was only making things worse, but found himself unable to pull out of an emotional tailspin.

Clearly, the turn-on they had hoped to get from their vacation had not materialized on cue. They would have to deliberately investigate what was missing and how to supply that needed magic in order to have their vacation be a romantic success.

Set up the Conditions for Turn-on

Wouldn't it be convenient if we could turn ourselves on as easily as we turn on a lamp? Then, even if we had a miserable day, or felt low energy, or were mad at our partner for not taking out the garbage, we could simply put our state of mind aside, flick on our turn-on, and have a great time, knowing that afterwards we could return to our previous state if we wanted to.

It only takes a few botched special evenings to convince most expanded orgasm practitioners to spend the time to learn how to generate turn-on deliberately, as well as spontaneously. Turn-on provides the dynamics to make the date sweet, juicy, and high-octane for both you and your partner. I'd bet every one of you are reading this book at least in part because you want much more turn-on in your lives.

To deliberately heat up your dates, set up in advance the optimum conditions for allowing the turn-on to flow. Now I know as well as you do that this is a tall order! It is akin to asking a poet, on the spot, to evoke the mystery of an experience. Nonetheless, this is the kind of order that will pay dividends of the best kind imaginable.

Like Rick and Suzanne, many people come to us not to learn technique as much to reawaken themselves to their ability to feel the turn-on they remember from those magical earlier days. They want to know: does turn-on come from within or without? Is it something you do to yourself—I turned myself on, and everything turned me on as a result—or is it something someone does to you, from the outside? It is confusing; after all, if you're not turned on, then no matter what someone else does, will it help? On the other hand, we all have had the experience of someone—or something outside us—turning us on, so we know it's possible.

The answer is both. You need both internal *and* external stimuli to maximize turn-on. What does this mean? Internally, you will want to find ways to honor the desires, wishes, and dreams that make your life a radiant work of art, in and of itself. (This is a state of being we call *coherence*.) Externally, you want to surround yourself with the people, places, and things that most light your fire. So the path to turn-on is powered with knowing what and where those internal and external qualities and things are—and where they live.

When your inner and outer lives are powerfully and pleasurably aligned, you act and feel unified, coherent, and turned-on. In coherence, you know what most lights your fire because you can feel in your body what you are thinking about in your mind. Aligned, then, you will always know what you most truly desire, because your body/mind feedback system will all be saying "Yes! This is exactly what I want!"

Consider the following questions. They will all refer to your sensual and sexual turn-on specifically.

Do you turn yourself on?

Do others turn you on?

Do you find that as you turn on more, your world turns you on more?

Do you find that as the world turns you on more, your own turn-on increases, too?

Sometimes, the questions can be more interesting than the answers! We suggest you ponder these questions frequently, and take notes whenever possible.

The Turn-on Life Cycle

While it is our natural birthright, turn-on is fragile and easily turned off. As children get older, stern voices, cold shoulders, unfair blame, repeated failure, and countless traumas lurk in the wings, waiting to diminish the promise of a life of miracles and magic. Rather than being a fun, wonderful existence, life appears increasingly to be an oppressive game, demanding we shut down our pure, unedited turn-on. Parents, and even children themselves, reproach the spirit that feels too much, or acts too happy.

Eventually, all of us learn, through ubiquitous social messages, that it's easier and less painful to feel less and not more. We repeatedly choose safety over risk, at the grave expense of our ability to feel full turn-on in life.

The same patterns that erode turn-on in other areas of our life can impact our sexual and sensual life as well. It doesn't have to be like this, but too often this is what happens.

Activity #48: Where Are You in the Sensual and Sexual Turn-on Life Cycle?

We realize that not everyone is at a point in their lives where it is appropriate to put a high priority on turn-on. But for those who wish to consider this possibility just for fun, or, as a potent mental exercise in setting intentions, ask yourself these questions:

Is the pleasure you derive from connecting sensually with your partner increasing or decreasing overall? Answer both from your point of view and what you believe your partner's to be.

Compared to six months ago, describe your orgasmic experience, in terms of frequency, intensity, duration, and expansion (the area of your body over which you experience orgasm). Compare again for two years ago.

Do you see yourself having more, less, or about the same orgasmic pleasure in the future (in six months and in two years)?

How has getting older affected your ability to enjoy sex, orgasm, and expanded orgasm? Explore what you believe about aging and your ability to enjoy sex, orgasm, and expanded orgasm.

Looking back, what standards have you set for your sexual and sensual life? How have these standards changed with time? Are there changes you would like to make?

If you could make the changes in your sensual and sexual life that you would like to make, would you find it easy or difficult to live by these changes? Why or why not?

What would have to change in order for you to fully live by a standard of maximizing your sensual turn-on? How do you really feel about living by such a standard? How do you think your partner feels about it?

What standards would you like to see your partner set?

What standards do you think your partner wants you to set?

Again, considering your most-valued sensual and sexual standards, how do these compare with and interact with standards for turn-on that you could set in other areas of your life?

Share your responses, if appropriate, with your partner. If your answers are not what you wish they were, what could you do to make them more to your exact desires?

The Conditions of Turn-on

Like one car battery getting a charge from another car, turn-on can be jump-started, given one or more of the right inputs. Let us consider in greater detail the "starters" that can inspire your natural turn-on to flourish. Any one of these ingredients may be enough for a single surge. Over time, as all these factors can be attended to, and optimized, the more turn-on you will impart to your everyday, moment-to-moment living.

Sensual and sexual turn-on can be started from outside, using the following ingredients. But, remember, it can also trickle down. As your life gets more turned on, each of your dates will ooze with this energy already present elsewhere in your life. As far as we're concerned, the more genuine turn-on you can get from within and outside yourself, the more fun you'll have on your expanded orgasm dates!

Novelty

We seek out the new and different. Detailed physiological and neurological studies have shown that we preferentially perceive and respond to motion and novelty. We are biologically rewarded with sensations of pleasure when we learn new things. Mental and emotional growth and learning actually feel good! Little children are always in a state of learning new things. You can watch their faces light up in sheer joy in the process. Unlike adults, when children are in a learning process, they do not regard all the times they don't get it right as failure. They stumble and brush themselves off and keep exploring. Successful business people and inventors follow the same process. As we described in Step One, they continue to regard the emotions and physical feelings as associated with developing competence, or as an integral part of the exploratory and learning process.

Even adults light up when they encounter novelty. Whether it's a new joke, or a new outfit, a new car, or a new lover, the mind and body delight in the new and different.

This principle has great significance to expanded orgasm. It explains why partners no longer thrill at the same moves and strategies that once sent them into ecstasy. Simply put, their mind/body stopped registering this action or set of actions as "new." As Rick and Suzanne discovered, what was great—for a while—can fade. The demotion from "new" to "everyday" sent a signal to the brain: no longer "new." Look for the new "new."

You've heard this advice a thousand times: do something new in sex. Change the room, the music, the time of day. Some people even change their personas temporarily, adopting, for example, dominant or submissive attitudes for fun and novelty. While we know this approach can be very useful, we also know from extensive experience that superficial types of novelty are not as powerful as the more personally generated ones—the ones that come from those that are generated from the moment-to-moment flow in your *state of being*.

Our approach to novelty, then, is to focus more on *who you are* sensually and sexually, than on *what you do*. It is very useful to build up a library of things to do, but not very useful merely to pull things at random from that library in the service of novelty. It is much more effective to stay in touch with yourself and your partner in each moment. Then, you will find yourself knowing where to go in your library. You will intuitively know what to do.

Now you can understand why I've been harping on knowing what turn-on feels like to you, and knowing what turns you on. Without this connection to your (and your partner's) sources of juiciness, you will stay mired in the strategy of novelty for novelty's sake.

How can you infuse your experience with appropriate novelty?

1. *You can do new things in each moment.* Like skilled dancers, skilled expanded orgasm practitioners know how to give pleasure by reading their partner's energy. They enter into a free-form cocreative interaction. Their creations combine structure and ingenuity. They know to vary their moves, heighten nuance, and deliver input in all four dimensions of heart, body, spirit, and mind.

Rick and Suzanne are not alone in finding time-tested techniques no longer working. Earlier, and more than once, we've cautioned against too heavy a reliance on technique. Just because it worked before is no guarantee it will work again.

2. *You can yourself be someone new in each moment.* "What am I supposed to do, give up my identity?" Well, yes and no.

We first of all never expect anyone to change—that is, as they live in the everyday, ordinary house of their relationship. That house is the best house most people have been able to create over their time together, and there are always beautiful and profound ways in which that house comes together to serve its occupants.

However, you will change in the process of living in the house of expanded orgasm. Your focus expands from the *what* and *how* to the *being of life*; from who you are, what you do, how you do it, to who you are in every moment.

In the space of expanded orgasm, in each moment, we are all potentially someone new. Life is lived moment to moment. Even though we think about a past and future, we think about them in present time. What makes us truly new in each moment (and exciting to our partner) is when, out of our authentic turn-on and passion for life, we honor ourselves, take joy in our circumstances, discover and acknowledge the good and even the painfully hard truths, and, overall, engage in personal growth. Personal growth is a massive turn-on for every person I have ever worked with.

In the space of expanded orgasm, who you are can be described by wording ending in "ing": growing, learning, lusting, hoping, desiring, giving, feeling, and receiving. Your identity becomes identical with your actions, expanding beyond a fixed definition of who you are.

This is why we can so confidently predict the success of couples who closely follow expanded orgasm lessons. In expanded orgasm, as someone breaks down the fixed structures of identity in which they have lived for many years, someone new emerges. And they find that their partners will find them irresistibly desirable. They want to chase this stranger a bit. When both partners are engaged in a process of personal evolution, passions can become torrid, often in a remarkably short period time.

In fact, as Janice and Dirk discovered, even the idea that it's possible to *be new*—to reinvent oneself and the interaction—can rekindle long-hibernating turn-on.

Janice and Dirk were bright, accomplished, and successful, the center of an upbeat and upwardly mobile circle. Everything in their lives seemed perfect, except for one thing. The passion had drained out of their twenty-eight year marriage many years ago. What their circle of friends didn't know was how lonely each of them felt in the other's presence. Their children grown and on their own, Janice and Dirk were considering a breakup.

They had built a solid house of a relationship over the years and yet slowly the house had become a prison. Therapy helped them understand how the house was built, but what they yearned for was to find a new and magical and unexpected place in it.

What mattered was who they could be in the new space. I thought the two of them remarkable, conscientious persons. Could they create a room of expanded orgasm in their relationship in which to try out some new behaviors? I advised them that it was important to go very, very slowly into building their foundation. For some, just a taste of "being"—in which they reveal even one moment of deeper truth—can overturn a lifetime of other behaviors. To taste this new way of being can tap deeply into one's reservoir of courage and energy.

Here's the point: once they got the idea that they were to bring someone new, some new aspect of themselves, into the space of expanded orgasm, they agreed to embark on the program, step by tiny step. Not surprisingly, just in agreeing to embark, they had already begun to transform into new partners. They were already beginning to regard each other with a sense of wonder and curiosity. Who is this "new person" that my mate is going to reveal to me? Will I like this person? How will I respond? As each of them asked such questions, the turn-on level grew more tangible to each of them.

Truth-Telling

Have you ever stopped short of telling the truth to your partner? Perhaps you wanted to look good, and not admit you didn't know something. Or perhaps you were afraid that the truth would hurt your partner more than he or she could tolerate, so you tried to protect them, or perhaps...and this is a biggie, you didn't want to rock the boat. Women with children or who are financially dependent often find themselves in this category.

What was the *effect* of withholding the truth? Especially in the long run? Did it make you more or less likely to get what you wanted? Did you harbor resentment at feeling you were unable to express or be yourself? Did it make the turn-on in your relationship go up or down?

Maybe you were at a loss for words, and maybe, you didn't even know yourself what the truth really was. At least if you didn't know what was true for you, you didn't have to face the risk of telling it—and thereby exposing yourself.

Most of us train to drive, to fly, and to do our jobs. But how many of us ever train to be in a long-term relationship? Instead we learn by trial and error. For most people the error they most regret was: *I wasn't honest from the beginning and so I never got a chance later on.* The habits and compelling reasonableness of look-good, cover-up, and don't-rock-the-boat became firmly established. All this is in the service of safety, security, and commitment—until every ounce of passion had been drained and we became prisoners in the house of relationship. Paradoxically, many people resist expressing truth because they fear the consequences; yet, it is this failure to speak honestly that does the damage. Sometimes, a truth may be hard to tell, but, in the long run, far more healthy than the alternative. This is what I tell myself when I have to take a deep breath, close my eyes, and take the truth-telling risk in my own life.

I have experienced first hand that self-disclosure not only saves relationships from disasters and slow death, but also liberates turn-on. As you will see from a personal story shortly, the clue that it's time for self-disclosure often comes when one or both partners find themselves in apathy during a date. That's the moment to explore what thoughts or concerns might be keeping you from feeling connected to yourself or to your partner.

So, in the name of liberating your most precious turn-on, let's examine several categories of truth telling.

- Telling the truth to yourself (self-knowledge)
- Telling the truth to your partner
- Telling the truth about your relationship

We'll consider all three areas as fodder for the truth process, courtesy of Bill Lamond, developer of the Pleasure of Business workshops.

The truth process goes as follows:

Ask, regarding _____, what is the truth that:

Is about me and only about me.

Is something I have never thought before.

Is better than I thought.

Leaves me feeling lighter and happier once discovered.

Recently, I was agonizing over whether or not to move to another city where Allen had received a spectacular job offer. Both the job and the money were practically irresistible. There was only one problem. As much as I wanted the money and security, I wasn't juiced about the idea of a move to this city. For a month, Allen and I both watched my level of turn-on sink lower and lower. Neither of us could figure out why. Was it a medical condition? Was it seasonal? It is not uncommon in times like this that obvious remedies seem too obvious to consider seriously. I found myself wondering day and night whether we should take the offer. As my turn-on dropped to new lows, my suspicion increased that perhaps this move was not right, but my logical mind could not see a way to let go of the idea of lifelong security and economic improvement.

Finally we did a several day truth process. We kept examining possibilities and then pretending that each was our decision. Whenever I thought we would tell the company *no*, we weren't moving, my joy resurfaced with a vengeance. But then my fear would set in and I would back away from this decision.

Finally, two days before our decision was due, I went on a daylong private spiritual retreat in order to connect deeply with my inner guidance. Again, my spirit soared as I "pretended" that I wouldn't have to move. Finally, it hit me. I was not for sale at the level of my soul. I would rather struggle, if need be, than be in an environment which did not nourish me. Yes, logically this was an insane decision, but my heart spoke loud and clear.

Once my mind, emotions, and spirit were aligned with this decision, I was on fire with the joy of not having to go, even though I felt great fear at the uncertainty my decision was sure to bring. I recognized clearly that my turn-on had been a casualty of this process. I vowed to connect with, enjoy, and turn up my turn-on, and to fuel Allen with it. I would risk betting everything on my turn-on. If I was right, we would juice each other so powerfully that this energy would spread into the rest of our lives and make Allen a magnet for other, even better offers. With each of us honoring and being fueled by our own and each other's turn-on, I became certain that his star would rise far beyond where it was at that time.

As I returned home, my mind was finally clear. My body was finally clear. My heart was finally clear. The process had been a long one but my unwillingness to compromise the crown jewel of my life and our relationship created a new and powerful coherence that carried me forward. Allen called the company the next morning, grateful for my truth, and withdrew his candidacy for the position.

We were flying on turn-on! We knew that we had done the right thing, even though it seemed so risky. And then, something interesting happened. Two days later, Allen received an incredible offer, a better offer from a new company out of the blue.

Before proceeding to the truth process exercise, review my story in light of the four earmarks of truth:

It is about me and only about me. I had to come to know what *I* wanted most.

It is something I have never thought before. The idea that turn-on was more nourishing to me than the opportunity for security was—at this level of certainty—something I'd never "thought" before.

It is better than I thought. This is self-evident!

It leaves me feeling lighter and happier once discovered. Once I recognized what was true for me, my body, mind, emotions, and spirit all lined up—producing a deep sense of release, freedom, and coherence.

Activity #49: Turn on with the Truth Process

Do some truth processes for yourselves and your relationship. Again, here are the four earmarks of a truth:

1. The truth is about you and only about you. If you start with, "My truth is that you are…" Stop! Your truth is that "I am" or "I desire" or "I feel."

2. It is something you have never thought before, at least it has not occurred to you on a deep level of impact. If you had already thought of it, you would solidly recognize the truth and stop obsessing about your issue.

If your truth starts to sound like this, "How come we never go to Miami to visit our relatives?" and you have said this thousands of times, try going deeper. Perhaps you are realizing that you want to see your aunt before she gets too ill to enjoy you, or perhaps, you really just want a Florida vacation nowhere near your relatives.

3. It is better than you thought. But don't take my word for it—find out for yourself! Even if you uncover a painful or unpleasant truth, fully knowing, facing, and dealing with it has got to be better than the alternative. If what you come up with doesn't resonate as better than what you've thought, keep peeling the onion.

4. It will leave you feeling lighter and happier once you have told it. In other words, you will literally experience that the truth sets you free.

Every truth you tell is fire for your expanded orgasm practice, since truth is turn-on. Turn-on is not ossified, predictable, and socially convenient. Sometimes it will not be pretty, but it will be intimate and ignite great fires.

Some truths may seem impossible to admit. You feel stifled. You feel expected to perform sexually. You feel you give more than you receive. You feel unacknowledged for all that you do give and thus uninspired to give more. Find a way to tell them anyway. The truth under, "I feel I give more than I receive," might be, "I would be a lot more fun to be with if I experienced myself as being receiver as well as giver."

Start with yourself. Do not tell truths to blame anyone else. Tell them so that you can enroll your partner to help you solve your blockages, and offer to help him or her similarly confront theirs. Remember that you are both on the same side. You are going for more—more life, more self-expression, more freedom, more connection, more pleasure, more love. Act like it.

Sometimes, just the act of telling the truth, even about something for which there is no immediate solution, can be immensely freeing. This freedom has a funny way of making it into the expanded orgasm practice in the nicest way. In the end, it is often not what you have said, but that you have said it, that will bring the turn-on more fully into your life.

Many people feel shame about their deep down feelings, unaware that many of these truths are universal. I have repressed my truth on many occasions, as have all of our clients. Viewed in this light, the truth is not so much about the content as about the process and the context. Are your views and those of your partner welcomed or feared? To the extent they are feared, ask yourself why and what there is to gain from withholding truth from your partner.

In each moment of genuine truth telling, you are choosing exactly what you want in present time.

Activity #50: Discover Universal Truths

Take comfort: there are many "universal truths" about sex and relationships. Almost everyone has felt some or even many of these at some time. Make a list, using the list below as a starter set.

Then, evaluate how many of these truths apply to you, your partner, and your relationship.

If you are ambitious, you may make subcategories. For example, one category might be "Our relationship" and another category might be "Our sexual relating." Then of course you can subdivide into *me, you,* and *us.*

Some examples of universal truths:

I have not always been honest with you. (Relationship-Me)

There are areas of my life where I have said things to please you that didn't really please me. (Relationship-Me)

I have not told you consistently what pleases or does not please me in bed. (Sexual-Me)

I wish you would notice more when I am being unusually quiet and ask me what I am thinking. (Relationship-You)

There are times when you are manually stimulating me when you go too hard, and after the third time, I stop asking. (Sexual-You)

We could have a lot more fun if we planned more time away. (Relationship- and Sexual-Us)

I wish you would do more activities in personal growth. (General-You)

I am afraid I am working so hard that I am getting "stale" as a human being but don't know how to solve this problem. (General-Me)

You get the point. These truths are often easier to tell when you can see them as universal. I can't imagine how many people would read these and not see themselves and their partners in each and every one.

Each of the above is the opportunity for a truth process. Be patient! Sometimes, the final resolution only comes after some soul-searching.

As an additional exercise, now might be a good time to review the evaluation you gave of your sensual and sexual relationship in the first chapter. Are you willing to revisit that evaluation? If there are still items on that list, consider sharing them with your partner at this time now that you have grown emotionally closer.

Be Congruent with Your Desires

Magic happens during the truth process. Fully expressed, you know when you have fulfilled the requirements. Any sign of doubt is an indication that there is further to go!

However, during the process, you can often peel away the layers of truth, and that can feel very good. With every step you take closer to pure truth, you are entering into a state of biological coherence. Here, as mentioned earlier, your physical, mental, emotional, and spiritual desires all line up in the same direction. In the process, you can feel a deep sense of liberation as the energy required to orchestrate all those internal conflicts is released. When you feel coherent, you also feel congruent, consistent, and harmonious within yourself.

Often, by engaging in a stream of consciousness discussion, you give yourself and your partner the space to explore all the dimensions of an issue, and come to a new and unexpected resolution. Even when you don't, it still feels really good to explore. We often recommend couples use a truth-exploring ceremony for this purpose.

Activity #51: Hold a Truth-Sharing Council

A truth-sharing council can be done with two or more participants. It is a turn-on–liberating process. Often, we like to have a small ceremony before the council, in which we trade acknowledgments first. This helps create a safe and loving space. It also designates the council as a special time in which the two (or more of you) have a meaningful experience of connection.

So begin by trading a few heartfelt acknowledgments of each of the persons present for the council. Take turns of five minutes each, just talking in a stream of consciousness. The listener should listen with full attention. The talker most benefits from approaching the ceremony with a sense of risk taking.

You may switch back and forth several times during this process. Go until each person feels emptied (for the moment).

Once you have developed a comfort with the truth-sharing council, you may decide to do a more specialized one on a particular topic, such as your desires to find more special time to spend together. When you do want to focus on just one topic, communicate this in advance and get everyone's agreement to focus there. This is a practice that benefits from being done often; many couples enjoy doing this at the beginning of an expanded orgasm date, just to make sure they have a chance to clear their minds and emotions of whatever is in the way of connecting fully. It is a good thing to do often, as it develops the habit of speaking freely and looking forward to being fully heard without interruption.

Allen and I like to have a truth-sharing council at least once a week, even if we don't have any burning issues to discuss. Sometimes, we discover during the process just how much we really did want to say and hear that might not otherwise have been expressed. As a result, we feel close and in good, current communication with one another. Sometimes, these seemingly "not-urgent" councils are the sweetest and juiciest ones of all.

Live in Gratitude

Many of our clients have a common problem. One or both members of the couple feel that their partner never seems to "have enough" of them. Their time together is never enough. Their sexual encounters are not adequate or frequent enough. These complaints of "never enough" seem very real, but they are not helping this partner get more!

Most people who hear the words "never enough" feel that whatever they have been giving has been diminished and discredited. That makes them feel even less motivated to give more. Often they give even less than they were giving. Who wants to give to someone who just complains? After all, if they had given them all they had, and the partner didn't like that, well, then, why should they go out of their way to make an even greater effort?

Going from "not enough" to an attitude of gratitude really is like throwing a switch. If you have a spiritual program, you have a big leg up if you want to learn to increase your gratitude level. My advice: pay attention and say thanks. Appreciate. Acknowledge. You are awakening a muscle that very definitely grows with exercise.

What would it take for you to switch from "never enough" to "unbelievably grateful," for the identical quality and quantity of sex, sensuality, love, attention, and caring? Would this switch be easier to make, knowing that in so doing, you have invariably started down the path to getting way more pleasure in your life?

Relationships are like rivers sculpted over many years. Some rivers of relationship are characterized by logjams at every turn. Other rivers have the power to clear out logjams periodically so that the river can surge smoothly ahead. Which kind of river is yours?

Surround Yourself with Turned-on People

Another way to keep yourself new is to socialize with others who are turned on. We become someone new with each person in the sense that we express and develop different facets of ourselves. With a varied social group that reflects your own patterns of personal growth, you will find that you and your partner will find each other more interesting, as well. You will have new stories to tell, new adventures to plan, and new challenges to encounter.

Turn-on is highly contagious. Are you ready to make a point of keeping company with those who fuel your own sense of turn-on? If you are, you will fill your room full of turned on people. These others can infuse you and your partner with high energy that can last long after you and your partner have returned home.

Infuse Your Partner with Turn-on

With all of Allen's pampering, I am sweeter, mellower, nicer, and overall, more turned on. And, with my turn-on, I give Allen reasons to shine from morning to night. We make a point of sending each other as much turn-on as possible. It's kind of like putting money in the bank and seeing the interest grow over time. Naturally, the more withdrawals of turn-on you make, the more additions you'll want to make. What could be a more fun investment program than this?

Is all this talk about acknowledging, showing gratitude, and sending your partner turn-on making you think we are promoting co-dependent relating?

We are biologically wired to care about each other. Many people feel that any form of co-dependence—a concern for another's well being so deep that it impacts one's own happiness—is bad. I am in favor of healthy co-dependence, one bolstered at every turn by liberating truth-telling processes.

Are you ready to feed and water your partner's turn-on at every possible opportunity? If so, your partner will be most turned on when you honor him for who he really is, and he will be turned on to you—you as deeply connected to yourself, and aware of your desires.

Flirt with your partner for no reason at all. Draw a finger lightly across her lips and wink at her. Call her terms of endearment. Brag about her in front of an attractive friend. Find other ways to juice her, just because it feels good.

Take Scheduled Time to Be Alone

Many people fail to please the one person who matters most: themselves. In times of singlehood, or times when your turn-on feels low, why not give yourself the erotic pleasures you would give gladly to a partner? Or which you wish a partner would give to you? Often people are stingier with themselves than with anyone else.

As within, so without. How willing are you develop your inner turn-on? How will you feel, knowing that the more your inner turn-on grows, the more it will shine in the outer world, too? Are you ready to have friends and lovers clamor to be around you when you are clearly having a such a good time?

Schedule some pleasurable alone time for yourself and notice the effect this has on your overall level of turn-on.

Nurture Your Turn-on

Long-term expanded orgasm successful practitioners make turn-on a priority. They have seen this magical energy powerfully influence the entire quality of their lives. In its absence, life has fallen flat. For those of you who have experienced this truth first hand, it will make sense to connect with and expand your turn-on endlessly. With this degree of intention, your turn-on will never fall too low before you—or your partner or your friend—rush in to lend a hand!

Let's return to Sam and Linda's dream vacation. It had taken three days for them to reach this conclusion, but they finally realized that something was seriously amiss.

Sam had been caressing Linda's shoulders, and was finding her unresponsive. "Linda, you're not responding. What is going on? You used to be more responsive before we ever took an expanded orgasm lesson. I've done everything I can humanly think of to make this trip our best ever, and yet, all I get is your brush-off. I think I am ready to hear another level of truth from you."

Linda paused, realizing the opportunity to go deeper than her resistance. After a few moments, she replied, "I guess you're right. I have been wondering myself what is going on. I'm still not really clear, but let me just get something out.

"All the while when we were planning for the trip, you kept talking about how great it was going to be. In the process, I felt you ignored me! You talked, but didn't touch. You planned, but didn't ask me what I wanted. I felt increasingly hurt by this, but you didn't even notice! I felt like you were talking to yourself more than me, and it hurt. For some reason, even though you are touching me now, I can't get this out of my mind. It brings up so many other hurts and pains, all the times in our past when all you wanted was sex, and didn't notice how I yearned for romance. Somehow, I can't stop remembering these things."

Sam was boiling inside. But, he remained silent, not wanting to say the first, and probably, stupidest thing that came into his mind. He spoke after a long pause. "Linda, I can hardly believe what I am hearing. All this time, you had these thoughts about what you wanted, and yet, you didn't say anything to me? You withheld all these requests? After all we've learned about cocreative communication? Can you blame me for expecting you to speak up when you want something? Am I the only one around here who is responsible for this relationship?"

Linda felt rising defensiveness. This vacation had stirred so many emotions in her. Why had they waited so long to take one? Had they let most of their lives slip away? She was very tempted to lash out at Sam, blaming him for not taking better care of her and not appreciating the amount of sex they had enjoyed. Instead, she let go of this particular resentment and hung her head. "You're right," she said. "I guess I just haven't felt very much. I wanted so much for you to stop and touch me and be romantic all those years, not just now. Even in the last week, I wanted you to notice that these emotions were coming up, and ask me about them. I didn't think it would feel as good if I had to ask you to do these things. It would have taken away the romance."

Sam responded immediately. "Linda, this relationship is a two-way street. Until I master the art of mindreading, do you really want to risk never connecting deeply just because you want something and don't ask for it at a time I am not aware of it? Not only that, but are you always going to wait for me to initiate everything? How I would love it if you touched me or if you planned something romantic for me! If you only knew for one minute how hard it is for me to do all the work, all the time, and then get blamed because it isn't just the way you wanted it. Where are you in this equation?"

They sat a long while in silence.

Finally, Linda lightly stroked Sam's face, inviting him to gaze into her eyes.

"Come here, tiger," she said in her sexiest voice. Her eyes watered from tears. The electricity of her first touch sent a shock wave through them both. Without further words, they began to touch each other, guided by the current flowing between them. And in that moment they began the second honeymoon of their dreams.

Grow Your Turn-on over Time

What you focus on, you create. We've all seen that principle at work. This book began as a twinkle in my eye one day, two years ago. What if…that new car you're driving similarly began one day in the past, as you imagined owning it?…the man you married was one day in the past, just another guy, before your visions and dreams went to work?

Turn-on grows and builds over time just like all other dreams blessed with constant nurturing. Think of your development of your turn-on as a process that yields both instant results and is also constantly making deposits into your turn-on bank. Over time, with continual deposits, you will discover yourself an increasingly wealthy man or woman. Just like the truly wealthy everywhere, you will have oodles of turn-on to send to others and also to re-invest in enriching your own life in all ways imaginable.

Expanded Orgasm Is Ever-changing

Months after Suzanne and Rick began their expanded orgasm training, Suzanne had begun writing a book on modeling specifically for professionals. Her dream, once fully formed, was to help models avoid the burnout that had almost cost her her career and had certainly cost her happiness in relationships. Rick enjoyed helping her with the book on weekends—they had made this into a joint project and their emotional and spiritual exchange was fueling their already skyrocketing expanded orgasm program.

Suzanne's journaling expressed the extent to which she had made turn-on a priority in her life:

I watch with never-ending wonder as the turn-on in my expanded orgasm practice rises and falls like waves in the ocean. Sometimes there are storms on the sea. At other times it is sunny and still. Sometimes weeks of high turn-on follow periods of introspection and a going inward, where my turn-on can go very deep and expand more inside than out. Throughout it all, the expanded orgasm continues, developing in ways that always amaze and delight.

Sometimes it seems the expanded orgasm is keeping my life energy fully activated. At other times, it seems that life is fueling my expanded orgasm practice. As long as my energy stays vibrant, I don't really care which feeds which. It's only when my life energy feels persistently down that my wise inner elders call a council to see what is off track and what can be done to return to the course of truth, energy, and passion.

Thank you, Suzanne, for saying it so well.

Bring Your Energetic Connection to Your Date

Have you ever looked across the room, locked eyes with someone, and blissfully melted? If so, who was it that was doing the "melting"? Did this person (a stranger, a partner, or whomever) melt you? Were you a neutral bystander, with no thought of melting before your eyes met? Or were you already a fertile bed of potential melting just waiting, perhaps even scanning, for just the right signal to go ahead and melt?

This inquiry raises more questions than answers. Some things, people say, just seem to happen without words or explanation. Some energy connection, often called *chemistry*, just happens. A meeting of two beings sparks a surge of desire. Where one begins and the other ends is unclear. Two potentially meltable people met…and melted! Both of you played your part.

Melting with strangers sells romantic pulp fiction. It keeps us going to movies. Oh, how we yearn for the chemistry! But wouldn't you really like to have it with *your partner*?

At a deep level, energy is what is present. Even the distinction of giver and receiver slips away. All that matters is the connection that converts both into givers and receivers simultaneously, regardless of who is doing the initiating and who is doing the following. In the energetic flow state, in fact, am I initiating, or am I exquisitely responding to your desire? All differences—giver, receiver, gender, desire level, and degree of enjoyment—gradually fade away into the strengthening connection. The connection becomes consuming. It is the energy that flows inside one person; it is the energy that flows between two people. It is the sum of one's heart, mind, spirit, and body, and the expression of the dance with another unique being in the ever-changing moment.

Take a ten-minute break with your partner to feel their energy without words, five minutes in each direction. Place your hand over his or her heart. See if you can tell what your partner is thinking, feeling, and requesting of you nonverbally. Afterwards, check your accuracy. Also, did you notice yourself becoming more tuned in to your partner as you relaxed into the experience?

Jason had set up a routine date with Kelly. In one of those mysteries of turn-on, having done nothing special, he thought, he had carried her to a place where she sailed over edge after edge in a series of orgasmic rolling. Amazingly, all this had occurred in ten minutes. Jason had mentally prepared himself to spend at least a half-hour giving Kelly pleasure, and thus was eager with his surplus of remaining time to push ahead, to "go for that blowout orgasm."

Oddly, every time he tried to push her to that higher level of pleasure, he met with Kelly's resistance. At first he was puzzled, and assumed he must not be reading something about Kelly's desire. Kelly seemed to be having a fabulous time; in fact, he was reluctant to ask her what she wanted since she seemed so far out in her pleasure world.

Soon, rather than feeling more pleasure himself, he began getting flustered. Kelly wavered too. He sensed that he was going to drop Kelly down, and short-circuit Kelly's expanded orgasm experience if he didn't change something soon.

Rather than ask Kelly, he scanned his body and released his own building tension. Suddenly it hit him. Kelly didn't want to go any higher than this! She was already enjoying the ride intensely and wanted to hang out where she was. What she wanted Jason to do was to accept her own pleasure as "enough" and just keep her exactly where she was just then.

He eased off on his attempts to have her climb, and Kelly stabilized, resuming her expanded orgasmic coasting. Within moments, Kelly, sensing the coherence between her deepest desire and Jason's action, reached for yet a new and even higher level of sensation. She wanted to continue to taste the edges she had gone over—and she wanted to continue coasting. Somehow, Jason was giving her all of this, and she wanted even more—more of the same—whatever it was. Her reaching was so spontaneous, so effortless, so guided by desire, that her edge expanded further, enabling her to coast and yet climb to yet higher levels.

Jason continued giving her this "coasting" experience and witnessed her extend what he called a rolling expanding edge for another twenty minutes. He thought, "This is a kind of edge I've never seen. Usually Kelly wants to explode by now, but since she's having such a good time—and so am I!—that all I want to do is stay with her desire. This is an edge that goes very wide, and keeps getting wider, and then because it's wider, gets higher, too. Wow!"

When he finally brought her down, taking an extra ten minutes to ease her from the dizzying heights, she raved about this unusually fun date. Calling him a psychic wizard, she begged him to do this again, many times over.

Knowing better than to expect this exact set of circumstances to occur again, he wisely answered, "Kelly, the next time you want this, I'll be there. All you have to do is send the signal through your true appetite and desire."

Kelly promised several times that day to send such clear signals. Jason simply basked in the praise. Usually he'd share with her exactly what happened to make his giving really special, but this time, he gleefully treasured his little secret. "Sometimes," he mused, "the less you talk, the better," thinking of the near miss that preceded his stroke of genius. Who said he couldn't tease her with a little mystery every now and then?

Reflecting, he was very clear about what had happened. He had wanted to take her higher with an idea in mind about how the date should look; but she wanted to "coast." Her biofeedback had told him this, and once he could finally hear her, and not his own mind, he backed off instead of going higher. He had let go of giving her want he wanted her to have, and truly given her what she was asking for. This resulted in her "surprise" expansion. Their coasting expanded orgasm at the very high level was truly a dual achievement. She had communicated, he had listened, she had received, and both of them sailed the heavens together.

In Turned-on States, Boundaries Dissolve

Turned on, boundaries that once seemed necessary to define our identity seem to dissolve. In everyday life, we have and identify with roles—wife, mother, engineer, artist, blonde, young (or middle-aged or old), and so on.

Can we say this too many times? As your lover gently touches you and you shiver with delighted anticipation, who is giver and who is receiver? You both are. In receiving, you give the gift of your pleasure and turn-on to your partner, and in giving to you, your partner receives joy, as well. And as your lover touches even deeper into your core, skillfully unlocking your orgasmic current and leading you into blissful surrender, so that your entire body now vibrates in ecstasy, where do you begin and end, and where does your lover begin and end?

And it's more than that: for me to *give* to your desire requires that I *receive* you, that I immerse in the endless biofeedback loop of me feeling you feeling me feeling you.

In the turned on state, fantasy, hopes, and dreams intermingle playfully with reality. Creativity seems to flow easily. New ways of viewing the same everyday circumstances seem to emerge of their own accord, usually carrying messages of healing and of promoting greater good to oneself, one's friends, and even one's larger environment. Anger and resentment melt away in the presence of love, compassion, and deeper awareness.

Expanded orgasm practitioners Dan and Sherry understand the significance of turn-on in their lives and they also know the importance of keeping up the practices that tap into its wellsprings. They have long loved the natural dissolving of boundaries that occurs in highly aroused states.

Dan is a high-powered telecommunications executive who travels extensively. Sherry is a public relations consultant for large corporations. Both of them rely on their wits every day for survival in highly competitive workplaces. Neither of them has much time in their lives for meditation, long walks in the woods, and the like. Realizing this, they worked with us to develop a regular schedule so that their relationship wouldn't fall victim to their ongoing time shortages.

They started out communicating a fair amount over the phone, and having two-hour expanded orgasm dates once a week, usually on the weekends. In this time they put significant energy on sandboxes and communication. Over the course of their first six months, they had progressed to where both could easily give expanded orgasmic experiences. And that's when they began to notice unusual occurrences in the expanded orgasm state of arousal.

Dan and Sherry started to compare notes. Dan noticed that during expanded orgasm sessions in which he was both giving and receiving, he had been able to solve difficult problems simply by rising to another level of perspective in the expanded orgasm state. In one example, he saw that in a contract dispute his company was fighting, the other side was making some fair points that he had never fully understood. In the expanded orgasm state, a flash of insight had hit him. It's as if the insight awaited his deep and coherent relaxation.

Relationship issues fared similarly. Things Sherry had asked for that Dan hadn't heard before would flash into his mind so that he could grasp their meaning. Sherry, too, began generating fresh ideas for her work as a publicist. "In the expanded orgasm state," she told us enthusiastically, "I'm so relaxed that my mind, my body, my heart, and my spirit stop being separate departments. Not only do I resolve paradoxes—like how Dan and I are going to do something when neither one of us is home to do it—but I also find that the turn-on generated in the expanded orgasm unleashes my creativity.

"I laugh at how I have come up with exciting new PR campaigns during our sessions together! Sex, pleasure, relationship, life all seem to flow together in expanded orgasm. Since both Dan and I are getting so much out of our sessions, we have stepped up our practice. It is a source of ongoing renewal, compassion, and creativity that really works for us in our busy lives."

Dan and Sherry's experiences are typical, and not unusual. Expanded orgasm practitioners find that the benefits of going into expanded orgasm range from healing emotional wounds to finding new sources of love, caring, and connection to oneself and the outer world, and even generating creative solutions and new ideas. These developments all flow from the relaxation of boundaries in the presence of the generative magic of turn-on.

I bring these kinds of experiences to your attention to show you more of the range of what's possible in expanded orgasm. The bliss, the dramatically enhanced capacity for pleasure, the deeper bonding with your partner—all these are enough reason to do expanded orgasm!

The Mystery of It All

Like Suzanne, I too have often wondered what feeds my orgasmic nature over time. Why is it that sometimes when I am touched, sleepy, and wanting only the warmth and love of another person's skin next to mine, I find a deep fire igniting, a kindling that must have lain in wait for that touch? And why is it that on another occasion, I am counting the minutes until I have a date, only to find, when the time comes, my body strangely unresponsive to the pleas and orders to turn-on being issued by my mind?

In the end, turn-on has always been a mystery, and I suspect that it always will be. Science will no doubt unravel much of its biochemical and neuroelectric concomitants, but I believe these new "understandings" will only point to ever greater mystery, for it is the glory of the mind and spirit to wonder and to stand in awe. I thrill to make sense of its many mysteries while finding more mysteries ever deeper. I cherish those moments when I find even more life inside me than I had thought: I love that the truth is better than I thought. I still wonder how much of turn-on is external, and how much is internal. I wonder if it can even be sensibly termed "my" turn-on, or whether I am allowing some greater force to come through me.

One thing I know: turn-on is the direct experience of the current of life. To taste it, I must be willing to face fear, insecurity, challenges, and rejection. To live in it, I must also desire to have pleasure greater than my wildest dreams, and to find ways to enlarge my container so as to hold even more turn-on.

The only thing I have to show for all my inquiry and practice is, in fact, my turn-on. By looking for it everywhere I can, I have kept it at the center of my focus and have found it far more often than perhaps I had any hope to expect.

In addition to feeling it within myself, I love to see turn-on reflected back to me. I tingle when people ask us if Allen and I are on our honeymoon, as they often do. I glow when I get compliments about how I look ten years younger than I did ten years ago. I feel on top of the world when I walk down the street, having had the greatest, most passionate sex of my life ever, with my husband and partner of sixteen years. I share my turn-on everywhere I can with other people, even people I don't know, like salespeople, shopkeepers, and new acquaintances. I share it by radiating enough turn-on that they feel it too and even send some back my way.

What We've Explored

Those who master an art know that superlative performance is only 20 percent about technique. Yet mastering technique is absolutely essential before you can invent the new. The first eight steps have been mostly about technique. You need to know how to sit, how and where to touch, how to give and receive feedback, how to do a sandbox, how to coordinate your hands (and ultimately your entire body) in delivering expanded orgasm and in making love.

Yet it must have been apparent to you from the very beginning that the path of expanded orgasm was not going to be only about learning some techniques. The path of expanded orgasm is as much about *being* as it is about *knowing* and *doing*. Ultimately it is about who you are as much as it is about what you know and what you do.

From our standpoint as teachers, this step is the most difficult to deliver because it is not about what to know and what to do. It is about something that is at its very core ineffable: about energy and flow and intimate biofeedback loops and communicating bi-directionally with your whole being—with body, mind, emotions, and spirit. We can't tell you how to do that. But the good news is that you already know how, so we see our job as reawakening your longing to be turned-on. We've laid out several methods for exploring what you already long to do.

Who does one turn on, anyway? Many think turn-on is something one does for a partner in order to look sexy and score points in marital heaven. This thinking is expensive. Unrequited turn-on exposes the person experiencing it to loss, rejection, and pain—certainly none of which are powerful motivators.

Turn-on must be done for oneself, and to oneself, and for its own sake. It is its own reward. It is the ultimate fruit you have to share with someone else, but if this other person doesn't want it, it is not invalidated. You still have it and, if you are smart, will guard it with your life, for that is what it reflects.

Turn-on that is other-dependent is bound to get you hurt, and that kind of turn-on is diminished and withers away, just as self-esteem that requires someone else to validate it makes no sense. Look inside and see if you can find those places where your turn-on was hurt, not by you, but by someone else, and ask yourself: for how long am I going to give that person power over my precious life energy?

Once you are turned on, turn-on can be other-fed. I am amazed at the power couples have to infuse their partner with turn-on. Here's how it happens. Turn yourself on. Share one moment of this turn-on with your beloved, and leave the door open for more.

You bring yourself into every date. What the mind craves most is novelty. If you bring yourself into present time, then in that moment, you are new, and your experiences will be fresh. Your partner will also be new. Imagine what fun you can have with a partner who is new and already cherished!

10

Step Ten: From Here to Further Mastery

Michelle lay on her bed, thinking that her entire body must be smiling with pure pleasure.

She was in an expanded orgasmic state, but not actually having an orgasm. She hadn't planned for this. She had cancelled her expanded orgasm session with Matt when her energy had dropped. The massage was a last minute idea on Matt's part. After all, since now they had the time to connect, why not use it?

Responding to his velvety touches upon her forehead and face, she had slipped into this state of effortless and timeless bliss, instinctively going even deeper. Her body flooded with a sense of pure fulfillment. In her dreamlike state, she fell in love with Matt, with pleasure, with her greatly expanded ability to *feel*.

Matt drank in her face. He had but touched her gently on the temples for only a few moments before she had started to contract. Now, she was climbing higher into expanded orgasm, unaware, perhaps, that if he didn't do something to pull her back, she just might go over the edge into a full-blown orgasm.

Michelle's reverie resonated into Matt as well. He had been exquisitely focusing on the fine details of every part of a stroke that crossed her forehead. Suddenly, he too, was swept away. He imagined his last day on earth. He felt his mind, emotions, and body enter a superlative lightness of being. Everything felt just perfect.

He traced a finger inquisitively across Michelle's gorgeous high cheekbones. Her eyes were shut, but she gently purred and arched her back a little, like a cat reaching for the next pet. Her energy seemed to be picking up all the while she lay in the dreamlike state. Curious, Matt peaked her by stopping for just a moment before resuming his stroke on her face. Her vibrations grew more intense, and spread from her pelvis to her abdomen.

It felt so good to Michelle to lie there and not have to do anything, even not to have a climax. Paradoxically, her body was responding anyway, even as her mind slipped more deeply into a cloud-like world, soft, tender, and peaceful.

"How good it feels to pause long enough to feel the texture of the time that lives between moments," thought Michelle. She experimented with letting time stretch out further. She found that in the reverie state, time was hers to play with. She took each stroke of Matt's, and stretched it in time, like pulling out warm taffy. Suddenly, in her experience, each stroke took ten times as long to complete. And that gave her that much more time to experience the space between the moments.

Matt felt that he was conversing with Michelle in this land between times. "You know, Michelle," he said, in his mind, but knowing she was thinking this too, "in the end, the cost of living won't matter…only the pleasure will. And we will be happy to have found so much pleasure filling our lives."

Michelle surged with another pure smile, once again filling the room with the energy of pleasure. She moved a little and moaned a little. Her entire body began to vibrate and to pulsate in deeper, orgasmically generated waves. She finally took Matt's hand away from her forehead and placed it firmly on her mons pubis. She wanted, even craved, more of Matt's touch now.

Matt's hand followed her desire for genital pleasure without breaking his train of attention. He knew exactly where to go; how softly to press; and most assuredly, to stretch time in every stroke so that each stroke seemed like ten.

His touch startled Michelle in its intensity. Picture a fiery ball of pleasure racing down the mountain, growing rapidly and effortlessly, until it is a star… picture a tiny stream starting in the tips of the Himalayas as it makes its way into a mighty river…and that is how quickly and easily her pleasure grew, from a first little moment to a magnificent throbbing universe.

Michelle and Matt's date thus entered their relationship hall of fame. Once again, they had turned a half-hour into an event worthy of framing forever. Such events were becoming increasingly frequent, while at the same time increasingly powerful and special.

They both felt a moment of gratitude that their focus had shifted from orgasm to the ever-expanding bowl of pleasure they knew was possible in the expanded orgasm state. Their agreement to spend the time together in this way had become a potent generator for deepening love, passion, and turn-on.

Have you ever slipped into an orgasmic state of bliss without even trying? Have you brought a partner along with you? What was it like?

The expanded orgasm space is a magical place indeed. It enables you to *feel* what another person thinks. You can modulate intensity simply with your intention. You can play with energy as skillfully as a concert musician plays his instrument. In mastery, expanded orgasm students embrace not only the goal of giving and receiving expanded orgasm, but also the understanding that expanded orgasm is a path to be traveled. It's a journey. Masters have learned to value visits to that state— independent of what happens during the visit—as importantly as they value the outcomes of those visits.

Expanded orgasm masters train themselves to observe carefully the degree of pleasure that they can feel in each moment. They observe, in ongoing truth processes in all areas of their lives, what will bring them less pleasure and what will bring them more pleasure. They fill themselves with the pleasure from feeling and relating deeply, knowing that in so doing, they generate so much more love to give everyone else.

Did you notice how Michelle and Matt entered an expanded orgasm state and enjoyed a shared fantasy? Both of them had experienced going into many expanded orgasm states. The more you enter expanded orgasm, the easier and more pervasive it becomes. With enough practice, in fact, you can learn to enter the expanded orgasm state almost instantly, and you can build from there. That is why the slightest breeze, or subtlest smile, can send a well-trained expanded orgasm practitioner into an orgasmic state so easily.

Can you pull together all you have learned about expanded orgasm into a greater cohesive picture, so that you too can begin to follow the path to mastery? Up to this point, we have been breaking down expanded orgasm into its component parts. We have been focused on building out the space of expanded orgasm, and finding the planks and nails with which to do so. Now, we wish to reverse the process to give you the bigger picture, so that you can integrate the room of expanded orgasm into the rest of your life, and so that you can gracefully enter and exit the expanded orgasm space, often, and whenever appropriate. With this bigger picture, we can offer you some advanced techniques to practice and enjoy.

In this step, we'll explore putting all we've learned together by paying a final visit with our two couples, Sam and Linda, and Jason and Kelly. We have followed them as they have shared with us some of the trials and successes of their journey through their expanded orgasm lessons.

We conclude our final step with some suggestions as to how you can continue in your practice.

Live Both in the Everyday World and in the Expanded Orgasm Space

We are born largely undifferentiated. We are in the world, and of the world, as potentially fully developed humans, but that is it. Over the process of maturing into adults, we go from being a generic member of the world, to having a specific planet, country, name, address, and zip code. We develop preferences, idiosyncrasies, habits, and behaviors that make each one of us unique. I call this process a deepening of identity. It is simultaneously a narrowing of identity, as we transform from an undifferentiated child who could be or do anything, into someone who is very concretely defined by a set of roles—mental images, attitudes, beliefs, and expectations.

The everyday world, then, is a world in which we acquire more and more details about who we are. These details define us, but they also separate us, as we become ever more different from everyone else we know.

Prior to their expanded orgasm training, Matt and Michelle had operated almost exclusively in their everyday world. Matt was a father, a husband, an assistant professor at an Ivy League college, a part-time sports coach for his son's baseball team, and a mostly dutiful son. Michelle, his wife, was also a mother, a daughter and daughter-in-law, a part-time editor at a local magazine, and a homemaker.

When they had met, they had spent hours together making love, talking, laughing, and sharing their lives, hopes, and dreams together. In the past few years, however, sex had become an infrequent and sometimes awkward event that rarely exceeded fifteen minutes from start to finish. They worried that at this rate, they might soon stop connecting sexually altogether.

It should not have surprised them that the signs of a drop in connection had begun showing up in the rest of their lives. Matt felt Michelle could not understand, for example, his need to attend so many professional meetings at the expense of his home life. Michelle felt Matt could not understand why she could not make an effortless transition from editor to mother to wife to lover on demand. Both felt hurt and misunderstood by the other. They felt "trapped" in their everyday world.

When Matt and Michelle came to visit us, they had already decided that expanded orgasm could help them strengthen their own bond, their marriage, even their ability to relate to others in their lives. In order to accomplish their goals, they would have to enter a process of "letting go" of the identities that they had so carefully crafted in their everyday lives.

They were startled to find aspects of themselves they never knew existed or which they feared had withered forever—parts of themselves that were whimsical, silly, genius, romantic, sexy, daring, and adventuresome. Engaging in the practice of expanded orgasm released the constraints of their historical identity.

Since they were fully committed to the program, their main concern was simply time. Neither one of them felt they had the hours to dedicate to yet another project! (It's amazing how we can even perceive "connecting," or "orgasms," as a project, isn't it?) We emphasized right then that the program was more about a process than a series of tasks to be performed. The overarching goal of the program was to learn to optimize their pleasurable time spent together—rather than to demonstrate yet another domain of personal prowess.

We wanted a time commitment up front. Even if it was fifteen minutes twice a week, we would agree to work with them. But we asked them to think long and hard about a commitment they could win with, and stick with, for ten lessons, plus homework. They needed to very specifically toss their hats into the ring. They were to discuss this and respond to us within the week.

Bravely, yet somehow still fearing the burden of yet another obligation, they decided to commit one hour, twice a week, and fifteen minutes a day on the other five days. We were pleased—that would certainly be more than enough time to begin to build out their expanded orgasm space.

In the one-hour blocks, they were to explore the series of sensual exercises outlined in this book, as well as a few developed specifically for them. In the fifteen-minute segments, we asked them to connect in a variety of other ways: They were to trade acknowledgments, do truth councils together, and decide upon joint truth processes.

The sensual discovery exercises seemed the easier, since they embodied non-verbal, and hence, seemingly more "foreign" behaviors. These experiences helped them transfer needed cooperation and cocreation skills from their sensual, nonverbal types of communication, to their verbal communication.

Each couple seems to have their characteristic way of resisting intimacy. As both Matt and Michelle prized themselves as professional thinkers, they had developed a pattern of debating at every point of discussion. It was a struggle for them to learn how to communicate cooperatively rather than competitively. For them, this was more challenging than anything they learned about nonverbal communication, or about how to go into purely feeling states.

In time, as their sessions progressed, they learned how to share themselves deeply at a feeling, connecting level—the level at which competition doesn't make sense. By the end of their lessons, they had become skilled at shifting into "expanded orgasm time" (as they called it) within minutes. In a sense, what they had learned was how to spend their time together.

Could you commit to communicating with a partner a little bit each day so that you develop and maintain the skill of connecting? If you find yourself saying "Yes, but…" at this suggestion, ask yourself how important connecting with your beloved is to you.

Sexual Narrowing and Expansion

During one of their earliest sessions, we asked Matt and Michelle the following questions:

When receiving sexual pleasure, have you ever "shut down" in order to protect yourself from feeling too much at a time when you were feeling vulnerable? Did you learn, for one reason or another, to narrow your feeling to just the body part that was being stimulated? Do you ever feel with your body, instead of with your entire being?

When giving sexual pleasure, have you ever narrowed your giving down to just a body part—your hands, penis, or mouth? Have you ever restricted what you gave with your being, your attention, your focus, your intention, and your love, in order to protect yourself from being vulnerable, and also to protect the person you were being sexual with? We call the process of shutting down one's range of responses "narrowing."

Matt and Michelle answered most of these questions in the affirmative, revealing that they had unknowingly narrowed their sexual responses. This unintentional, yet damaging and habitual narrowing had, over time, dramatically limited the pleasure of their intimacy.

Michelle told us how they had acquired this habit. "We'd try something new. Maybe it was a new position or a new way of him touching me. If it didn't work out or feel good right away, we'd get spooked and wouldn't try it again. There were other times, in a tender and vulnerable moment, when I'd offer my heart and soul to Matt. If Matt didn't notice or care, I'd withdraw, and promise myself not to take that risk again."

Matt elaborated. "Progressively, during our intimate time, we became more focused on avoiding what went wrong in the past, rather than on creating fun in the present. I walked on pins and needles trying to give Michelle just the right type of pleasure that wouldn't bother her too much. The tension was pretty thick."

Looking back on these earlier days, Matt commented, "The real problem is that our heads were in the way, in more ways than one. We couldn't communicate very well, but we also weren't together in present time enough to generate fun and interesting things to talk about."

Michelle jumped in, "It really helps to have learned to keep our intimate focus in present time." She reached over and squeezed Matt's hand, and held it for a moment, feeling its warmth, and celebrating the brief connection the two of them had just snuck in.

Matt nodded his head vigorously. He continued, "Now I ask, what can I give Michelle today? I simply relax, and then relax some more. At each level of relaxation my mind lets go of its tight grip on navigating through experiences. With each new wave of relaxation, the texture of how I relate with Michelle shifts. As my mind becomes soft, I become soft. By the time I touch Michelle, I do so in ways that always seem to bring her pleasure. I keep a certain kind of softness in my mind and in my body, even when we build the intensity to extremely high levels."

Michelle and Matt proved to be exceptional in how they learned to spend quality time together. After completing the ten lesson series, they weren't any less busy, nor had they claimed more time for expanded orgasm in their lives. Still, they were maintaining their original expanded orgasm schedule faithfully, and consistently improving the quality of time spent together. This had become their private sanctuary time.

Why else have expanded orgasm if not for the pleasure it provides?

Imagine having a lifetime that is a cornucopia filled with one unique and delicious expanded orgasm after another, each with its own flavor, intensity, and pleasure profile. What a goal that is!

And yet, on the path of pleasure, each moment is all there is. The goal itself is not what matters most. What matters most is simply being in present time.

True masters have learned to embrace each moment of expanded orgasm as complete experience in itself. They have learned to let every stroke be "the one" that sends them into rapture. In a sense, every moment in present time is orgasmic. No matter what the moment is, the master is so full of gratitude and joy that this moment is the best one ever.

Activity #52: Make Every Moment Count

This exercise is both short and sweet. Take five minutes or longer, if you have the time. Start by breathing deeply but slowly and relaxing until you can feel the energy circulating through your own body.

Then begin to give attention to your partner, while your partner just receives. Let go of all your goals, even the goal of giving your partner pleasure. Simply explore what it feels like to be so fully present that even you don't know what you will do or feel in the next moment.

Then, switch giver and receiver roles. Notice, after both sets have been completed: were there any differences between giving and receiving?

You might want to try this exercise as an icebreaker before an expanded orgasm session if one or both of you has had a hectic day before arriving.

Can going into expanded orgasm states *really* resolve problems? Yes, and no! Couples will always face problems. Often, they are problems of separating out the "me" from the "you" and both "me" and "you" from the "us." Such problems are inherent in the everyday world. The creative tension between differentiation and connection forever will be essential to the dance of relationship.

Still, in the expanded orgasm space partners get together to lose their smaller identities, at least temporarily. The problems of the everyday world don't seem to make much sense here.

Of course, the space of expanded orgasm carries with it new kinds of "problems." Just how does one maximize cooperation or the quality of time spent together here? How great can our capacities to feel pleasure become? How far am

I willing and able to lose myself in the service of the sublime? What if we encounter experiences that are far better than we expected? What implications would that have for how we live our lives? On the expanded orgasm path, you trade one set of problems for new—and far more pleasurable—problems that are wonderful to address!

What problems would you like to solve with a new way of looking at them?

Advanced Techniques

The following exercises will invite you to bring more of yourselves as both giver and receiver into the expanded orgasm experience. We will share with you the master practitioner approach.

Discover Your Range

People easily get into sexual ruts. If you've been used to doing something a certain way for years, you may come to believe you're almost incapable of changing that pattern on request, even if you wish you could. The rut can be either mental or physical. More often than not, it is mental.

For example, when a person changes partners and the new partner likes a very different stroke or speed, the new partner might ask for the giver to slow down dozens of times. The partner thinks that he or she *is* slowing down; but from the receiver's perspective it's just not slow enough. Physically, this makes no sense. We are all capable of slowing down; but our mind doesn't have the new pattern locked in. The limitation is not physical, but mental.

Even partners who have been together awhile find that they have a hard time "hearing" their partner's requests for a significantly different approach. Many, many clients have commented that they reach a major roadblock when an "out-of-range" request was made.

Rick reported recently, "Suzanne wanted me to go way up above her clitoris, practically on the very top of her shaft." Rick admitted his first reaction was anxiety. "She's never asked for that before! She had to ask me ten times before I heard her request, and even then it was only because she put my hand in the place she wanted it to go a few times. I was having such a hard time getting out of my mental rut that I might as well have been deaf."

Masters open their minds to expand their range. As receiver, you can train yourself not to feel upset making the same request many times. Realize that in making out-of-range requests you may be breaking very ingrained mental habits. And, realize that some requests may have to be made repeatedly over time.

Sometimes, even the same word means something different to two people. Marie couldn't get her partner Chris to go hard enough. It seemed that with each request, Chris would go faster, or too hard, but not "hard" the way she wanted. Even when she showed him on herself, he didn't seem able to translate her request into the exact action she was looking for. After a few months of this, she had given up asking, but then resented him for not giving her what she wanted.

We suggested that the next time Marie gave Chris pleasure, she demonstrate what she meant by "hard," by doing the desired stroke on him. After several times, Chris finally understood what she meant by "hard." Her desire for hardness wasn't really a request for more pressure. What she really wanted was a *deeper type of contact* achieved by having Chris press her clitoris using more surface area of his hand, coupled with a mental image or intention, in which he "sent" more contact mentally through his body to hers. Once understood at the mind/body level, it was as if he had thrown a switch—from then on, he was able to deliver. And this pleased him not only because he was able to please her more fully, but also because the increased sense of contact felt really good *to him.*

Expanded orgasm masters don't give up communication just because it didn't hold on one occasion; they see themselves in a lifelong process of communication, and understand that expanding range requires the reshaping of mind/body habits over time.

Activity #53: Expand Your Range

Each of you lists what you know about your preferences as receiver. Then, use sandboxes to challenge each assumption.

For example, how would you evaluate your current range as receiver? Do you like light or heavy pressure? Where would you say is your growing edge of desire? What do you find yourself attracted to exploring more? Would you be willing to spend time in sandboxes exploring ways to increase the range?

As giver, what are your strengths? Are you better at delivering light or heavy pressure (or do you feel most comfortable in the midrange)? Set up sandboxes to explore ways to give that are outside your current range. This exercise is deceptively simple. It might take several sessions to learn how to expand the ranges in which you are most comfortable.

Another way to expand range is to expand the number of body positions that you use to give and receive pleasure.

Ask yourselves: what positions haven't we tried? Get some books or some videos, and explore how you can adapt other people's positions to your own practice of expanded orgasm.

Develop Your Intuition

Have you ever given pleasure by following the energy rather than leading it? To the giver, this might feel like you are following a oiuja board. When you give in this way, you operate out of intuition.

Because expanded orgasm is an art, your mind alone is never going to fully lead you to deliver or to receive truly magical expanded orgasm sessions. Here, mind and intuition must be partners. You can easily practice following your intuition by attending to the messages of your non-rational mind.

The dissolving of boundaries that you explore in expanded orgasm enhances your ability to advance in your expanded orgasm practice. Your ability to deliver variety will expand. Your abilities to spread sensation will expand. You will learn how to see what you feel, think what you see, feel what your partner feels, predict what your partner wants next, and even respond to your partner before a request is even made. The path of mastery in expanded orgasm is profoundly about your ongoing expansion of talents in both physical and non-physical domains.

Activity #54: Awaken Your Intuition

To awaken your intuition in expanded orgasm, allow your thoughts and feelings to intermingle freely with your physical actions. You might do one or more of the following:

- Experiment with mixing thoughts and emotions with bodily motions.
- Send (and let yourself receive) love through your stroke.
- Feel your attentive focus as an energetic spot in your hand (or other giving part).
- Play with fantasies that allow you feel more turn-on in your own body.

For example, you could imagine your own being fully saturated with turn-on, or that your partner's genitals have vastly expanded in size.

When learning to develop your intuition, observe your partner's reactions without telling them what you have just done and see for yourself the profound impact this can have.

Activity #55: Stroke up the Center

In this exercise, practice delivering the first of the three opening strokes outlined in Step Five. This time, men, rather than using your mind or your vision, allow your intuition to guide you up the center of your partner's introitus. Have as a goal letting your intuition follow perfectly up the center without veering to the left or the right. Givers might imagine that the receiver is actually "calling forth" their path as they make their way up the center. They might feel this call as a warm line or just a place where it feels sweetest and most compelling to touch.

Dylan gave Judy one very long stroke. He started at the base of her vagina, with his hands cupping her lips gently. He let his hand rest there for a while, doing nothing but feeling Judy's energy. With this high degree of contact and feeling, he made micro-adjustments in his position, barely perceptible visually, but which allowed her to free increasing energy, until Judy was subtly streaming, highly aroused from the contact alone.

Develop Your Integrity

As people advance in their expanded orgasm practice, they learn to have complete integrity in both delivering and receiving every stroke. If the last stroke took her up, but not quite as much as the previous stroke, notice this. If the last stroke took her down, notice this too—perhaps it is time to switch to another kind. If the last stroke took your partner up, this should make you want to deliver another, relishing feeling her enjoying your delivery.

Most people have not trained themselves mentally to notice the fine distinctions that occur from one stroke to the next. They know logically that in expanded orgasm, this practice is essential; but they have not developed the discipline it takes to stay that focused, without getting swept away by expanded orgasm's rising tide of energy.

Expanded orgasm lives in present time. Overenthusiastic givers often fall into the trap of falling out of present time. It's an easy and seductive mistake to make. The giver mistakes the *state* of expanded orgasm for the *stimulation* of expanded orgasm.

Here's how it works. As the receiver climbs ever higher into expanded orgasm, the energy builds. The giver is delivering a continual stream of stimulation, with adequate peaking to allow the receiver to remain in expanded orgasm and climb further. When the stimulation stops, whether intentionally or unintentionally, the receiver will stay in the state for just a few moments longer. The giver may then be fooled into thinking that what he's doing is OK. But, unless the receiver has reached a very expanded state, the expanded orgasm state will start to drop again within a few strokes.

With training, the giver can learn to notice this (at first) subtle drop, change what he is doing, and bring the partner up again. But too often the giver doesn't notice until the partner has dropped so low that precious time has been lost; rather than taking her higher he must now bring her back up to her previous level.

Ideally, new expanded orgasm practitioners learn from their mistakes. But, even master expanded orgasm practitioners make lots of mistakes. Perhaps the biggest separation between the novices and the masters is how they recover.

When the energy drops, novices race ahead or try to make up for the energy drop; in so doing, they lose contact with their partner and get out of present time. When expanded orgasm masters lose contact, they notice, within a few strokes, and return to what worked before, with a minimum of emotional reaction. They are more focused on the goal of pleasure than turning attention away from the receiver and onto themselves and their egos.

You could say that in expanded orgasm, both the giver and receiver are in an ongoing truth process in every moment.

You can develop an ongoing truth process with yourself. Ask yourself the following questions:

Are you judging yourself or your partner? Let that judgment go.

Are you focused on pleasure or success? Let the success focus go, too.

Are you judging your judgments? Let them go too. Just immerse in the glorious Now.

Activity #56: Revisit the First Three Strokes

This deceptively simple exercise is one of our most advanced. Many students found it was this exercise that catapulted them in the paradigm shift from technique to mastery.

You are to create a complete experience out of giving your partner the three opening strokes you learned in Step Five. The goal is to create a complete expanded orgasm experience in just three strokes. This is the practice for that goal.

For each of the three strokes, do the same stroke ten times, each of you commenting each time on its straightness, speed, pressure, accuracy, and what you felt of the orgasmic energy. You will do the first stroke ten times, then the second, and then the third. Here are some things for both the men and the women to consider.

Men: You can, in the first few strokes, use a little more pressure than you would later, in order to stimulate engorgement. With your hand remaining in starting position, don't even begin until you can feel your partner is streaming and you can feel a very sweet spot. Get used to the feeling of how total control and total relaxation feed, not compete with, each other.

Women: Report each time on each stroke. You want to have complete integrity on communicating about how each stroke affected you.

Once you have practiced, on another occasion, see if you can bring your partner over the edge in just three strokes.

Intensifying the Climaxes

In order to take your partner into a powerful and sustained climax, review *peaking* and make sure you have a comfortable grasp of the concepts discussed in Step Six. It is with masterful peaking that you can build a large base from which to intensify the climaxes.

Masters at peaking form an energy picture or map. They have a sense of how they want the date to "feel." This picture, then, is not something they force on their partner, but rather it is the map and direction derived from "reading" their partner's desire. They let their intuition tell them the right timing for delivering intentional peaks. They have let go of counting each peak and engage in a direct feedback loop so that they are reading the energy moment to moment. Such mastery implies that the giver has mastered the art of avoiding unintentional peaks (which in itself is an achievement) and of delivering well-timed intentional ones. Master givers read a woman's energy so well that they are in perfect sync with her in present time. They read the energy so well that their hand feels energetically glued to her source; they cannot easily pull their hand away to stop delivering perfect strokes.

Now let's take the perspective of the master receiver, who notices when the stimulation is going down long before the orgasmic energy drops. She quickly informs her partner, so that they can resume the climb needed to sustain loft. Some receivers feel so intensely that they "energetically pull" the giver's hand back into the correct location and stroke.

This mutual experience—of feeling caught up in a flow of energy that seems to be directing the whole experience—can feel like a state of grace to both partners. The building of enormous expanded orgasm energy seems effortless.

Activity #57: Take Her over the Edge and Hold Her There

In this final exercise, you are going to build the base of your partner's pre-climax expanded orgasm so wide that when she goes over the edge, it will be with enormous intensity. (If she doesn't go over the edge, don't worry about it…this will still be a fun exercise!)

Think of a pyramid: the wider the base, the higher the top. Here are the objectives for this exercise.

Giver: Control the intensity of stimulation so that she can progressively accept greater amounts of sensation.

Let there be a conceptual center of focus to each hand, so that your attention centers on this focus, even though you are providing stimulation through a wider area of your hand.

Since each hand may be stroking at different rate, you won't be able to think, so don't even try.

Allow yourself to move to music, or otherwise get into a rhythm that bypasses your mind. With so much going on to occupy you, you'll be better able read her energy directly.

After taking her up through a series of peaks, you'll be able to sense that she's approaching an edge. Peak her just before you feel that she is going over the edge so as to build a broader base. This peak should give you the experience that you are pulling her back just a little from the brink; you want to deliver a series of climbs and peaks and pullbacks to help her expand the location of the edge outwards. Think of an expanding series of concentric circles.

When the time is right, take her all the way over the edge, and *now hold her there*. Again, your intuition will lead you perfectly, if you allow it to. Of course, she can give you verbal, as well as kinesthetic, feedback.

Once you've brought her over the edge, you may want to add pressure for a while, and then lighten up and slow down. You don't need to peak any more at this point. Now the pleasure-giving is at its easiest.

Receivers: At this point, if your partner is new at taking you over the edge and holding you there, give copious feedback so he learns just how you like to be kept over the edge. Experiment with staying over the edge for predetermined amounts of time, like five or ten minutes.

Don't give up just because you think you are done. Explore how far you can go in the extended expanded orgasmic state.

Men and women: Decide together whether or not you would like to take the woman over yet another edge. Women's sexual physiology is somewhat different than men's. Just because a woman has climaxed, it doesn't mean she is necessarily "spent." Often, there are one, two, or even more higher edges that she can go over if the offer is made and properly delivered!

Also, each woman is different. So, just because you have had success with other partners, don't expect this success to be perfectly duplicated in this one.

Michelle had noticed for some time that she and Matt always seemed to hit the same wall about twenty minutes into their expanded orgasm session. They set up a sandbox to address this apparent limitation.

Michelle commented first. Matt was *unintentionally* peaking her because his strokes were not smoothly distributed. At the top of the stroke, he exerted more pressure than at the bottom. She asked him to focus on smoothing out his strokes, and turning them into circles, so that he wouldn't peak her accidentally. Matt was thrilled to have this feedback and gladly complied. A little while later, he felt Michelle starting to space out. Determined to break their "twenty minute barrier," he starting talking to her, telling her how much he appreciated her input, and asking her questions. His talking reminded her to talk.

Returned from space, she began to give a rolling commentary: "Yes, you are keeping great contact with my favorite spot. I'd like to feel you create a center of focus on your bottom hand too, even if it is only conceptual. Yes, that made a world of difference. I'm really starting to climb now."

Her commentary allowed Matt to relax and focus on reading her energy, knowing that if something were amiss, she would let him know. Again, she asked for what she wanted from him. More variety, since her mind was starting to wander. This was a clear warning signal that without immediate change, her energy would drop.

Somewhere, with all the variety, Matt hit upon the perfect combination, and Michelle's pelvis began gently undulating. He knew he had captured her essence now and that he could easily take her over the edge at any point. With one hand glued to her favorite spot on her clitoris, and the other inside matching her movements, Michelle's experience of deep and unrestricted pleasure reached up to yet another level.

Up to now, he would speed up at this point, thrilled to be in such control. This would take her over the edge, and he'd be gratified that he was able to "deliver" a successful date. But, keeping with their plan, he peaked her, moments before she would have gone over. When he began stroking again a second later, her energy shot up dramatically to yet another level.

As Matt, still in perfect control, held her firmly, the need for coaching and feedback dissolved; her clitoris was literally sandwiched in between his upper and lower hands. It was impossible to escape him now. He told her, "I'm going to have my way with you, baby, and there's nothing you can do about it now."

Michelle responded, "Yes, take me, please, take me, keep going, please, and don't stop! What you're doing feels so, so good."

Matt recognized that he had attained that "state of grace" in which everything he did seemed completely effortless. He had never had so much fun with her! He was fully present to enjoy the experience right along with Michelle. And he didn't think he could stop now even if he wanted to. It's as if some energy current was running through Michelle and pulling him into every next stroke.

Michelle was also in the grips of a massive wave of energy that was moving her; while lying still, this wave rippled through her over and over again. She tossed away a little pillow to liberate her neck so that her whole body could move freely with the streaming current. Her knees were bent, hips rotated outward; her feet touching, giving her a heightened sense of both stability and grounding as she streamed higher.

Contractions spread powerfully throughout her entire body. She had but one thought, which was to reach for yet more pleasurable sensation. Her face grew fiery hot; then her neck. And then, her hands and feet splayed out as the fiery energy streamed through her fingertips and toe tips. The energy was rushing so quickly she needed to open her entire being up. With every new push toward opening, she bore down on her pelvic floor.

She was so conceptually "reached out" that her entire being felt settled into the sensation of being in one, steady-state push-out. Her physical body contracted and pushed out powerfully, without any conscious direction from her. She, too, had nothing else to do but to surrender and reach.

At some point, the intensity of the push outs seemed to reach a steady state, and now, the direction of energy shifted inwards, so that she lay contracting, reaching, undulating, and yet, strangely still. She hung blissfully suspended between the energy of the storm and a deep inner peace and calm. She realized that she, like Matt, had reached a certain "state of grace," in which her entire being was already over the edge, even though she hadn't quite gone over yet.

And then that moment came when she could take no more stimulation. A giant fireball welled up inside her and started rolling from deep within, pulsing outward from her pelvis. She was about to be engulfed in flames of ecstasy.

Matt was going very lightly now, but peaking her every third stroke. He could feel the final stroke come on, knowing, as she knew, that the next one would be It. He summoned up all the turn-on in his own body, and visualized a rocket taking off as he pressed the magic button. He was stunned to see how powerful this boost of intention blasted through his body, and into hers.

As she felt Matt taking her over the edge—finally—she was past the point of being able to move at all. She let the sensation from Matt's being pour into hers with no resistance anywhere. She felt first this perfect motionlessness, and then…she exploded.

Matt's hands instinctively held her down with a little more pressure to prevent her from flying off the bed. The energy gushed through her like a giant waterfall, unending, immense, streaming, and churning.

Michelle felt Matt place his hands more firmly on her now, and she used him to absorb some of the energy coursing through her. She could feel it transferring directly from her body into his. With this increase in pressure, she felt her energy rising yet again, going for yet another powerful edge. She went over this one, too. Matt noticed he was using considerable pressure just to keep her grounded; far more than he had ever remembered her enjoying. But, she was so engorged that her entire vaginal area had swelled to at least three times its original size, providing layers of extra cushioning.

As Michelle's throbbing contractions started to wind down, she started coaching Matt again. "Slow down now...don't move...no, move! But slowly...slowly!" She realized she was breathlessly issuing orders. A quick glance revealed that Matt was in ecstasy, so she continued, relying now entirely on her intuition to tell Matt what to do.

"Lighten up...that's perfect...stay there...stay there...," she called, and was also surprised at how she knew just what to say. "OK, let's go another five minutes. Use your intuition now, I'm lying back for this ride," she said, honoring their initial intention to extend their date.

Matt began to play. It was so easy now that she had gone over the edge. Every little touch sent her quivering and contracting over new edges. He felt that together, they had entered a new universe. Never had giving pleasure been this easy. He surrendered his final little piece of mind, and allowed his body to vibrate orgasmically, too, beyond all need or desire to deliver any more performance.

Matt felt Michelle's energy starting to drop. While he had lightened up to hold her over the last few edges, now he slowed his hand to complete stillness, and began pressing, ever so slightly. Michelle went over yet another edge.

Matt now held his hands motionless and firm. Within a few more minutes, Michelle stopped vibrating. Matt left his hand inside her for an extra several minutes, while she remained in a state of deep reverie. She could feel every molecule of his being in his every touch. She felt she was lying in clouds, loved, cherished, beautiful, not needing to go anywhere or do anything. Wave upon wave of relaxation bore her deeper and deeper into this profoundly meditative state.

She was overcome with bliss and gratitude. She wanted to thank Matt for just staying there, but could not even find a way to speak just yet.

There came a point where both of them recognized a perfect time to switch into deeper lovemaking. She wanted every particle of his being to merge with hers. She had never craved him so much as in this moment. Together they made flowing and profoundly connecting love until the long yet timeless afternoon shaded into evening.

Tap into the Positive Relationship Cycle

In the *space of the everyday world*, we find our roots, our family, our history, our hopes, our dreams, and all the details of our identity that make us unique and special individuals. This world gives us challenges to meet, families to love, projects to create and complete, and the other experiences that make our lives full of rich detail.

In the *expanded orgasm space*, we find our turn-on, our aliveness in the present moment, our creativity, and our connection to a sense of that which is greater than ourselves. We experience giving and receiving pleasure; we enlarge our ability to contain pleasure; we dream; we play; we grow.

Mastery embraces and includes both the everyday world and the expanded orgasm space. You can travel between them as you wish. You enrich each world by visiting the other. As this mutual illumination of each world in the other intensifies, the richer your overall experience of life. And, just as expanded orgasm benefits spread outward to enrich life, an enriched everyday life also cycles back to the expanded orgasm space, to enrich its experiences too.

This is how expanded orgasm feeds relationships over time, and keeps the passion alive and growing. In this positively reinforcing cycle, the more turn-on you feel, the more turn-on you share. Your partner welcomes your passion and returns it to you enhanced, feeding your relationship's generative core. As you feed one another, you find your "outer lives" expanding as well. And then, you have ever new experiences, feelings, and adventures to bring back to your expanded orgasm sessions.

Back and forth masters dance, infusing each space with the inspiration and turn-on found in the other. With each journey, they return a larger person for having made the trip. As you master this "dance between the worlds," you enhance both your ability to love yourself, and your ability to accept, appreciate, and love your partner.

Two Couples, Revisited

As our client couples complete their work with us, we ask them to reflect back and evaluate how learning expanded orgasm has gone for them. Below, let's find out what Linda and Sam, and Kelly and Jason, had to say. Linda spoke first:

During the expanded orgasm training, I came to realize that, above all else, I wanted some space to grow on my own. With the children gone, I wanted the freedom to get more involved with community activities or go back to school if I wanted to. Initially, Sam was against my desire for greater independence, fearing he was going to lose even more of me just when he was going to be home more. I was finding that his clinging was driving me further away.

I'm thrilled that Sam came to see that what he really wanted was quality, more than quantity, of time with me. I knew that by developing my own personal life, I could become even more exciting and interesting to both myself and to Sam.

Sam and I have a new standard for what we want with each other and for our relationship. Before, I think we clung to routine—that's really all we had to cling to. So, even though we were bored and stuck in a rut of patterns, we couldn't possibly find our way out. There just didn't seem to be enough motivation to change. Nor did we know what we wanted. There was an unsettled yearning—but for what? But doing expanded orgasm allowed us to change in the sweetest way. We had to communicate, after all, if we were going to get the first three strokes done correctly! We had to communicate way more about those three strokes than I think we did in an entire typical year of our marriage.

It's not just that we communicated, but that we revealed ourselves. I learned how to tell the truth to myself, as well as to Sam. In expanded orgasm, the feedback is immediate. You know whether you are telling the truth or not because you can actually feel the truth—and that's a skill I've been able to carry over to the rest of my life. Once I could tell the truth to myself, I could ask for what I wanted from others.

I think that as a result, I have become more interesting. I know Sam is happier that I am fulfilling my wishes to be more active outside home, even if that isn't what he used to say he wanted. Now, both of us are far more comfortable planning our lives cooperatively. We learned this in expanded orgasm and took it home with us to our everyday lives.

Oh yes, and the orgasms! I feared I was losing my sexuality when I started the lessons. Actually, I am certain this was happening. What I've learned is that my sexuality could be revived, and powerfully! Now, I still don't think I am the most orgasmic woman alive, but I feel good, knowing that I am highly orgasmic—far, far more orgasmic than I'd ever dreamed. I look in the mirror and I look and feel ten years younger than when I started. Often, I have a glow over my whole body. I like feeling young again. Sam and I are already planning our third honeymoon together, even though we just had our second one. When Sam and I are together, we have so much more fun. I have fallen in love with him in a whole new way.

Sam told us:

I must admit that I entered this program reluctantly. It seemed to be another one of Linda's get-better-quick programs. But since it was about sex, I agreed. Little did I know what I was getting myself into.

I have been going through lots of changes, and in a sense, this timing couldn't have been better for me. I was ready to take on a new identity. I had just stopped working day to day, and frankly, was feeling lost. I was hoping Linda would help me find myself, but now I see how ridiculous that plan was.

Doing expanded orgasm gave me a chance to experience myself as capable of learning significantly new things. It made me feel young again, and not stuck like an old man going into retirement. In fact, doing expanded orgasm made me feel like a teenager. I feel totally in love with Linda all over again. I even felt the way I did when I met her. I quivered with insecurity, hoping she would like what I was doing for her, and worried that I wasn't getting it right. But rather than just act like I used to and not admit it, I told her all of this. Rather than reject me, she loved it when I shared my deepest feelings with her. And do you know what? It felt good to be a little scared, a little challenged, a little not knowing what's next. What is life about if it isn't to be on a grand adventure? Who wants to feel so secure they never get to wonder and find out where their limits are? Certainly not me.

In many ways, this expanded orgasm training has pointed out many things I thought I knew and turned them upside down. Expanded orgasm, for example, is not about sex! It's about love, and pleasure, and discovery, and connection.

Don't get me wrong, our sex life has gone through the roof in terms of pleasure, and Linda's learned so much about expanded orgasm that her ability to give me pleasure has skyrocketed. But, in the end, expanded orgasm is about connection, pure and simple. I got what I most wanted from this—the true connection I have always wanted with Linda. That's how I can set her free now, with my blessings. I know that when we do come together, we will always be able to connect.

Kelly and Jason also were deeply impacted by their expanded orgasm training. Both of them had had to confront—and resolve—their own issues of freedom and security. They did so with breathtaking sophistication.

Jason was the first to volunteer his opinion:

I enrolled in this because I wanted to make sure that my marriage to Kelly was going to be sexually satisfying. In the beginning, I was really scared that I wasn't going to "get it." I only seemed to be a success at work, never with women. I thought of myself as a typical clumsy nerd, and even wondered deep down what Kelly saw in me. To be honest, if we hadn't done this, I'm not sure I could have kept Kelly.

Kelly is looking for someone who can meet her energetically, and not run away. I was both intrigued and terrified by her power. I certainly wasn't meeting it, though. My competitiveness seemed to plague me, and her, of course, to the point that I couldn't see Kelly as she was. All I could see were my own fears, projected onto her. I wouldn't have blamed her for leaving me for treating her so poorly. Who wants to be seen only through the haze of their partner's fears?

Luckily, I got to see just how I was doing this. No one pointed this out to me. Just by doing expanded orgasm, by being a different kind of person in that sandbox, and by communicating and cooperating, I became someone else, at least for a while. I became someone who listened, who felt, and who loved. My mind, my income, and even my ego didn't seem to be of any help in giving Kelly pleasure. In the end, I learned, that more than anything else, Kelly wanted me, the "me" behind the face, the me who is fun, and creative, and adventuresome. Expanded orgasm brought these things out in me.

And, as promised, I have been able to bring these gifts of being back into my day-to-day space. Kelly and I are having way more fun now than when we dated.

Finally I think I understand how good marriages operate. They get increasingly better over time! I love Kelly more every day. I know I'll never let her go, and I know how to keep her happy. Now I feel truly masculine and I know I am becoming a great husband.

Kelly listened to Jason tearfully. He had touched on her own issues and said things she'd never heard him say before. Then she added:

I don't know if I could have understood at the beginning what was really possible. You would have used words that wouldn't have made much sense to me before I had the experiences to go along with them. I was too afraid to ask for what I really wanted, which was love.

I have been beautiful since the day I was born. Men have always clamored to give me all sorts of attention. But in order to keep that attention, I have had to sell off little pieces of my soul. I had to look a certain way, act a certain way, and think a certain way, to continue buying their approval.

When Jason and I began, I was already starting to do the Kelly-for-sale routine. I could feel the passion slipping away and I didn't understand that my routine was doing far more harm than good. Jason doesn't want a doll for a wife. He wants to meet me, and go the distance with me, to slog through the piles of stuff that cover up the truth, and go for that truth, and that turn-on and fire and joy that lie at the heart of my being totally honest, real, and truthful.

So, here's the truth. I am on fire! I am just starting to discover my sexual and sensual nature, and I love to unleash my passions. I won't hide any more. I want to be loved and accepted for who I am. But it gets even better than that. Who I am in my full turn-on is far more magnificent than the Kelly doll I was parading around as. The Kelly doll is dull. The real Kelly, me—I am a flame that burns brightly, and I know that Jason is, too. We fuel each other's flames. I have already watched him unlock a passion that I never dreamed any man could unleash.

Maybe with another woman Jason would never have felt this passion. I want to think I have set his passion free just as I have set myself free. I want him to set himself free forever, free to live out of his passion and desire, just as I want to do this myself. I also want to develop his expanded orgasm, too! I see so clearly how both of us go into this state for renewal as well as pleasure.

At first, I wondered if I should feel bad—that it took so long for me to under-stand what I learned in expanded orgasm. But, I know I have to love myself, and see my entire learning curve as being perfect. I couldn't have known too much about all these discoveries before I began the program. The expanded orgasm sessions helped me build the container I needed to hold all the advances I've made.

The best part is that I have a security now I never had before. I know that as I grow older, I will never lose my looks. I will only grow ever more beautiful, since the beauty I get from my turn-on surpasses all other. And I also know that love is the greatest possible security of all for my marriage. Finally, I feel truly secure, at home in the world, in love with myself, and blissful in my marriage with Jason.

Begin at the Beginning...and Stay There

I conclude not with a final ending point, but with an invitation to get into present time. There is no end to the depth to which you can take this material.

True masters of expanded orgasm acquire a beginner's mind. They have learned to be someone new in every moment. They embody the wonder and surprise of someone who is so truly present to each moment, that each one is an orgasm in itself.

In truly present time, masters can never become old; they become part of the river of being, never the same being twice, always someone new. Imagine having an expanded orgasm master for a partner with whom to go through life. With this person, you will perpetually learn, discover, grow, and develop.

I have given you the tools, and now you can rediscover and reinvent how you will understand and apply them for as long as you keep this practice alive.

I encourage you to read through and dip into these steps more than once. If you can approach each with beginner's mind, I guarantee you will never do the same step twice. Since you are unlimited, you will always find something new to learn. Allen and I have been practicing these very lessons ourselves for more than ten years, and are still amazing ourselves at all there remains for us to learn. May you be as fortunate and blessed in your pursuit of expanded orgasm mastery.

If you feel that in going through these ten lessons that you have found more questions than answers, then surely I have done my job well. Keep wondering, and keep discovering. There is no limit to what you can learn about expanded orgasm.

About the Author

Patricia Taylor holds a Ph.D. in psychology and an M.B.A. She has taught expanded orgasm for both women and men for the past twelve years. Patricia's teaching organization offers relationship counseling and expanded orgasm trainings privately and through workshops. She lives with her husband and cat near San Francisco. For further information on her public offerings you may visit her website at www.expanded-orgasm.com, or write to: info@expanded-orgasm.com